To: Tony & A

My two faithful pastors

II Timothy 4:2

Wayne

MW01265138

I

II

Dedication

Dedications are difficult to write. There are so many individuals that have made an impact on our lives that to ferret out those most worthy of recognition is almost impossible.

First, and foremost, I dedicate this book to my Lord and Savior, Jesus the promised Messiah, who died in my place freeing me from the penalty of sin and death.

This book is dedicated to all who have honest doubts or questions regarding Jesus of Nazareth being the Messiah prophesied in the Old Testament. My prayer is that all who read this book will find answers to that question.

If the reader is already a believer in Jesus the Messiah this book will provide inspiration and materials suitable for Sermon material and Bible classes.

I could not have written this book without the patience of my wife, Cammie, allowing me many hours of solitude while composing this book. She also spent many hours editing manuscripts and making constructive criticism.

I am deeply grateful to my daughter Carol and her husband Olie who first encouraged me to begin this work. Their deep spiritual lives, and the times of evening devotions together, encouraged me to continue the laborious work known by all authors.

To my daughter-in-law Judy a special thanks for proof reading and formatting while on her vacation.

Finally, my deep gratitude to my daughter-in-law Gerrie, who worked her computer magic to meet the requirements of the publisher, and spending many hours as a proof reader.

Table of Content

1. Seed of Woman
2. Seed of Abraham
3. Seed of Isaac
4. Seed of Jacob
5. Descendant of Judah
6. Descendant of King David
7. Have eternal existence
8. Be the Son of God
9. Have God's own name
10. 483 Years
11. Born of a virgin
12. Born in Bethlehem in Judah
13. Adored by great persons
14. Have one who would announce Him
15. Anointed with the Spirit of God
16. Be a prophet like Moses
17. Binding up the broken hearted
18. The ministry of healing
19. The ministry in Galilee
20. Tender and Compassionate
21. Meek and unpretentious
22. Sinless and without guile
23. Bear the reproach due others
24. Be a priest
25. Enter Jerusalem on a donkey

26. Enter the Temple with authority
27. Hated without cause
28. Undesired and rejected by His own people
29. Rejected by the Jewish leadership
30. Plotted against by Jews and Gentiles together
31. Betrayed by a friend
32. Sold for thirty pieces of silver
33. His price thrown on the Temple floor
34. Forsaken by His disciples
35. Struck on the cheek
36. Spit on
37. Mocked
38. Beaten
39. Hands and Feet Pierced
40. Thirty during His execution
41. Given vinegar to quench his thirst
42. Executed without having a bone broken
43. Considered a transgressor
44. His death atoned for the sins of mankind
45. Buried with the rich
46. Raised from the dead
47. Ascended to the right hand of God
48. Exercise His priestly office in Heaven
49. Sought after by Gentiles and Jews
50. Be the King

INTRODUCTION

The book market has been flooded with Biblical Prophecy. This is a good and necessary subject in these troubled times, known as the Last Days.

I have seen little prophecy that centers solely on the Messiah Jesus. Jesus is the center of all prophecy. While it is important to learn the prophecies of the Last Days, it is also beneficial for us to authenticate that Jesus is the promised Jewish Messiah.

While the proof is overwhelming, that Jesus is the Messiah, many millions are still in a state of denial. To deny Jesus as the Messiah is to deny the authority of the Old Testament.

It is my desire to show that Jesus of Nazareth came to offer the Jewish nation a new covenant, as promised in the Old Covenant. The Old Covenant (Law) could only condemn and offer nothing but death. The New Covenant was made available on a cross at Calvary.

This Covenant offers eternal salvation to all who will accept Jesus as the Messiah. For those who understand the ceremony of the sacrificial covenant, I suggest that meeting God in the middle will cause that one to believe that Jesus of Nazareth is the Messiah for whom the Jewish nation has been awaiting.

"Believe on the Lord Jesus Christ and thou shalt be saved."

As you read each chapter bear in mind that each one has the unwritten prefix: The Messiah was prophesied to be...

Text were taken from the King James Version of the Bible.

VIII

Chapter 1

"Seed of Woman"

In the very beginning we find God to be the first to prophesy in Scripture. After the Original Fall God told Eve, the first woman, "and I will put enmity between thee and the woman, and between thy seed and her seed; it shall bruise thy head, and thou shalt bruise his heel." [1] The Messiah was destined to be the "seed of woman." The "seed" is the posterity, or descendent, of Eve. This reveals to us that the Messiah would be clothed in human flesh and dwell among mankind.

The New Testament grants ample proof that this prophesy, given by God Himself, was literally fulfilled. The apostle John, having been taught by Messiah, said, "He that committeth sin is of the devil; for the devil sinneth from the beginning. For this purpose the Son of God was manifested, that he might destroy the works of the devil." [2] Paul, in his epistle to the Galatians gave further testimony to the fact that Messiah was the seed of woman.

"But when the fulness of the time was come, God sent forth his Son, made of a woman, made under the law," [3]

From the beginning God so constructed the plan of salvation that it is utterly impossible for any man to cause himself to appear to be the Messiah.

---

[1] Genesis 3:15
[2] 1John 3:8
[3] Galatians 3:8

Only the Lamb, slain from the foundation of the world [4] is capable of fulfilling each prophecy exactly. God made it impossible for man, and possible for Jesus our Messiah. As you read each chapter in this book about the Messiah Jesus you will be awed at how impossible it would have been for a counterfeit Messiah to appear and deceive those who are familiar with the entire Word of God.

We begin where it became necessary for a Messiah, One who would be capable of carrying our burden of sin to the grave, and to experience the miracle of the resurrection. His death and resurrection sounded the death of sin and its penalty for all those who would believe.

Without the advent of Messiah mankind would be hopelessly lost, condemned to the eternal terrors and torments of Hell, a place prepared only for Satan and his evil angels. Man can only be condemned to Hell if he chooses to go there rather than accept the sacrifice of Messiah as being performed in his behalf.

Because God ordained that the Messiah would be the seed of woman we have a means of escape and an avenue of safety taking us into the very arms of a Holy God, a God of love.

We know the story of the Original Fall quite well, but it will serve our purpose to review it to help us recall why we need to understand the significance of the seed of the woman and the seed of the serpent.

We will begin after Adam and Eve have submitted to the deception of Satan as he possessed the serpent and spoke to Eve. The first mistake was to go into conversation with Satan, rather than flee from him.

---

[4] Revelation 13:8

We go now to the scene where Adam and Eve are hiding from God. It had been their habit to meet with God in the pleasant cool of the evening to praise Him for His wonderful provision and care.

Their fellowship was something they must have looked forward to, that is, until now.

Adam & Eve Knew They Were Naked!

Take note of how they behave now that they know they are naked. They surely knew they could not hide from the presence of the God that created the heavens, the earth, and that He was their creator. Their attitude now is that they were afraid of the very God in whom they previously found great pleasure.

This is the true nature of sinners, to cover their nakedness [sins] with their own self-righteousness [fig leaves], cut off their association with their Maker [church attendance], and tend to blame God for their sins. They rationalize something in this manner: 'You made me the way I am. You gave me these passions and they are too strong for me to resist, now you condemn me for your mistake.'

Adam & Eve, as do all sinners, hid themselves from God!

God called out, "Adam, where art thou?" God is aware that the sinner will not call out to him while indulging in his sin. But here is a lesson for us in soul winning.

Perhaps Eve sinned in the morning, and Adam sinned in the afternoon. They now had time to indulge in self-righteousness by hiding their symbol of disobedience, their nakedness. They sewed together fig leaves, making themselves the first to attempt to secure self-salvation, or salvation by works.

God did not come down hard on them the moment they sinned. God waited until the cool of the evening to confront them with their sinful action.

God's Question for Adam was, "Adam, where art thou?"[5] Why did you not come out to offer your devotion to Me as usual? God knew where Adam was, and He knew why Adam was unwilling to come face-to-face with God and praise Him and offer to Him his devotion.

God wanted Adam to admit his guilt of eating the forbidden fruit. It is necessary for the sinner to honestly and humbly confess their sins before God.

God was aware that Adam was now a sinner, and sinners know where they are spiritually.

They know how miserable, how spiritually blind, how naked they are before God.

God is also knowledgeable of the fact that pride is the portion of all of us who are recipients of the effect of the fall.

That pride causes one to refuse to accept the shame of their sins; they become reluctant to humble themselves before the Almighty, and are unwilling to confess their sinfulness. Until their hearts are broken over their sinful life, realizing that God has called us to be holy, because He is holy, [6]they will not come to Him. Therefore, as He called out to Adam, so He calls out to us, and what He is saying is "What is this that you have done? What a flood of misery you have brought on yourself. What prevents you from coming to me instead of hiding from me?"

---

[5] Genesis 3:9
[6] 1 Peter 1:16

4

We need to consider the Seed of the Woman and the seed of the serpent.

The seed of the woman would break the serpent's head and the serpent would only bruise the heel of her seed, the Messiah. Satan did bruise the heel of Messiah on five occasions.

1) Satan bruised his heel when he tempted him forty days in the wilderness.

2) He bruised his heel when he rose up strong persecution against him during the time of his public ministry.

3) He, in a special manner bruised his heel, when our Lord complained that his soul was exceeding sorrowful even unto death, and he sweat great drops of blood.

4) He bruised his heel, when he put it into the heart of Judas to betray him.

5) He bruised him, most of all, when the Romans nailed him to the cross and Jesus cried out, "My God, my God, why have you forsaken me."

The prophecies of God must come true because He can see the end from the beginning. As He proclaimed this prophecy in Genesis 3:15 He could look into the future and see these five terrible events awaiting His Messiah. Being truly and properly God, and truly and properly man, Jesus could be tempted, but as He was without sin, He chose not to succumb to the deception of Satan.

Since we too are the seed of the woman, with Jesus being the First Born, we will, like Him be tempted and persecuted by the seed of the serpent.

We have something in our favor, however. Satan has had little success with persecution of the Church. The more he persecutes, the more the Church grows.

Persecution of the individual will have the same effect if we remember that the "bruised heel" has "crushed the head" of the persecutor and his seed. Satan seems not to have come to the realization that his tactics only backfire on him and promotes the very thing he tries to destroy.

The seed of the woman will give the last and fatal blow; crushing the serpent's head. Satan, the accuser of the brethren, and all his accursed seed, shall be cast out, and never be allowed to bother the seed of the woman again. The righteous will shine as the sun in the kingdom of their Father, and sit with Christ on thrones in majesty on high.

The motivation of the dedicated Christian should be to help those in the grip of sin to realize their sin is a form of malice toward the God who loves them, and He is faithful to His promise to forgive and forget if they will only forsake all that is displeasing to Him. There are still so many "forbidden fruits" for us to claim as our own, but we must run from them as quickly as we would a poisonous serpent that is coiled up to strike us with it's venom. .

Let us not forget that our subject is centered on Messiah Jesus. Having a deep-seated love for my Jewish friends I have embarked on this study to verify the accuracy of the Old Testament, and the exact fulfillment of those prophecies as recorded in the New Testament. It is my earnest prayer that many Jewish believers will receive a copy of this study, and dare to read the truth as revealed in the Old Testament and the New Testament.

Chapter 2

"The Seed of Abraham"

One of the most revered personalities in Scripture is surely the man of faith, Abraham. Abraham was considered righteous because he believed God.[1] God called Abram, later to be renamed Abraham, out of the land of his birth, and go to a land that God did not reveal to him at that time. It was an act of faith for Abram to obey the call of God and separate himself from loved ones and close friends. God told Abram that if he would do as commanded He would make him a great nation, and He would bless them that would bless Abram, and curse him that cursed him.[2] Then God gave Abram a blessing that was prophetic, and one that offers hope eternal to our present world; "in thee shall all families of the earth be blessed."

This prophesied that not only would the people, who were to become known as Jews, be rescued from the penalty of sin and death, but also the Gentile as well.

Consider the man Abraham and His calling from the One true God:

The Lord spoke this prophecy to Abraham 2000 years after the fall of man. God had given the prophecy to Adam and Eve in Genesis "And I will put enmity between thee and the woman, and between thy seed and her seed; it shall bruise thy head, and thou shalt bruise his heel" [3]

---

[1] Galatians 3:6
[2] Genesis 12:3
[3] Genesis 3:15

The coming redeemer would be from the seed of Abraham.

It is significant that when God spoke to Abraham about his "seed" it is in the singular, and not in the plural.

"Now to Abraham and his seed were the promises made. He saith not, And to seeds, as of many; but as of one, And to thy seed, which is Christ." [4] God spoke of a great multitude of Abraham's descendants, but one seed.

The promise was spoken about 400 years after the flood.

The world had again turned to idolatry and wickedness. Idolatrous worshippers surrounded Abraham, living in the land of Ur of the Chaldees. Abraham however worshipped Jehovah. Abraham's belief in God secured him the recognition as being the first Hebrew.

We must never mistake the magnitude of this promise, because it included all the families of the earth, which included all Gentile nations.

The Israelites would ultimately become God's chosen people, but only for the purpose of sharing the Gospel of Salvation to the entire world.

The entire Bible is built upon this promise to Abraham. The promise was repeated to Abraham's son Isaac and his grandson Jacob. Ancient Rabbinic Judaism regarded this passage as Messianic.

Abram was obedient to the command of God and departed his homeland, a land of idol worshippers, to follow the One true God.

---

[4] Galatians 3:16

The inhabitants of Ur of the Chaldee worshipped Sin, or sometimes-called Nanna, the moon god. Abraham was born in Ur of the Chaldees, located on the mouth of the Euphrates on the Persian Gulf. This places Ur of the Chaldees in modern Iraq. As Abram departed, he took with him Sarai his wife, his nephew Lot and his servants, as well as his father Terah. Abrams father Terah went as far as Haran where he died. Abram was seventy-five years old as he left Haran. His wife Sarai, who would be renamed Sarah, his nephew Lot and all their possessions were packed for the journey, one that was yet a mystery to them.

We may assume that friends and relatives asked why he was leaving Haran questioned Abram. We might also imagine the ridicule as he revealed to them that he was going to a land, but he had no idea where this journey would take him.

As they left Haran they traveled in the direction of the land of Canaan, and in time arrived there. Going through Canaan they came to Sichem in the plain of Moreh.

The land of Canaan was inhabited at that time, but God promised Abram "Unto thy seed will I give this land: and there builded he an altar unto the Lord, who appeared unto him."[5] Take note of the fact that God did not promise this man of faith that he would possess the land of Canaan, but rather his descendants. Abram recognized the magnitude of the promise and built an altar that he might worship his God.

---

[5] Genesis 12:7

Abraham and his assemblage arrived in Haran, twenty-four miles from the Syrian border. The Tanakh, Old Testament, records that Jacob spent twenty years in Haran working for his uncle Laban.

The New Testament records the fact that the Messiah indeed was the seed of Abraham. The Messiah was the promised One in whom the families of the earth be blessed. Matthew, another apostle of Jesus, wrote "The book of the generations of Jesus Christ, the son of David, the son of Abraham."[6]

In the book of Acts, Luke wrote "Ye are the children of the prophets, and of the covenant which God made with our fathers, saying unto Abraham, And in thy seed shall all the kindreds of the earth be blessed." The apostle Paul wrote in his epistle to the church in Galatia "Now to Abraham and his seed were the promises made. He saith not, And to seeds, as of many; but as of one, And to thy seed, which is Christ."[7]

In our continuing search for the truth concerning whether Jesus is the true Messiah, we turn to the Word of Truth and find a promise regarding the coming Messiah in the first book of the Bible.

In Genesis we read "And I will bless them that bless thee, and curse him that curseth thee: and in thee shall all families of the earth be blessed." [8]

---

[6] Matthew 1:1
[7] Galatians 3:16
[8] Genesis 12:3

In thee— In thy posterity, in the Messiah, who shall spring from thee, shall all families of the earth be blessed. He shall take on him human nature from the posterity of Abraham, he shall taste death for every man, his Gospel shall be preached throughout the world, and innumerable blessings be derived on all mankind through his death and intercession.

The Gospel according to Matthew, "The book of the generation of Jesus Christ, the son of David, the son of Abraham." [9]

"All The Families of the Earth Shall Be Blessed." There is no nation on earth that has not benefited from Christianity:

1) Missionaries taking the truth of the Gospel to non-Christian countries, Christians collected money sent in forms of disaster relief, even nations opposed to Christianity have been unable to ignore the existence of Christianity and Christ, whether they accept Him as the Messiah or not.

2) Christianity has brought to civilization hospitals, reformatories for making good citizens from criminals (although modern society turned the reformatories into criminal warehouses).Volumes of intellectual literature, scientific journals, many of which were composed and printed in Christian countries. In short, little that benefits this world has come from heathen nations when compared to that, which came from Christian countries.

:

---

[9] Matthew 1:1

The word 'families' translated from the Hebrew refers to the circle of relatives, tribes, or people. It begins with the smaller of groupings and extends to larger (tribes) and even larger (people, meaning nationalities).

If God told Abraham that, his posterity [descendents or future generations] would bless all these, it is exactly what He meant. No one person, no tribe, no nation would be excluded, unless they chose to exclude themselves.

Jesus prophesied that the Gospel will be preached in all the world, and then the end will come. Every person will have the opportunity to hear and respond to the Gospel of Peace, peace between God and man. [10]

As is typical with sinful man, some will attempt to excuse their sinfulness by saying they never heard of the Gospel of Peace, but God will not leave one person with that excuse. We read in the book of Revelation "And I saw another angel fly in the midst of heaven, having the everlasting gospel to preach unto them that dwell on the earth, and to every nation, and kindred, and tongue, and people,"[11] God will not leave one person with an excuse, saying I never heard the Gospel.

The word 'angel' (ανγγελλω) has more than one word when translated from the Greek. It can mean that God will literally send an angelic being fly around the earth proclaiming the Gospel.

---

[10] Matthew 24:14
[11] Revelation 14:6

It can also mean that a messenger, who is also the meaning of angel in the Greek, could fly on aircraft as missionaries worldwide to spread the Gospel. Missionaries have translated the Gospel into numerous languages.

I am a spiritual romantic, and I tend to believe that God will literally send a heavenly being to earth to be certain that mankind has not missed anyone.

An angel could proclaim the Gospel in such a manner that every person would hear it in their own language, just as did the people gathered in Jerusalem on that first day of Pentecost when the Holy Spirit came upon the disciples.

Either interpretation would verify what God told Abraham concerning his descendant blessing all the nations of earth. The proof that Messiah comes from the Lineage of Abraham is beyond dispute. The Jews will dispute this because they choose not to believe in Jesus. To believe in Jesus brings up the question of the Trinity, and to the Jew that is polytheism.

It is essential that we understand the full meaning of Genesis 1:1 "In the beginning God created the heaven and the earth."

The Hebrew word for God in this verse is Elohiym, plural, as it ends in 'im'. This indicated a three in one God. When this word is used with an article, it specifically refers to the supreme God, and not to some lesser idol gods.

We also read "And God said, Let us make man in our image, after our likeness: and let them have dominion over the fish of the sea, and over the fowl of the air, and over the cattle, and over all the earth, and over every creeping thing that creepeth upon the earth "[12]

The Jews have chosen to either ignore this interpretation, or find some illogical rendering of it. It is my prayer that my Jewish friends will hear the voice of God rather than the teachings of mortal man.

The Quran says that the lineage of Abraham goes to Ishmael rather than to Isaac. This, of course, would eliminate Jesus as the Messiah because he was of the lineage coming from Isaac, not Ishmael. In this manner, they acknowledge Jesus as no more than a prophet, and he is listed about seventh in rank with the other prophets mentioned.

I see no way the Islamic can justify the words spoken to Abraham when they see that the nations of the world are not blessed by Islam, but rather oppressed by that religion.

Even in this world that is so far removed from the holiness that God expects from mankind we can still see the prophecy God gave to Abraham as being true.

Persecution of the Christian has not eliminated Christianity; in fact, it has spread it around the world.

This was true in the day of the first century Christians, and it is true today in non-Christian countries where believers worship Messiah at the cost of their lives.

---

[12] Genesis 1:26

In Judaism we see anti Semitism, hatred toward the Jews. The name 'Jew' has become a by-word in the world even today. "And thou shalt become an astonishment, a proverb, and a byword, among all nations whither the LORD shall lead thee." [13]

An astonishment: a consternation or ruin; byword: a taunt, something pointed. If I plan to take unmerited advantage of ones finances I will "Jew" him out of it. What a derogatory statement!

In Islam, we see no salvation for forgiveness of sins. We only see reward for following the hateful instruction of "holy jihad", which is far from holy. The intent is plainly spelled out in the Quran; they are to kill all Jews and Christians. No Moslem is to have a Jew or a Christian as a friend. This is far from blessing ALL the families on earth, as it leaves out the Jew and the Christians.

This was spoken to Abraham, and the Moslems claim Abraham as their ancestor. We take great consolation from the fact that the Old Testament clearly points out that the Messiah Jesus would be the seed of Abraham, and that all the nations of the earth would be blessed through him. That includes us, and that makes it supremely personal. This, no one, no religion, can ever take away from us.

For that, we can honestly praise our God and Savior Jesus Christ for His sacrifice in our behalf and the fact that one-day we will go to be with Him for all eternity.

---

[13] Deuteronomy 28:37

I take great joy in knowing that Christians are "grafted in Jews." It is true that in times past some of the Jews were subject to the wrath of God and cast away, but He has always reserved a remnant. The Jews are God's chosen people and we Christians wish to share in the promises made to Abraham, because it included all nations.

The epistle to the Romans gives better explanation than would I and I present it here.

"God hath not cast away his people which he foreknew. Wot know ye not what the scripture saith of Elias? how he maketh intercession to God against Israel saying, Lord, they have killed thy prophets, and digged down thine altars; and I am left alone, and they seek my life. But what saith the answer of God unto him? I have reserved to myself seven thousand men, who have not bowed the knee to the image of Baal. Even so then at this present time also there is a remnant according to the election of grace. And if by grace, then is it no more of works: otherwise grace is no more grace.

But if it be of works, then it is no more grace: otherwise work is no more work. What then? Israel hath not obtained that which he seeketh for; but the election hath obtained it, and the rest were blinded." [14]

(According as it is written, God hath given them the spirit of slumber, eyes that they should not see, and ears that they should not hear;) unto this day.

---

[14] Romans 11:2-8

And David saith, Let their table be made a snare, and a trap, and a stumblingblock, and a recompence unto them: Let their eyes be darkened, that they may not see, and bow down their back alway. I say then, Have they stumbled that they should fall? God forbid: but rather through their fall salvation is come unto the Gentiles, for to provoke them to jealousy. Now if the fall of them be the riches of the world, and the diminishing of them the riches of the Gentiles; how much more their fulness? For I speak to you Gentiles, inasmuch as I am the apostle of the Gentiles, I magnify mine office: If by any means I may provoke to emulation them which are my flesh, and might save some of them. For if the casting away of them be the reconciling of the world, what shall the receiving of them be, but life from the dead? For if the firstfruit be holy, the lump is also holy: and if the root be holy, so are the branches.

And if some of the branches be broken off, and thou, being a wild olive tree, wert graffed in among them, and with them partakest of the root and fatness of the olive tree;

Boast not against the branches. But if thou boast, thou bearest not the root, but the root thee. Thou wilt say then, The branches were broken off, that I might be graffed in. Well; because of unbelief they were broken off, and thou standest by faith. Be not highminded, but fear: For if God spared not the natural branches, take heed lest he also spare not thee." [15]

---

[15] Romans 11:9-21

If this chapter has not erased all doubts about the Messiah Jesus, I urge you to read on, there is much evidence to follow. Read with an open mind, considering the fact that what you have been taught, and what you believe may not be what God has revealed in the Scriptures.

Chapter 3

"Seed of Isaac"

This chapter begins with the unfolding of the prophecies regarding the promised Messiah. It beginning with God promising Abraham a son in his old age. Scripture tells us that Abraham laughed in his heart, saying, "Shall a child be born unto him that is an hundred years old? And shall Sarah, that is ninety years old, bear?" [1]

And God said unto Abraham, As for Sarai your wife, you shalt not call her name Sarai, but Sarah shall her name be. And I will bless her, and give you a son also of her: yea, I will bless her, and she shall be a mother of nations; kings of people shall be of her. - Gen. 17:15-16

God promised to give Abram and Sarai a son but they evidently thought God needed some human assistance. Sarai gave Abram her handmaid, Hagar, that she might bear him a son. At this time, Sarai had not yet conceived.

Abraham then turns his affection to his son Ishmael, whose mother was an Egyptian. In effect, Abraham said to God that it was his wish that his son, Ishmael, might be the head of a prosperous and powerful people. [2]

God answered that prayer in verse 20.

God promised that Ishmael would have twelve sons; all would be princes.

---

[1] Genesis 17:17
[2] Genesis 17:18

This was fulfilled as God gave Ishmael Nebajoth, Kedar, Adbeel, Mibsam, Mishma, Dumah, Massa, Hadad, Tema, Jetur, Nephish, and Kedemah. They did become a very prosperous and powerful people whom we know as the Moslems.

God was very specific as he told Abraham that his son's name should be Isaac.

He also told Abraham that He would establish an everlasting covenant with Isaac and with his seed after him. [3]

Ishmael was never promised to enter into an everlasting covenant with God, but God did promise to make Ishmael fruitful and multiply exceedingly.

We can attest to the fact that his prophecy has been fulfilled.

God then restates what He had earlier said about Isaac, "But my covenant will I establish with Isaac." This is a key verse, as God intended the nation of Israel to be the one through whom the Lord God, the Almighty Creator of the universe would be made known.

The heathen nations must come to know Jehovah, and Israel was chosen to proclaim His name. [4]

The heathen must know God because it was His intention to bless all the nations of the earth through one of Abraham's descendants.

That "one", of course, is the promised Messiah, the One proclaimed in the New Testament as Jesus.

---

[3] Genesis 17:17
[4] Genesis 12:3

20

Jesus of Nazareth is the promised Messiah, and as we continue to research the Old Testament, we will find proof positive that only Jesus could ever fulfill all the prophecies written regarding the Messiah.

Man, with his limited knowledge, often turns to emotions to voice his prayers or make decisions. Abraham would have chosen to see Ishmael be the chosen one through whom the everlasting covenant would be established.

His human emotions told him that he and Sarah were too old to have a son, and desiring that the covenant promise with God would come through his lineage he decided to take the certain route. He already had a son, Ishmael, but Ishmael was the son of his flesh, and not the son of the promise.

Sarah had been greatly dismayed because Ishmael had been taunting Isaac, who was much younger that he. We have no way of knowing what this "taunting" was, some suppose disparaging remarks were made to Isaac about the age of his mother, as compared to his much younger mother.

Others, such as Jonathan ben Uzziel and the Jerusalem Targum represent Ishmael as performing some idolatrous rite on this occasion, and these offended Sarah.

We have no scriptural verification of this, however, and must discount this as pure conjecture.

When she complained to Abraham, he told her that Hagar was her handmaid, do as you wish with her.

Hagar was not only Sarah's handmaid, she was also Abraham's concubine, but Abraham relinquished that privilege and turned Hagar's destiny over to Sarah.

Sarah decided that Hagar and Ishmael must be sent away and Abraham provided necessary items for their journey. It grieved Abraham to do this, but God assured him it was the proper thing to do. It was then that God reminded Abraham that it was the son of promise, not the son of the flesh that would enter into an everlasting covenant with Him.

God told Abraham, "Abraham, Let it not be grievous in thy sight because of the lad, and because of thy bondwoman; in all that Sarah hath said unto thee, hearken unto her voice; for in Isaac shall thy seed be called." [5]

How often we have our own ideas about how God should govern this Planet, but God, in His wisdom, always has a better plan. What a terrible mess would this world be if God listened to the advice man might give Him.

The Moslems today will tell us that Ishmael was the son of promise, and not Isaac. It is true that Ishmael came from the seed of Abraham, but it was not through his lineage that the promised Messiah would come.

There is no one in the history of the world that has evolved through the lineage of Ishmael that could, or did, fulfill all the prophecies set down by God for the Messiah to fulfill.

---

[5] Genesis 21:12

These prophecies were given to assure the world that the one that claimed to be the Messiah would have a scriptural reference point to prove He indeed is Emmanuel [God with us]. No man has ever fulfilled the prophecies we will consider as we research the Old Testament, no man that is, except Jesus of Nazareth.

The very fact that Abraham was promised that his 'seed', singular, would be the heir of the promise, tells us that it is not a nation, which would need to be called the 'seeds' of Abraham. The 'seed' God was referencing was one that was to be much misunderstood, maltreated, and rejected by many. Only one sent from God would be capable of enduring the kind of rejection that would be facing Jesus.

Christians today can claim to be descendants of Abraham though faith. We are "grafted" into Judaism through our acceptance of the Jewish Messiah, Jesus. We are heirs of all the promises and curses that were given Israel. Blessings will be ours if we obey God; if we are disobedient we will be subject to all the curses God promised Israel.

The New Testament verifies that Jesus is a descendant of Abraham. Follow the lineage of Jesus in the New Testament and you will soon see proof positive.

There are still those today that have never attempted to understand the Triune God, acknowledging there is only one God, generally referred to as Jehovah. Jehovah, however, does not possess the limitations of finite man, and is in reality Three in One, The Father, the Son, and the Holy Spirit.

Before this study has been completed we will delve deeper into the doctrine of the Trinity in the hope that should one read this, not accepting the fact of a Triune God, will have the eyes of their understanding opened by Jehovah Himself.

Chapter 4

"Seed of Jacob"

Scripture is very clear regarding the genealogy of Jesus. There is no doubt that Jesus was a descendant of Jacob. Perhaps what we need examine here is the life of Jacob, since the genealogy is not in doubt. I believe a "thumb nail" sketch will be sufficient.

Perhaps a fitting opening remark should come from Sir Walter Scott: "Oh what a tangled web we weave, when first we practice to deceive!"[1] The Scriptures are scrupulous in recording both the bad, as well as the good, of the various men of God as they play out their role. This Isaac, soon to become Jacob, was a supplanter, somebody who takes the place or position of somebody by force or intrigue.

That is a good description of the man Isaac before the Messiah Jesus, as a Theophany, changed both his character and his name.

"And Isaac intreated the LORD for his wife, because she was barren: and the LORD was intreated of him, and Rebekah his wife conceived. And the children struggled together within her; and she said, If it be so, why am I thus? And she went to enquire of the LORD. And the LORD said unto her, Two nations are in thy womb, and two manner of people shall be separated from thy bowels; and the one people shall be stronger than the other people; and the elder shall serve the younger.

---

[1] Sir Walter Scott 1771-1832

And when her days to be delivered were fulfilled, behold, there were twins in her womb. And the first came out red, all over like an hairy garment; and they called his name Esau. And after that came his brother out, and his hand took hold on Esau's heel; and his name was called Jacob: and Isaac was threescore years old when she bare them." [2]

The struggle between Israel (the lineage of Messiah) and the Moslem nation began in the womb of Rebekah.

God told Rebekah there were two nations in her womb, and one nation will be stronger than the other, with the elder (Esau) serving the younger (Jacob).

As if to prove the reality of this prophecy, when Jacob was delivered from his mother, he took hold of Esau's heel. This was a sign of aggressiveness and dominance.

As the two boys grew into manhood we find Esau willing to sell his birthright for a bowl of beans, something he would later regret. [3] Esau had obviously been on an extended hunting trip without success. The sun had beat down upon his body sapping his strength, and he had doubtlessly walked many miles through the barren wilderness seeking venison. Coming home he found Jacob, the more domestic of the two, preparing a pot of beans, red lentils.

Esau, in his weakened condition was more concerned with the present than the future, and when Jacob bartered with Esau for his birthright, Esau consented.

---

[2] Genesis 25:21-26
[3] Genesis 25:27&34

Later, we find Jacob living up to his name, which means 'supplanter'; he took the place of Esau by deception. His mother, Rebekah, devised a clever, but devious plan to put her favorite son in a position to inherit the legacy of the firstborn.

Esau had become a cunning hunter and his venison had become a favorite of his father Isaac. Jacob, under the direction of his mother Rebekah, carried out a scheming plan to deceive Isaac into believing that Jacob was Esau, the firstborn.

Covering his hands and forearms with the skin of an animal and wearing the clothing of Esau that had the smell of the field on them, he went into Isaac for a blessing. At first Isaac was skeptical because the voice was that of Jacob, but upon feeling the "hairy" arms and smelling the aroma of the field in the clothing, Isaac was convinced.

Isaac gave Esau's blessing to Jacob without realizing the fraud being worked on him.

Upon returning from the hunt for venison for his father, Esau prepared it in the manner preferred by Isaac. As he presented his offering to his father, Esau received a shock that would turn his heart to murder. Isaac explained that he had already eaten of the "venison" and given the blessing.

When Esau heard the words of his father, Esau became bitter and asked if Isaac had not kept at least one blessing for him. [4]

---

[4] Genesis 27:34

The animosity between these two brothers was now a present reality, and down through the ages their descendants have been bitter enemies even though, in time to come, the brothers departed each other in peace.

How long Esau harbored the bitterness in his heart, planning to murder Jacob is not known.

Many years later King David wrote "A brother offended is harder to be won than a strong city: and their contentions are like the bars of a castle." [5]   It would appear that King David might have been thinking of these two brothers, knowing the contention that still existed between their descendants.

It is no speculation that Esau was planning a murder. It would seem that he had uttered his intent to kill Jacob in the hearing of servants. Rebekah was told of the plan of Esau and she immediately sent Jacob to her brother Laban, at least until Esau's desire for murder was past.[6] [7]

It was the intention of Esau to await the death of Isaac and then regain his right to the title of the first born with all its privileges.

Had only Jacob known the verse, "Oh what a tangled web we weave when first we practice to deceive." [8] This deception is a false reality based on a true reality.

---

[5] Proverbs 18:19
[6] Genesis 2741
[7] Genesis 27:43
[8] Sir Walter Scott: "Marmion"

Once the web has been weaved the weaver finds the lie has entrapped him, and the more he struggles with it in his mind, the more it becomes an instrument of destruction for him.

As time passed, Jacob and Esau were once again to meet face-to-face. It was now time for Jacob to surrender or die.

Knowing that Esau was on his way to meet Jacob, Jacob felt it only reasonable to meet Esau in a submissive attitude. In effect, his plan of separating his family into groups, sending a "peace offering" before him, was raising the white flag of truce. For Jacob this could well be "panic time" as Esau was approaching with four hundred men.

This is obviously a war party, not just security guard patrol for Esau's journey "So went the present over before him: and himself lodged that night in the company. And he rose up that night, and took his two wives, and his two women servants, and his eleven sons, and passed over the ford [shallow crossing place in the water] Jabbok. And he took them, and sent them over the brook, and sent over that he had. And Jacob was left alone; and there wrestled a man with him until the breaking of the day. And when he saw that he prevailed not against him, he touched the hollow of his thigh; and the hollow of Jacob's thigh was out of joint, as he wrestled with him.

And he said, Let me go, for the day breaketh. And he said, I will not let thee go, except thou bless me. And he said unto him, What is thy name? And he said, Jacob.

And he said, Thy name shall be called no more Jacob, but Israel: for as a prince hast thou power with God and with men, and hast prevailed. And Jacob asked him, and said, Tell me, I pray thee, thy name. And he said, Wherefore is it that thou dost ask after my name? And he blessed him there." [9]

Jacob was on his journey to his homeland when he was informed that his brother Esau was moving toward him with an army of four hundred men. All the emotions pent up over the years, fearing this very confrontation, have now become a present reality.

Jacob wisely broke his caravan into sections, each one carrying a reconciliation gift for Esau. Jacob stayed behind, at the brook Jabbok, taking his two wives, women servants and his eleven sons with him. He sent this group across the brook, but he stayed on the other side in solitude. Jacob had much to consider, especially his speech to Esau when once they met face-to-face.

Jacob had not counted on an encounter with a theophany [an Old Testament of the Messiah Jesus]. Scriptures tell us he "wrestled" with "a man" until the breaking of the day. We do not know if this grappling was mental or physical, what we do know is that Jacob would not give in until he received a blessing. It is obvious that Jacob recognized this "man" as being a supernatural being.

---

[9] Genesis 32:21-29

The word "angel" [αγγελοσ] has an interesting meaning in the original Greek. This, according to the scholars, was αγγελοσ Βουλησ αγγελοσ (the Messenger of the Great Counsel). Also means the one designed to bring fallen men from death, and bring him to eternal glory.

This is the same αγγελοσ (angel) that provided water for Hagar and Ishmael when they assumed they were dying in the desert after Abraham had cast out (divorced) Hagar.

The "angel" changed Jacob's name from one who took the position of another by intrigue (Supplanter), to Israel. This was a custom in the East when some event of importance happened in the life of a person. Abram, a prince among men, was changed to Abraham, the father of nations. Sarai was also changed to Sarah, Saul to Paul, Cephas to Peter, etc.

The prophet Malachi wrote concerning these two brothers. [10] "The burden of the word of the LORD to Israel by Malachi. I have loved you, saith the LORD. Yet ye say, Wherein hast thou loved us? Was not Esau Jacob's brother? saith the LORD: yet I loved Jacob, And I hated Esau, and laid his mountains and his heritage waste for the dragons of the wilderness.

Whereas Edom saith, We are impoverished, but we will return and build the desolate places; thus saith the LORD of hosts, They shall build, but I will throw down; and they shall call them, The border of wickedness, and, The people against whom the LORD hath indignation for ever.

---

[10] MalachI 1:1-5

And your eyes shall see, and ye shall say, The LORD will be magnified from the border of Israel."

It is a proven fact that Jesus the Messiah was to be a descendant of Jacob, but we have seen in this portion that Jacob actually met with Jesus and received His blessings. It is unlikely that Jacob realized who this "angel of the Lord" was, but the record is certain.

This will lay a heavy emphasis on the fact that Jesus the Christ is from the lineage of Jacob. God promised Malachi, the Jew, that he has loved Israel, but He will hold indignation against Esau (the Moslem nation) forever.

It is with adequate justification that we say that Jesus the Messiah was descended from the Patriarch Jacob, who's name was changed to Israel.

As we translate the word "Israel" into English we find it means, "He will rule as God." Israel (Jacob) did rule as though he was God over his people and was greatly revered by other surrounding nations. It is most appropriate that Jesus, the Messiah, came as Emmanuel (God with us) to the tiny nation of Israel to fulfill His role as the Lamb that was sacrificed from the foundation of the world.

"And all that dwell upon the earth shall worship him, whose names are not written in the book of life of the Lamb slain from the foundation of the world." [11]

---

[11] Revelation 13:8

Knowing that Jesus, the anointed One, fulfilled the prophecy that He would be a descendant of Jacob we now have further proof that Jesus is who He said He is, He is the Son of God come to bring salvation to a sinful world, making provision for the repentant sinner to live for all eternity in the presence of the Almighty, Holy, Righteous, Pure, Perfect and Loving God.

Chapter 5

"A Descendant of Judah"

The Scriptures are convincing by the extreme honest of accounts. Scriptures bring into view all sin, scandal, incest, etc. without exception. This is also true in the genealogy of Jesus.

Consider just a few items showing the lineage of Jesus was full of trouble. Is it any wonder God sent Jesus to be a man and become our sacrifice for sin?

Example; God chose a Moabite widow, Ruth. Moab was a man born of incest between Lot and his daughter (Gen. 19:30-37); the Moabites were given his name. Before that, a Canaanite harlot (Rahab), then an unprincipled son of Jacob, (Judah who got his daughter-in-law pregnant, and King David committed adultery and murder to have Bathsheba as his wife, and a son born to her became a great king (Solomon).

There were others, but this should be sufficient to show that God reveals both the good and the bad in the Scriptures. Can we doubt that He will do the same in the judgment?

Even the sinless Jesus could not escape a sin-laden lineage, since all humanity was under the curse of sin. Original sin did not infect Jesus; but how can that be?

We need to remember that lineage goes through the male, not the female. The original sin was transmitted from the First Adam down though his first-born, etc.

Mary was but a receptacle, a chosen holy vessel, to receive the embryo of the Messiah. The Holy Spirit implanter her with the "seed" promised to Abraham. This "seed" made Jesus the first born of His Father, the Almighty God. Therefore, no sin curse was upon Jesus even though as man He could be tempted, but not made to sin.

There were some extreme problems in the lineage of Jesus, but God always protected both the Blood Line and the Royal Line for Messiah.

Consider Ruth, the Moabite widow. The son born to the daughter of Lot gave rise to the nation of the Moabites. (Gen. 19:28-38) This made Ruth a descendant of incest.

The Book of Ruth starts with Perez. The nature of his birth is the reason Perez is seldom mentioned. Ruth ultimately married Boaz and Boaz was a descendant of Perez. Perez was the son born to Tamar, the daughter-in-law of Judah.

Judah was the father (although unwittingly and due to not keeping a promise to Tamar).

It is also significant that Boaz was the son of Rahab, the Harlot (Matt.1: 5) Scripture scholars tell us that in the East the word "harlot" was often used for those who were innkeepers. This aptly describes Rahab. She was not a prostitute, but rather an innkeeper.

We need to consider the ancestor of Jesus, the man Judah

1) Judah was one of the 12 sons of Jacob.

2) Judah saved the life of Joseph, which was important to future events. Joseph became the father of Ephraim and Manassah. Judah, playing on the greed of his 10 brothers saved Joseph's life. They had thrown Joseph in a dry well pit, planning to kill him and lie to their father Jacob, saying a wild animal killed Joseph. Judah convinced the brothers to sell Joseph to some Midianites passing by in a caravan headed for Egypt. The men who bought him for 20 pieces of silver sold Joseph to Potiphar.

The tribe of Judah was named for this heroic brother of Joseph and the New Testament gives proof of this fact: "Abraham begat Isaac; and Isaac begat Jacob; and Jacob begat Judas and his brethren; And Judas begat Phares and Zara of Thamar; and Phares begat Esrom; and Esrom begat Aram;"

Which was the son of Aminadab, which was the son of Aram, which was the son of Esrom, which was the son of Phares, which was the son of Juda." [1]

3) Before Jacob died, he gave a prophecy to each of his 12 sons. See chapter 49th of Genesis to see his comments regarding each son, especially Judah.

4) Gen. 43, 44, 46 reveals that Judah had good leadership qualities. The Egypt incident finds Judah at the head of every main event.

5) The tribe of Judah became the greatest of the Israelite tribes, just as Jacob prophesied.

---

[1] Luke 3:33

6) Judah became the recipient of the position of the first-born, not the first three sons.

Reuben had slept with his father's concubine Bilhah (Genesis 35:22). which was normally an act of dominance over the one in leadership position?

Simeon and Levi murdered a nobleman and all the males in his tribe. Schechem (Gen 34th chapter) raped the daughter of Leah, Dinah.

This angered her two brothers, and when Schechem came to offer a dowry for her so he could marry her, the two brothers plotted to kill him. They said no Israeli woman could marry an uncircumcised male.

They agreed to the dowry, if, Schechem and all his males would first be circumcised. They agreed, and on the third day when they were too sore to defend themselves the two brothers came with swords and killed every male in that tribe. This meant Jacob would have to move his family out of Canaan because the other tribes of Canaanites outnumbered them and would come and kill them.

7) Judah would rule over the land of Israel: "The sceptre shall not depart from Judah, nor a law-giver from between his feet, until Shiloh come, and unto him shall belong the gathering of the people." [2]

---

[2] Genesis 49:10

8) The sceptre would not depart from Judah until Shiloah (Messiah) come. The patriarch Jacob did hereby prophesy the coming of Jesus, whom he (Jacob) called Shiloh, and through him (Jesus) the prophecy was fulfilled; for the sceptre did not depart from the Jews until Jesus appeared.

9) The sceptre represented the right of the Jews to rule their civil and religious government. The Romans were in power in Israel when Jesus came, and with Him was the fulfillment of this prophecy

10) After the revolt of Bar Khokba by Hadrian AD 135, the use of the name Judah passed out of use.

This took place in 132-136 under the commander, Simon Bar Kokhba as he revolted against Rome.

He established an independent state of Israel over   parts of Judea over 2 years, but the Roman army of 12 legions with auxiliaries crushed the revolt.   After that, the Jews could not enter Jerusalem except to celebrate Tisha B'Av, which is the ninth of Av, an annual fast day in Jerusalem (Tisha-ninth; Av-the month of the Hebrew calendar). This commemorates the destruction of the first and second Temple in Jerusalem and is the saddest day in Jewish history, even though the events were 656 years apart.

11) See Revelation 7:7. Judah is at the top of the lineage of Israel. The elimination of Dan was due to that tribe being the first to bring idolatry into Judaism. Ephraim is included with Joseph.

12)   Since Judah had been prophesied to "rule over the land of Israel) #7 above, we need further reference to this rule. "The sceptre shall not depart from Judah, nor a lawgiver from between his feet, until Shiloh come; and unto him shall the gathering of the people"[3]

This prophesied that although Judah would rule over the land of Israel, the "sceptre", the symbol of ruling authority, would not be forcefully taken away from the Jews by an invading army until the appearance of Messiah.

The Jewish population was well educated in this prophecy and must have been in great sorrow to think it will come to pass.

We know through history that Jesus was born during the occupation of Roman troops and had a king over them, taking away the Jewish right to rule Israel.

In Matthew 20:18 Jesus prophesied that the Jewish rulers would condemn Him to death. He did not say they would execute Him, only condemn Him. To carry out the death sentence they must go to the Roman leaders to have them condemn Jesus to death. "Then said Pilate unto them, Take ye him, and judge him according to your law.

The Jews therefore said unto him, It is not lawful for us to put any man to death" [4] "That the saying of Jesus might be fulfilled, which he spake, signifying what death he should die."

---

[3] Genesis 49:10
[4] John 18:31

"His body shall not remain all night upon the tree, but thou shalt in any wise bury him that day; (for he that is hanged is accursed of God) that thy land be not defiled, which the LORD thy God giveth thee for an inheritance." [5]

"And after threescore and two weeks shall Messiah be cut off, but not for himself: and the people of the prince that shall come shall destroy the city and the sanctuary; and the end thereof shall be with a flood, and unto the end of the war desolations are determined." [6]

Messiah will be cut off, executed, and that during the time when governmental rule has been taken from the Jews. The ruling forces were now the Romans, and their method of execution, death by way of crucifixion on a cross, was unheard of in Israel until the Romans began executions.

Jesus was to die on a tree, a cross made from a tree, and therefore He would be considered a curse. "Christ hath redeemed us from the curse of the law, being made a curse for us: for it is written, Cursed is every one that hangeth on a tree:" [7]

The curse that Jesus bore was our curse. "We have sinned and come short of the glory of God." [8]

The curse embodies the fact that the soul that sinneth, it shall surely die. [9] Jesus became our substitute in death so that we might live.

---

[5] Deuteronomy 21:23
[6] Daniel 9:26
[7] Galatians 3:13
[8] Romans 3:23
[9] Ezekiel 18:4

41

The Messiah was definitely much in need, if His ancestry was so affected by the sin principle, how much more the heathen world. Consider what has been written regarding Messiah Jesus and decide if you are beginning to see that He is the promised anointed One.

Chapter 6

"Descendant of King David"

What a marvellous promise God gave to King David. He promised David that a descendant of his would occupy the throne of David forever. I wonder if David ever wondered about those words "for ever." That is a long time, and it far exceeds the ability of mere mortal to fulfill it. Only One who is Divine, the Ancient of Days, can fulfill that prophecy.

"And when thy days be fulfilled, and thou shalt sleep with thy fathers, I will set up thy seed after thee, which shall proceed out of thy bowels, and I will establish his kingdom. He shall build an house for my name, and I will stablish the throne of his kingdom for ever." [1]

"For every battle of the warrior is with confused noise, and garments rolled in blood; but this shall be with burning and fuel of fire. For unto us a child is born, unto us a son is given: and the government shall be upon his shoulder: and his name shall be called Wonderful, Counsellor, The mighty God, The everlasting Father, The Prince of Peace.

---

[1] 2 Samuel 7:12-13

Of the increase of his government and peace there shall be no end, upon the throne of David, and upon his kingdom, to order it, and to establish it with judgment and with justice from henceforth even for ever. The zeal of the LORD of hosts will perform this." [2]

"And there shall come forth a rod out of the stem of Jesse, and a Branch shall grow out of his roots: And the spirit of the LORD shall rest upon him, the spirit of wisdom and understanding, the spirit of counsel and might, the spirit of knowledge and of the fear of the LORD;

And shall make him of quick understanding in the fear of the LORD: and he shall not judge after the sight of his eyes, neither reprove after the hearing of his ears: But with righteousness shall he judge the poor, and reprove with equity for the meek of the earth: and he shall smite the earth: with the rod of his mouth, and with the breath of his lips shall he slay the wicked. And righteousness shall be the girdle of his loins, and faithfulness the girdle of his reins." [3]

"Behold, the days come, saith the LORD, that I will raise unto David a righteous Branch, and a King shall reign and prosper, and shall execute judgment and justice in the earth." [4]

---

[2] Isaiah 9:5-7
[3] Isaiah 11:1-5
[4] Jeremiah 23:5

"The book of the generation of Jesus Christ, the son of David, the son of Abraham. Abraham begat Isaac; and Isaac begat Jacob; and Jacob begat Judas and his brethren; And Judas begat Phares and Zara of Thamar; and Phares begat Esrom; and Esrom begat Aram; And Aram begat Aminadab; and Aminadab begat Naasson; and Naasson begat Salmon; And Salmon begat Booz of Rachab; and Booz begat Obed of Ruth; and Obed begat Jesse; And Jesse begat David the king; and David the king begat Solomon of her that had been the wife of Urias;" [5]

"And when he had removed him, he raised up unto them David to be their king; to whom also he gave their testimony, and said, I have found David the son of Jesse, a man after mine own heart, which shall fulfil all my will.

Of this man's seed hath God according to his promise raised unto Israel a Savior, Jesus:" [6]

"Concerning his Son Jesus Christ our Lord, which was made of the seed of David according to the flesh;" [7]

It is obvious that God was telling David that a descendant would rule the kingdom forever.

It would be somewhat impossible for a human lineage to fulfill this prophecy since kings and they families were often murdered during a coup.

---

[5] Matthew 1:1 - 6
[6] Acts 13:22-23
[7] Romans 1:3

Here, then, are the Scriptures and events proving that Jesus was both prophesied and fulfilled the prophecy that He would become the heir to the throne of David.

Four verses in the Old Testament give us absolute assurance that the Messiah, Jesus, would one day be enthroned on the throne of David.[8] and re-confirms this prophecy, "And King Solomon shall be blessed, and the throne of David shall be established before the LORD for ever." [9]

The verses in the New Testament confirm these were historically fulfilled. [10]

David, translated means "beloved." Even with all his faults and sinful actions, God loved David.

David once prayed in Psalm 17:8 "Keep me as the apple of the eye," When translated, the "apple of the eye" is the pupil of the eye, sometimes called the "little man of the eye."

David was the second king of the united Kingdom of Israel. He was a righteous king, although he had his share of faults. David was a powerful warrior, musician and poet. His reign was from 1040 - 970 BC, his reign in Judah c1005-1000 BC.

His predecessor, King Saul, refused to carry out the ban against the Amalekites and God withdrew His favor from Saul.

---

[8] 2 Samuel 7:12-13; Isa. 9:5-7; Isa 11:1-5; Jere. 23:5
[9] 1 Kings 2:45
[10] Matt. 1:1,6; Acts 13:22,23; Ro. 1:3

Amalek was the son of Eliphaz, and the grandson of Esau (Ge. 36:12; 1 Chron 1:36). He was a chief of an Edomite tribe (Ge 36:16). At the battle of Michmesh, sinned during his war against the Philistines (1 Sam 14 ch).

Two things were displeasing to God:

1) Saul, not wanting the warriors to take time to eat, thus allowing the Philistines to get away, made it a capital offence for any of his men to eat anything before morning. This was a bad decision, because the men would not have the strength necessary to do vigorous battle.

When they finally did go into battle, and won, they were so hungry they slaughtered cattle and sheep and ate the meat with the blood still in it. Had Saul not made such a decree this would never have come to pass.

2) Saul then decided that his men should surprise the Philistines in the middle of the night and therefore win the victory by surprise. This would be displeasing to God because many innocent people would also be slain in the darkness of night.

When Saul wanted to get a decision from God he built an altar of sacrifice. He obviously did not think that was wrong for him to do, because when he was with Samuel he had built an altar.

However, on that occasion he also offered a sacrifice because Samuel did not come to him as soon as he had expected. Samuel informed him that he had no right to offer a sacrifice.

When Jonathan and his servant went into the Philistine camp and began to kill their guards, it awoke the camp and confusion reigned. The Philistines thought the Israelite army was attacking and they were so frightened that they killed each other in the confusion.

To further excite the Philistines we read "And there was trembling in the host, in the field, and among all the people: the garrison, and the spoilers, they also trembled, and the earth quaked: so it was a very great trembling." [11]

Adam Clarke tells us that this was not an earthquake, but only a form of speech saying there was confusion.

However, other commentaries take the wording literally declaring that God sent a divinely ordained earthquake to assist Jonathan and his servant.

Saul continued to displease God, and when God would no longer give him answers. Samuel was now dead and there was no prophet in Israel to inquire for Saul. Saul went to ask advice of a medium, (1 Samuel 28 chapter), God, of course, forbade this.

The Philistine army had recruited help from other nations and again was coming against Israel. Saul asked the medium to bring up Samuel, but when Samuel came up she was frightened, because she had expected to see her familiar.

---

[11] 1 Samuel 14:15

She did not bring up Samuel; God brought him up to give a message to Saul. Tomorrow both you and your son will be with me, that is, you will both be dead.

Saul and Jonathan were both killed in battle just as Samuel had told him.

Before his death Samuel was sent by God to seek a new king from the family of Jesse, an ancestor of the Messiah.

David was chosen, and the legends held by the Jews tell us that when the oil from Samuel's flask was poured out upon David it turned into diamonds and pearls. This was to give Samuel assurance that he had chosen the son of Jesse that God intended.

David began his career as a warrior while still a young lad. He had gone to take food to his elder brothers and to inquire as to their safety. While there he heard the blasphemy coming from the giant called Goliath.

He was so large that no one would take his challenge to fight him. Whichever man won, that nation would be the winner of the battle.

Goliath taunted the Israelites for forty days (the Jews were in the wilderness for forty years. David's defeat over Goliath made him a type of the new Joshua as he now has delivered Israel.

Saul was of the tribe of Benjamin, and that tribe was noted for their excellence with the sling. Saul could have taken up the challenge, but chose not to do so.

Goliath was dressed like a serpent with his scale armor, and he died like a serpent with a head wound. Dagon, the Philistines fish god also suffered a crushed head when God threw it down before the captured Ark of the Covenant.

David took the severed head of Goliath back to Jerusalem as a warning to the Jebusites who ruled there.

It is interesting that David's stone killed Goliath. The Law specified that blasphemy was a capital crime punishable by stoning to death.

David was then promoted to be the commander of Saul's army. He was also given the promise to marry Saul's daughter, Michael.

When God sent an evil spirit to Saul to bring about the beginning of the end for him David had to flee from Saul. While David was in hiding, Saul gave Michael to a man from Laish by the name of Phaltiel.

When David finally became king, and Saul's son, Ishbosheth was king of Judah; David insisted that Michael be returned to him.

The king honored his request and Scripture tells us that Phaltiel followed behind weeping all the way to Bahurim.

Abner, the General for David's army, turned him back.

According to the Talmud, Phaltieli never consummated his marriage to Michael but slept in the same bed with her with a sword between them to keep them separate. Difficult to believe.

The name, Bahurim means "youth" and infers that they both had remained unmarried youths and never consummated their marriage. (Again, difficult to believe).

Once settled in his kingdom David committed a grievous sin against Uriah and God. David had seen Bathsheba bathing on her rooftop. His castle overlooked their house and David became infatuated with her.

David sent for Bathsheba and committed adultery with her. When she discovered she was pregnant, and her husband Uriah was at war and could not be the father, David planned an evil scheme.

David sent for Uriah to come into his palace where he ordered Uriah to rest and spend the night with his wife. Uriah, however, slept outside, because the other warriors were outside in the battle zone.

David then ordered that Uriah be placed in harms way during the next battle and then withdraw all the support troops from him. Uriah was killed in this battle and David took Bathsheba for his wife.

The Talmud says that David did not commit adultery with Bathsheba because the night before going to battle a warrior would give his wife a bill of divorcement, because he might be killed.

Also, it says David was not guilty of murder because Uriah had disobeyed an order from the king by not sleeping with his wife when David told him to do so.

When David was nearing his own death he was told that his son Adonijah had declared himself king. The agreement David had with Bathsheba was that Solomon would be king, and that was also the command of God.

Adonijah secured a chariot, horses and fifty men to run before him proclaiming him as king. He then called all the kings' sons, servants, etc. to himself and made a great feast. While feasting word came to him that David had made Solomon king. Fear fell upon the assembly and they left Adonijah.

Later, Solomon the king pronounced the death sentence on Adonijah.

Just a thought or two regarding King David:

1) He was a descendant of Ruth the Moabite widow that married Boaz, the son of the Harlot Rahab.

2) The Jewish Midrash says Adam gave up seventy years of his life for the life of David.

3) Bathsheba was not only the wife of one of David's trusted warriors, but also the daughter of one of the men in his "thirty." These were the thirty chiefs of David's army.

4) David was thirty years old when he became king and reigned for forty years.

These are some of the interesting events in the life of King David, an ancestor of the Messiah. One day King Jesus will be enthroned on the throne of David and will reign over planet Earth with a rod of iron during the millennial reign.

"And out of his mouth goeth a sharp sword, that with it he should smite the nations: and he shall rule them with a rod of iron: and he treadeth the winepress of the fierceness and wrath of Almighty God." [12]

It is during this Millennial Reign that the Church, the born again Christians, will realize their role as Priest and Kings "And hath made us kings and priests unto God and his Father; to him be glory and dominion for ever and ever. Amen." [13]

"Moreover if thy brother shall trespass against thee, go and tell him his fault between thee and him alone: if he shall hear thee, thou hast gained thy brother. But if he will not hear thee, then take with thee one or two more, that in the mouth of two or three witnesses every word may be established." [14]

"This is the third time I am coming to you. In the mouth of two or three witnesses shall every word be established." [15]

Jesus and Paul both quoted Levitical Law stating that it requires two witnesses to establish a thing. We have seen one witness in Revelation 1:6, now we see the second witness to the fact that we are Priest and Kings, and shall reign on Earth with King Jesus.

---

[12] Revelation 19:15
[13] Revelation 1:6
[14] Matthew 18:15-16
[15] 2 Corinthians 13:1

"And hast made us unto our God kings and priests: and we shall reign on the earth." [16] The word "shall" indicates that a thing will happen in the future.

Christmas this year should remind us, not only did Jesus come to Earth over two thousand years ago to bring salvation to mankind, but also that He is coming again.

"And out of his mouth goeth a sharp sword, that with it he should smite the nations: and he shall rule them with a rod of iron: and he treadeth the winepress of the fierceness and wrath of Almighty God." [17] The sharp sword is the Word of God that will be obeyed, or else! Also, He will rule over the inhabitants of Earth with a rod (instrument of punishment) of iron. That is, sin will have a zero tolerance. Obey King Jesus and live for a thousand years, sin and you die.

During this period, you and I will assume the role we now have as Priest and Kings. We will receive our assignments, authority, and the location over which we will reside.

Keeping this in mind next Christmas we can accept this promise as one of the greatest Christmas gifts Jesus gave us. He gave us His salvation, and adopted us as children of God, being the only other thing greater.

---

[16] Revelation 5:10 ; 17 Revelation 19:15
[17] Revelation 19:15

O Come, let us adore him, He who is a descendant of King David, and who will sit on the throne of authority for all eternity.

Chapter 7

"Have Eternal Existence"

Faith in God starts with a belief in His self-existence. God exists in Himself and exists always in the present. The self-existence of God implies there is no fundamental difference between time and space. Because God exists above time, He is able to leave us totally free to make choices yet direct the consequences of these choices according to a plan made before the creation of the world.

Up to this point, I have referred only to God, yet my subject is "Messiah Must Have Eternal Existence." Why then did I not begin with Messiah? The answer, for me, is simple: Messiah is Emmanuel, God with us. Jesus, the Messiah is God clothed in human flesh for two important reasons:

1) To help humanity understand God as more than a Law giver and One who issues punishment for breaking that Law; 2) To be the perfect sacrifice for sin; a sacrifice to end all sacrifices. This required a sacrifice that is spotless, and without blemish, no sin   for which He must die.

"In the beginning was the Word, and the Word was with God, and the Word was God. The same was in the beginning with God. All things were made by him; and without him was not any thing made that was made. In him was life; and the life was the light of men." [1]

---

[1] John 1:1-4

Jesus, the Messiah of God, is amply recorded in the Old Testament and the New Testament as has been revealed in previous chapters in the history of Messiah.

Consider these verses in the Old Testament. [2] Now, consider the fulfillment in the Old Testament before we proceed with further documentation [3]

When Moses was attracted to the bush in the wilderness that was burning, but was not consumed, he had conversation with God "And Moses said unto God, Behold, when I come unto the children of Israel, and shall say unto them, The God of your fathers hath sent me unto you; and they shall say to me, What is his name? what shall I say unto them? 3:14 And God said unto Moses, I AM THAT I AM: and he said, Thus shalt thou say unto the children of Israel, I AM hath sent me unto you."[4]

The Septuagint reads: εγω ειμι ο ων, I am he who exists. The vulgate reads, Sum Qui Sum, I am who I am.

Parmenides, where he treats sublimely of the nature of God, says: υδ αρα οσομα εστιν αυτω, "nothing can express his nature, therefore no name can be attributed to him." Basically, that is very true.

We call God, Jehovah, but that is only what we use to refer to Him.

---

[2] Micah 5:1 & 2
[3] John 1:1,14; John 8:58; Ephesians 1:3,4; Col. 1:15-19; Rev. 1:18
[4] Exodus 3:13 & 14

The book of Revelation reveals God in the role of man, the man Christ Jesus, as He returns to Planet Earth for His Second Coming: "And I saw heaven opened, and behold a white horse; and he that sat upon him was called Faithful and True, and in righteousness he doth judge and make war. His eyes were as a flame of fire, and on his head were many crowns; and he had a name written, that no man knew, but he himself." [5]

It might be profitable at this point to restate the intent of our consideration at this time. Our subject is Messiah Must Have Eternal Existence. Since there is only one God, although He appears shrouded in a mystery we refer to as the Trinity, we know that Messiah is God.

I cannot separate God from the Messiah, Jesus, or the Holy Spirit. Therefore, whenever I refer to any one of the three, I refer also to the Almighty, self-existing, eternal God.

Not all scientists are atheists; however, those who do not believe in God have, for years, argued the finer points of the Universe.

They question, "Is the Universe Eternal?" "Why is there something rather than nothing?" "The Universe is a contingent entity, and "every effect has a forerunner cause."

Some scientists claim the Universe is expanding. They suggest that at points in space called 'irtrons', hydrogen was coming into existence from nothing. Hydrogen had to go somewhere and it displaced matter already in existence, causing the Universe to expand.

---

[5] Revelation 19:11-12

The clouds of hydrogen gradually condensed into clouds of "virgin matter", within which new stars and galaxies formed.

For scientists to admit to Creation is to admit to the "winding up of the Universe." If that theory is true, the question is who wound up the Universe.

Today scientists clearly state the Universe had a beginning and something eternal things do not have. "No matter can create itself."

Logic says, "The Universe was created, not the Creator."

Many are beginning to believe that all evidence indicates that the Universe did have a beginning, "something must be self-existent."

We will leave these hollow philosophies to those who have no faith. As for my house, and me we believe in a self-existing, eternal God.

Consider the words of Micah: "Now gather thyself in troops, O daughter of troops: he hath laid siege against us: they shall smite the judge of Israel with a rod upon the cheek.

But thou, Bethlehem Ephratah, though thou be little among the thousands of Judah, yet out of thee shall he come forth unto me that is to be ruler in Israel; whose goings forth have been from of old, from everlasting." [6]

The Almighty God made certain that Messiah could be recognized without controversy concerning His place of birth. There is a Bethlehem in the tribe of Zebulum, and it was necessary to identify exactly which Bethlehem would be the birthplace of Messiah.

---

[6] Micah 5:1-2

The word Beth lehem has a double meaning in Hebrew. It means the "house of bread" and speaks of the "Bread of Life", the Messiah Jesus.

It can also be translated as lehem, flesh. This refers to that portion of flesh that was burned representing a crucifixion cross.

It is also noteworthy that one of the ancestors of Jesus resided in Bethlehem, "And the name of the man was Elimelech, and the name of his wife Naomi, and the name of his two sons Mahlon and Chilion, Ephrathites of Bethlehem Judah. And they came into the country of Moab, and continued there."[7]

Naomi suggested that Ruth make herself ready for marriage to Boaz, a near relative who could qualify as the kinsman redeemer for Ruth's husband, a son born to Naomi and Elimelech.

I believe we have had ample proof from the Old Testament to convince one that the Messiah is God in the flesh, and He was born exactly where Scripture prophesied.

Turning now to the New Testament we find the Apostle Paul writing these words to the church at Ephesus: "Blessed be the God and Father of our Lord Jesus Christ, who hath blessed us with all spiritual blessings in heavenly places in Christ: According as he hath chosen us in him before the foundation of the world, that we should be holy and without blame before him in love:"[8]

---

[7] Ruth 1:2
[8] Ephesians 1:3-4

Paul also wrote to the church of Colosse, "Who is the image of the invisible God, the firstborn of every creature: For by him were all things created, that are in heaven, and that are in earth, visible and invisible, whether they be thrones, or dominions, or principalities, or powers: all things were created by him, and for him:

And he is before all things, and by him all things consist.

And he is the head of the body, the church: who is the beginning, the firstborn from the dead; that in all things he might have the preeminence. For it pleased the Father that in him should all fulness dwell;" [9]

Consider those phrases. then consider the last verse that tells us "that in him should all fulness dwell. That word 'fulness' πληρωμα refers here to the Divine nature dwelling in the man Christ Jesus.

This includes all the majesty, power and goodness of God.

Since credible witnesses testify all this we can easily believe that Messiah possesses eternal existence.

In the book of Revelation the Apostle John wrote "I am he that liveth, and was dead; and, behold, I am alive for evermore, Amen; and have the keys of hell and of death." [10]

King Jesus not only died for our sins, but He was resurrected to life to assure us that we too shall be resurrected to eternal life.

---

[9] Colossians 1:15-19
[10] Revelation 1:18

He is alive for evermore, and He, and He alone, has the keys of hell and of death.

So what can be said to bring all this together? Those who study the Scriptures in depth soon realize that the sixty-six books are all one book, dictated to forty scribes, by one author. The books of the Old Testament and the New Testament are one book, complimenting each other, and never contradicting the other.

It was prophesied that the Messiah must have eternal existence, and we see this fulfilled in Jesus, the Messiah.

When we celebrate the Advent, the arrival of Messiah, we acknowledge that He is God in the flesh. He is self-existing, and eternal in nature.

There is still great mystery surrounding the God of Israel and the Christian Church. We call Him Jehovah (JHVH), but He has a name unknown to any man. Dare I suggest that His name is so marvelous that if we heard it, and understood its full meaning, we would not be capable of containing that thought while in the flesh?

Perhaps one day, when God calls his children home, He will reveal His name, and at that time reveal to us our "new name." I wonder what my new name will be, since a name should indicate something about the nature or spirit of the individual.

"He that hath an ear, let him hear what the Spirit saith unto the churches; To him that overcometh will I give to eat of the hidden manna, and will give him a white stone, and in the stone a new name written, which no man knoweth saving he that receiveth it." [11]

---

[11] Revelation 2:17

Chapter 8

"Be the Son of God"

The Word of God tells us that the Gospel shall first be preached on the holy hill of Zion, and the kingdom of Christ shall be founded there. From here, the doctrine of the Lord goes out into all the earth. Scripture tells us that the Messiah must be the Son of God. Strange thought, that the Almighty God, the Creator, Preserver and Governor of all things would declare that He has a Son. For many, this is a difficult concept to accept, therefore we need to delve deeper into the Sonship of the Messiah.

Not forgetting the Scriptures recorded in the Old Testament we need to examine the action of the Sanhedrin at Yavneh in 80 CE. The title, Son of God, was used so frequently in the book of Enoch and Esdras, both being rejected by the Jews and Christians, that the term Son of God was also rejected by the Jews.

The Jews now consider Jesus as a "pious" holy man that by divine intervention performs miracles and exorcisms. To deny that Jesus is the Son of God, and relegate Him to this lesser position is to confess their lack of knowledge of Biblical prophecy regarding the Messiah. "Who is a liar but he that denieth that Jesus is the Christ? He is antichrist, that denieth the Father and the Son." [1]

---

[1] 1 John 2:22

"For unto us a child is born, unto us a son is given: and the government shall be upon his shoulder: and his name shall be called Wonderful, Counsellor, The mighty God, The everlasting Father, The Prince of Peace. The Messiah is" the everlasting Father, The mighty God. " [2] To be called the Son of God includes the name given to Messiah Jesus, Emmanuel, God with us." To help us better understand how God could clothe Himself with human flesh He used the term, "son of God. " Mankind could better understand that term, but Scripture clarifies it by making it known that Jesus and God are one. The New Testament is replete with statements offered by credible witnesses.

The more convincing facts are the New Testament accounts of Jesus of Nazareth fulfilling every prophecy regarding the Messiah.

The rejection of the title "Son of God" by the Jews is based on frail arguments that contradict the Old Testament.

Consider the dual title attached to Jesus the Messiah. He is called the Son of God and the son of man. Why would Jesus be given this dual title? The incarnation did not involve a subtraction of deity, but the addition of humanity.

God became a man because sinful humanity needed a "kinsman redeemer" to free us from our sins and bring us back into fellowship with God the Father. (Leviticus 25:25-26; 48, 49; Ruth 3:13)

---

[2] Isaiah 9:6

In Judaism, the term "Son of God" was used of the expected "Jewish Messiah", the anointed king. God never changes, but it would appear that man changes whatever might suit his purposes.

The Son of God means he is God the Son. That makes it understandable, if one accepts the doctrine of the Trinity.

Proverbs is asking, "What is his son's name, if you canst tell?" [3]

A cursory reading of this verse will not divulge the true meaning or intent. Allow me to put it into contemporary language. The author is saying, in essence, "Who has gone up to heaven to learn the science of heaven" Who has come down from heaven to proclaim it?" Could it be that the science of the plan of salvation is part of the science of heaven? I am reminded of Deuteronomy: " For this commandment that I command thee this day, it is not hidden from thee, neither is it far off. It is not in heaven, that thou shouldest say, Who shall go up for us to heaven, and bring it unto us, that we may hear it, and do it? Neither is it beyond the sea, that thou shouldest say, Who shall go over the sea for us, and bring it unto us, that we may hear it, and do it?
 But the word is very nigh unto thee, in thy mouth, and in thy heart, that thou mayest do it." [4]

A quick translation of these verses tells us that the word of God is not too difficult for one to comprehend or obey.

---

[3] Proverbs 30:4
[4] Deuteronomy 30:11-14

The plan of salvation will not be offered in a far off land first, but in Israel. The Old Testament reveals the Messiah will be born in Bethlehem Ephratah (and He was!).

Verse 12 "It is not in heaven" but the Word, the Λογοσ (Logos), the Living Word of God shall be made flesh and live in your midst.

You do not have to travel to distant nations, because salvation through Messiah is for the Jews first. Verse 14: The apostles of Messiah will preach the doctrine of salvation and the promise of redemption will be fulfilled.

No one, except the living Son of God, that is, God the Son, could possibly fulfill all the prophecies, including providing a sacrifice to end all sacrifices.

The New Testament offers us ample proof of fulfillment of prophecy found in the Old Testament.

Turning to the Gospel according to John 1:1, 14; 8:58 we read words from one that was taught by the Messiah for three years. John speaks what he knew from first hand experience. " In the beginning was the Word, and the Word was with God, and the Word was God." [5]

"And the Word was made flesh, and dwelt among us, (and we beheld his glory, the glory as of the only begotten of the Father,) full of grace and truth." [6]

Familiar words, "In the beginning", as we have read it in Genesis 1:1. There God is said to be Elohim, the plural God.

---

[5] John 1:1; John 1:14
[6] John 1:14

We understand that to mean the Triune God, and careful study of Genesis the first chapter will reveal all three Persons of the Godhead referenced.

"Jesus said unto them, Verily, verily, I say unto you, Before Abraham was, I am." Here we find the great I AM statement God made when He spoke with Moses at the burning bush.

I AM who I AM, and Jesus is telling these Jewish rulers that He is the God of all, including Abraham, whom they declare to be their "father." [7]

Ephesians give further light on the Son of God, Jesus the Messiah: "Blessed be the God and Father of our Lord Jesus Christ, who hath blessed us with all spiritual blessings in heavenly places in Christ: According as he hath chosen us in him before the foundation of the world, that we should be holy and without blame before him in love:" [8]

Here Jesus is call the Son of God by saying that God is His Father. He further elaborates on the nature of Jesus the Messiah by saying that He is eternal in nature, because He existed before the foundation of the world. God determined within Himself, before He created this world, that He would come to Earth in the form of man, a man known as Emmanuel, God with us.

Whom but God the Son (the Son of God) could make this statement, and know that it has already been amply proven by reading the Old Testament?

---

[7] John 8:58
[8] Ephesians 1:3 & 4

I will conclude with a few observation of my own, gleaned from personal experience.

The Word of God assures us that if we accept the Son of God as our substitute for sin, dying when we should have lost our life because of sin, we would have absolute assurance. "The Spirit itself beareth witness with our spirit, that we are the children of God:" [9]

I can confess with absolute honesty, as I stand before the Holy Throne of God, that this verse is true in my life. When the world would attempt to cause me to doubt that Jesus is the Son of God, the one who provided eternal salvation for me, I can rely on the truth of this verse.

There are some in the world that still find it difficult to accept the fact that Jesus is the Son of God. That is because they are still what the Word calls the "natural man."

That means they are still in their sin nature, never having been born again by the precious blood of Christ. The New Testament says it best for me, "But the natural man receiveth not the things of the Spirit of God: for they are foolishness unto him: neither can he know them, because they are spiritually discerned." [10]

I have a deep love for the chosen people of God, Israel. My sentiment toward Israel is best recorded in Romans, "Brethren, my heart's desire and prayer to God for Israel is, that they might be saved." [11]

---

[9] Romans 8:16
[10] 1 Corinthians 2:14
[11] Romans 10:1

I might add that not only is it my heart's desire and prayer to God that Israel might be saved by the shed blood of the Son of God, Jesus, but also many others throughout the world that are not Jews. Even in our own country, which was founded on Christian principles, millions have never experienced the witness of God's spirit that they are the children of God.

Becoming the children of God can only be effected by being adopted into His family, and that requires forgiveness of sins by repentance and embracing the salvation made possible by God the Son, Jesus the Messiah.

It is imperative that every born again Christian become a zealous witness to the fact that Jesus Christ is the Son of God (God the Son). We must tell the world about the wonders of His salvation.

Chapter 9

"Have God's Own Name"

We open this chapter with verses from both the Old and New Testaments (Covenants), as this is a key subject regarding the Messiah. There must be no misunderstanding as to who the Messiah is, and the power and glory that is His.

The New Testament witnesses to the fact that Jesus, our Messiah, is God Himself; He has God's name, and God would not share that with any creature. Therefore, God and Jesus must be the same.

"Wherefore God also hath highly exalted him, and given him a name That at the name of Jesus every knee should bow, of things in heaven, and things in earth, and things under the earth; And that every tongue should confess that Jesus Christ is Lord, to the glory of God the Father." [1]

For some individuals, the thought that Messiah Jesus would be prophesied to have God's own name, is a puzzle. Surely, this cannot be fact, because only God is called by God's own name. That is true, and we will now investigate these prophetic Scriptures from the Old Testament to see if that is indeed, what is meant.

We start with Isaiah 9th chapter; the verses indicated Messiah Jesus is to be called "The mighty God" and the "everlasting Father." "For every battle of the warrior is with confused noise, and garments rolled in blood; but this shall be with burning and fuel of fire.

---

[1] Philippians 2:9-11

For unto us a child is born, unto us a son is given: and the government shall be upon his shoulder: and his name shall be called Wonderful, Counsellor, The mighty God, The everlasting Father, The Prince of Peace. Of the increase of his government and peace there shall be no end, upon the throne of David, and upon his kingdom, to order it, and to establish it with judgment and with justice from henceforth even for ever. The zeal of the LORD of hosts will perform this." [2] Now we must go to the Hebrew translation to determine if this means what it appears to declare.

The word mighty God = "the Almighty", and is used only with One who is deity.

Everlasting - perpetuity, eternal

Father - "chief, or principal one"

Going now to Jeremiah we find Jesus called "The Lord".

"Lord" in Hebrew - self-Existent, or eternal.

Perhaps now we are beginning to see that, try as one may, it is indisputable that the Old Testament has declared that the Messiah must have God's own name, because Messiah and God are one in the same. There is only one God, and when He clothed Himself in flesh as a human and came down to Earth, He came as Emmanuel, "God with us."

---

[2] Isaiah 9:5-7

A careful study of the seeming impossible feats that must be accomplished by Messiah should tell us that here is One who is more than mere man. One could say that even a prophet could have done most of the miraculous feats, and that would be true.

However, God made certain that all should know beyond any doubt that Messiah is God in the flesh. The proof is found in the crucifixion, which required a sacrifice that was without spot and blemish. Only God could fill that requirement. Next, the resurrection of Messiah proves his eternal existence.

It is true that others have been resurrected from the dead, such as Lazarus, but these all died again in due time. Only Jesus died and rose from the dead to live eternally. His victory over death assures the true believer in Messiah that they too shall live eternally in His presence.

For those who rely mainly on proof from a Hebrew source I offer the following. In the Targum (translation of part of the Bible in Aramic, a Semetic language dating from about 30 BC): "His name has been called from old, Wonderful Counselor, Mighty God, He who lives forever, the anointed One (Messiah), in whose days peace shall increase upon us."

The Midrash Mishle, S. Buber edition: "The Messiah is called by eight names: Yinnon, Tzemah, Pele ["Miracle"], Yo'etz [Counselor], Mashiah [Messiah], El ["God"], Gibbor ["Hero].

Yinnon requires a longer explanation: "the ideal king, His name shall enure forever, his name shall endure as long as the sun, and men shall bless Him, all nations shall call Him blessed." (Psa 72:17)

The name "Tzemah" means the Hebrew tzemah, the promised "Branch."(Isaiah 11:1). This speaks of the Messiah Jesus.

The New Testament confirms the accuracy of the Old Testament in Philippians, "being in the form of God, thought it not robbery to be equal with God: But made himself of no reputation, and took upon him the form of a servant, and was made in the likeness of men:
And being found in fashion as a man, he humbled himself, and became obedient unto death, even the death of the cross. Wherefore God also hath highly exalted him, and given him a name which is above every name:
That at the name of Jesus every knee should bow, of things in heaven, and things in earth, and things under the earth; And that every tongue should confess that Jesus Christ is Lord, to the glory of God the Father."[3]

The word "Lord" in the last verse speaks of Messiah Jesus as being "supreme", "God" "Eternal". This verifies what the Old Testament has long been telling us, Jesus the Messiah is God in human flesh.

The question arises, should one be offended to hear others refer to Messiah Jesus as being God? The answer is simple, yes, and no. Yes, if they still have not had their spiritual understanding opened by the Holy Spirit, and no, if He has opened their understanding. I come to this conclusion by the Scripture verse found in **Exodus 34:35** where the children of Israel could not look upon the face of Moses because it shone with the glory of the Lord.

---

[3] Philippians 2:6-11

"And it came to pass, when Moses came down from mount Sinai with the two tables of testimony in Moses' hand, when he came down from the mount, that Moses wist not that the skin of his face shone while he talked with him. And when Aaron and all the children of Israel saw Moses, behold, the skin of his face shone; and they were afraid to come nigh him. And till Moses had done speaking with them, he put a vail on his face." [4]

"Seeing then that we have such hope, we use great plainness of speech: And not as Moses, which put a vail over his face, that the children of Israel could not stedfastly look to the end of that which is abolished:

But their minds were blinded: for until this day remaineth the same vail untaken away in the reading of the old testament; which vail is done away in Christ. But even unto this day, when Moses is read, the vail is upon their heart. Nevertheless when it shall turn to the Lord, the vail shall be taken away." [5]

The last verse tells us that when "it" [Israel] shall "turn to the Lord [convert to the Lord God Messiah] the vail shall be removed, cast off, taken away.

In the Psalms we read "Pray for the peace of Jerusalem: they shall prosper that love thee." [6] Peace will not come to Jerusalem until the Prince of Peace, Jesus Messiah returns at the time known as His Second Coming. At that time, Israel will acknowledge Jesus as the true Messiah and Jesus will then restore peace.

---

[4] Exodus 34:29,30 & 33
[5] 2 Corinthians 3:12-16
[6] Psalm 122:6

One last word of encouragement to help some to believe that The Messiah Jesus must have the name of God: From Numbers Rabbah 14: "The honor and majesty with which David tells us (Psalm 104) that God Himself is clothed, He will bestow on the Messiah. As it is said, 'His glory is given in Thy salvation, honor and majesty hast Thou laid upon Him.'

Part of the honor and majesty of God is His name. This God, the Father, has also bestowed on Jesus the Son of God (God the son). There is no doubt to those who have had the vail lifted from their heart that Messiah Must Have God's Own Name.

Chapter 10

"483 Years"

Before we go into this subject in-depth, it will serve us well to read from the book of Daniel. "Seventy weeks are determined upon thy people and upon thy holy city, to finish the transgression, and to make an end of sins, and to make reconciliation for iniquity, and to bring in everlasting righteousness, and to seal up the vision and prophecy, and to anoint the most Holy. Know therefore and understand, that from the going forth of the commandment to restore and to build Jerusalem unto the Messiah the Prince shall be seven weeks, and threescore and two weeks: the street shall be built again, and the wall, even in troublous times.

And after threescore and two weeks shall Messiah be cut off, but not for himself: and the people of the prince that shall come shall destroy the city and the sanctuary; and the end thereof shall be with a flood, and unto the end of the war desolations are determined."[1]

This prophecy was fulfilled, with the exception of the last sentence regarding the "prince that shall come…" , to the exact day, as we shall see in the New Testament account.

Daniel the ninth chapter is the most important prophetic scripture in the Old Testament regarding the end time, beginning with Messiah and giving information up to the time of the Antichrist.

---

[1] Daniel 9:24-26

This is also one of the most misunderstood, if not neglected portions of scripture in the Old Testament.

The account of the burning of Jerusalem is found in II Kings

"And in the fifth month, on the seventh day of the month, which is the nineteenth year of king Nebuchadnezzar king of Babylon, came Nebuzaradan, captain of the guard, a servant of the king of Babylon, unto Jerusalem: And he burnt the house of the LORD, and the king's house, and all the houses of Jerusalem, and every great man's house burnt he with fire." [2]

Ezekiel prophesied that Zedekiah would go to Babylon, but he would not see it: "My net also will I spread upon him, and he shall be taken in my snare: and I will bring him to Babylon to the land of the Chaldeans; yet shall he not see it, though he shall die there." [3] In 2 Kings is an account of how Zedekiah could go to Babylon and yet not see it "And they slew the sons of Zedekiah before his eyes, and put out the eyes of Zedekiah, and bound him with fetters of brass, and carried him to Babylon." [4]

Zedekiah, the king of Jerusalem, watched in horror as his sons were slain before his eyes, then Nebuchadnezzar's soldier put out his eyes; the last thing he ever saw was the death of his sons.

Jerusalem was then burned to the ground, including the Temple.

---

[2] 2 Kings 25:8,9
[3] Ezekiel 12:13
[4] 2 Kings 25:7

Our topic is that the Messiah must come at a precise time after the walls of Jerusalem are restored.

It is necessary to understand the "week/year" concept of prophecy before this portion of scripture opens itself to our understanding.

A "week" is seven years, therefore seventy weeks x 7 days = 490 years.

The Jews were captives in Babylon after Nebuchadnezzar captured Jerusalem and brought the Jews to Babylon as slaves. The Prophet Jeremiah had prophesied they would be in captivity for 70 years. "And it shall come to pass, when seventy years are accomplished, that I will punish the king of Babylon, and that nation, saith the LORD, for their iniquity, and the land of the Chaldeans, and will make it perpetual desolations."[5] This relates to their disobedience to the command of God that every seven years the ground must not be planted, it must rest because God has declared this a Sabbath year for the land.

The Jews ignored this for seventy years, and thus the decree from God.

Nehemiah was the cupbearer for Artexerxes and after praying to God for good reception from the King, he asked permission to go to Jerusalem to begin the rebuilding of the city. The king agreed and gave him a letter and an escort of soldiers for safety.

The repairs were started, but Sanballat became distressed with their building project and it became necessary for the workers to keep their weapons with them.

---

[5] Jeremiah 25:12

The work became difficult because of impending danger, but this was a fulfillment of prophecy. The Jews completed the building of the walls and put in place the large doors of the wall.

The prophecy of Daniel tells us that it would take 7 weeks of 7 years, or 49 years for Ezra and Nehemiah to restore Jerusalem. From that day, there would be 62 weeks of 7 years until Messiah should come. This would indicate 62 x 7 = 434 years, and then Messiah will be killed ("cut off").

This date will correspond with the time when Herod was king in Jerusalem, appointed by the Roman government. "Now when Jesus was born in Bethlehem of Judea in the days of Herod the king, behold, there came wise men from the east to Jerusalem:

"Then Herod, when he saw that he was mocked of the wise men, was exceeding wroth, and sent forth, and slew all the children that were in Bethlehem, and in all the coasts thereof, from two years old and under, according to the time which he had diligently enquired of the wise men." [6]

"Now in the fifteenth year of the reign of Tiberius Caesar, Pontius Pilate being governor of Judea, and Herod being tetrarch of Galilee, and his brother Philip tetrarch of Ituraea and of the region of Trachonitis, and Lysanias the tetrarch of Abilene, And Jesus himself began to be about thirty years of age, being (as was supposed) the son of Joseph, which was the son of Heli," [7]

---

[6] Matthew 2:16
[7] Luke 3:1& 23

The next date given is after Messiah there will be a period of 1 week (7 years), which is the time of the antichrist and the time of Jacob's Troubles (the Tribulation period).

Add these together: 49 + 434 + 7 = 490 years, or 70 weeks (70 x 7 = 490) as prophesied by Daniel.

An interesting fact is that if we add the 49 years to build the city of Jerusalem to the 434 years until the Messiah is killed we have 483 years. Multiply that by the 360 days of the Babylonian calendar to arrive at 173,880 days.

King Jesus rode into Jerusalem on that first Palm Sunday in order to make Himself available to His enemies, knowing they would find Him guilty of false charges and on that exact day He would be crucified.

He died on the cross of Calvary on a Passover Friday, which we call "Good Friday", exactly 173,880 days as predicted.

At the same time as the "Lamb that was crucified from the foundation of the world" was being offered up as our "Passover Lamb" the Jews in the Temple were sacrificing the lambs for Passover.

No man could ever contrive to be born at the right time, in the right place, and fulfill all the miracles prophesied for Messiah, except the Son of God.

The fulfillment of Daniel the 9th chapter should give all that read it the confidence that Jesus is the promised Messiah of Scriptures.

For those who have difficulty believing that Jesus, born in Bethlehem of Judah, is the Messiah, I suggest you read this chapter again. This is one of the more powerful miracles proving Jesus is the Messiah.

Chapter 11

"Born of a Virgin"

Perhaps the most controversial issue surrounding the Messiah Jesus is that of the "virgin birth." Those who chose not to believe in the virgin birth must, by default, also not believe in the Omnipotent God. There is nothing too hard for God to perform. He who could create the Universe certainly has the ability to produce a virgin birth if He should so choose.

Since God, not man, is the authority whom we should believe, we turn to His written Word, about the Living Word, Jesus.

"And he said, Hear ye now, O house of David; Is it a small thing for you to weary men, but will ye weary my God also? Therefore the Lord himself shall give you a sign; Behold, a virgin shall conceive, and bear a son, and shall call his name Immanuel." [1]

The New Testament gives the account of the birth of Jesus, emphasizing the virgin birth.
"Now the birth of Jesus Christ was on this wise: When as his mother Mary was espoused to Joseph, before they came together, she was found with child of the Holy Ghost. Then Joseph her husband, being a just man, and not willing to make her a publick example, was minded to put her away privily.

---

[1] Isaiah 7:13, 14

But while he thought on these things, behold, the angel of the LORD appeared unto him in a dream, saying, Joseph, thou son of David, fear not to take unto thee Mary thy wife: for that which is conceived in her is of the Holy Ghost. And she shall bring forth a son, and thou shalt call his name JESUS: for he shall save his people from their sins. Now all this was done, that it might be fulfilled which was spoken of the Lord by the prophet, saying, Behold, a virgin shall be with child, and shall bring forth a son, and they shall call his name Emmanuel, which being interpreted is, God with us. Then Joseph being raised from sleep did as the angel of the Lord had bidden him, and took unto him his wife: And knew her not till she had brought forth her firstborn son: and he called his name JESUS." [2]

We need to realize that even faux (imitation), or pseudo (not authentic in spite of appearance) virgin births always produce a female, never a male embryo. Parthenogenesis, (Reproduction without fertilization: a form of reproduction, especially in plants, insects, and arthropods, in which a female gamete develops into a new individual without fertilization by a male gamete.") or virgin birth is an asexual form of reproduction found in females where growth and development of embryos occur without fertilization of a male. Usually found in fish, frogs, insects, lizards, but by default it does not occur in mammals such as humans.

---

[2] Matthew 1:18-25

Parthenogenesis in humans never produces viable embryos, though, because unfertilized eggs lack specific instructions about gene expression from a sperm. Therefore, if there is no sperm, certain genes will be over expressed, and the "embryo" will die when it is only about five days old.

Eclampsia is an illness during pregnancy: an illness that sometimes occurs during the later stages of pregnancy and involves high blood pressure and convulsions, sometimes followed by a coma.

Treatment of Eclampsia, involves controlling the blood pressure and delivering the fetus.

Scientists have tried to refute the legitimacy of the virgin birth by way of in vitro fertilization, embryonic transfer, and artificial insemination. However, none of these qualifies for a true Pathenogenesis because fertilization is present it is only artificially induced.

If we find it no problem to believe that angels appeared to man, in various situations, in the Old Testament then it should not shatter our belief system if one appeared during the time of the Law, before the New Testament. The New Testament does record the virgin birth, but until the Christ child was born, Israel was still under Law, not Grace.

In Matthew, we read that Joseph planned a quiet divorce, thus ending their engagement. "Then Joseph her husband, being a just man, and not willing to make her a publick example, was minded to put her away privily.

But while he thought on these things, behold, the angel of the LORD appeared unto him in a dream, saying, Joseph, thou son of David, fear not to take unto thee Mary thy wife: for that which is conceived in her is of the Holy Ghost." [3] Joseph had certainly read Isaiah, but at this time in his life he did not realize the prophecy was about to be fulfilled in Mary.

"Therefore the Lord himself shall give you a sign; Behold, a virgin

shall conceive, and bear a son, and shall call his name Immanuel." [4]

An espoused couple was not permitted to be in the same room alone until after the marriage ceremony. Therefore, it is impossible that Joseph was the paternal father of Jesus.

This chapter in Matthew confirms that Joseph and Mary had not been alone during their engagement period, or Joseph would never have suspected that Mary had been unfaithful to him.

It took an angel to convince Joseph that Mary would indeed have the Christ child, and that the father would be none other than God.

It was explained to Joseph that God the Holy Spirit, would implant a holy seed in the womb of Mary, and that fertilizing seed would produce a child that would be truly and properly God, and truly and properly man.

Jesus existed before creation, because He is the Triune God. That fertilizing seed, that living spirit implanted in Mary's womb was none other than the second person of the Trinity, Jesus the Messiah.

---

[3] Matthew 1:19,20; [4] Isaiah 7:14

Later chapters will verify and prove that there is only one God, however, that one God is Triune in His nature; He is God the Father, God the Son, and God the Holy Spirit.

In the events of the virgin birth, the entire Trinity was involved.

Is it any wonder that Isaiah proclaimed that the Messiah would be called "Immanuel", God with us?

I sometime wonder what it will take unbelieving humanity to realize that what God says God means. God said it very straight forth in Isaiah 7:14.

Since no other child has been born that fills this requirement it is only logical to accept the fact that Jesus is the Messiah.

Add to all this the fact that in 70 AD God allowed the Temple in Jerusalem to be completely destroyed with fire, along with all the genealogical records of the Jews, and we have further proof that Messiah had to be born before 70 AD.

A second reason for the complete destruction of the Temple was to proclaim that animal sacrifice was now ended, and that the perfect sacrifice had been born, crucified and resurrected according to ancient prophecies.

God foreordained that the sacrifice of animals would be a sign of the supreme sacrifice to end all sacrifices.

It is well said in Hebrews "But in those sacrifices there is a remembrance again made of sins every year. For it is not possible that the blood of bulls and of goats should take away sins.

Wherefore when he cometh into the world, he saith, Sacrifice and offering thou wouldest not, but a body hast thou prepared me: In burnt offerings and sacrifices for sin thou hast had no pleasure." [5]

The Messiah Jesus proclaimed to the nation of Israel that God would no longer accept animal sacrifices for their sins, but would only accept the sacrifice He had prepared before the foundation of the world. "But a body hast thou prepare me!" Jesus would be that sacrifice, no other would be acceptable.

Had the Messiah not been of virgin birth, He would have inherited the sin principle and therefore could die only for His own sin. "The wages of sin is death."

Messiah had a virgin birth, with God being the Father and Mary being only a human vessel to nurture the embryo.

Jesus was born sinless, and even though tempted, as would any human, He never sinned. The sin principle was transmitted through the male, not the female. Mary was but a holy vessel chose by God to bear the sinless Son of God.

The virgin birth of the Messiah Jesus is proof sufficient for those with a logical mind, and a spirit that is truly seeking the truth.

---

[5] Hebrews 10:3-6

Chapter 12

"Born in Bethlehem in Judea"

The Scriptures of the Old and New Testament will give us important facts relating to the birth of the Messiah. There is much background information that is often overlooked when the Scriptures are being examined. Leaving out just one word, or phrase, can change the meaning of what God is attempting to give us. Consider the verse found in Micah, "But thou, Bethlehem Ephratah, though thou be little among the thousands of Judah, yet out of thee shall he come forth unto me that is to be ruler in Israel; whose goings forth have been from of old, from everlasting." [1]

Bethlehem, not Ephratah, is located north of Jerusalem, near Nazareth in the territory of Zebulun. It is southwest of the Sea of Galilee.

Bethlehem Ephratah is first mentioned as the place where Rachael died (Genesis 35:19, 20) as they were traveling from Bethel to Ephrath. She went into labor, gave birth to Benjamin, and died during childbirth. She was buried in Bethlehem and her tomb is still there today.

It was no accident of historical events that a census was declared for all Jews. The males were all to go back to their place of birth and register for the census. It was also no accident that God chose Joseph, a man from Bethlehem, to marry the chosen woman to give birth to the Messiah.

---

[1] Micah 5:2

Bethlehem became the scene of a great slaughter of the innocents" (Mattiyahu 2:16-18).

Bethlehem in Zebulun is now in ruin, located about six miles NW of Nazareth. It is mentioned only once in the Scriptures, Joshua 19:15.

In the book of Judges, we read of a Levite from Bethlehem Ephrath as he went to mount Ephraim to find a ministry for himself. (Judges 17:7-13).

His concubine was also from there (Judges 19:1). We also read of the tragic end of these two in Gibeon in the territory of Benjamin.

The Levite's concubine had left him to take up prostitution.

He went looking for her and when he found her, they began traveling toward their birth home of Bethlehem.

The Levite and his concubine were traveling homeward, passing by Jerusalem, which was then not a part of Israel. The concubine did not want to spend the night there among "strangers" and they continued their journey. They came to Gibeah in the tribe of Benjamin and no one invited them into their home for the night. Finally, an elderly man invited them to spend the night with him. They were eating and having good fellowship when "men of Belial" pounded on the door demanding to be given the Levite for sex. The man refused, but offered his own daughter, or the Levites concubine. They took the concubine and sexually assaulted her all night.

The next morning we read "And her lord rose up in the morning, and opened the doors of the house, and went out to go his way: and, behold, the woman his concubine was fallen down at the door of the house, and her hands were upon the threshold." [2]

The concubine was dead, and the Levite cut her in pieces, sending a piece to each of the tribes of Israel, other than Benjamin. The matter was explained and the Israelites came against Benjamin, but inquired of God if they should go against their brother. God gave them permission and they won the victory.

The town was founded by Judah (1 Chronicles 2:50-51, 56 and 4:4). It has different spellings in some parts of Scripture because Hur, Salma, changed the sound and spelling to honor his mother.

Ephrath/Ephratah has a double meaning: "fruitfulness" and "double fruit."

In the book of Judges the 12th chapter, we read that the Gileadites defeated Ephraimites at the river Jordan.

They had gone to war because Jephthath and the Gileadites became jealous that the Ephraimites might become too powerful.

Jephthah, the Gileadite was a mighty warrior and was the son of a harlot. Gilead married a wife who bore him sons.

His sons expelled Jephthah because he was the son of a harlot and did not want him to share in the heritage of their father. He went to Tob and gathered some worthless men around him as an army.

---

[2] Judges 19:27

When Ammon made war against Israel, the Elders of Gilead went to find Jephthah to ask his assistance. He protested because they had expelled him but finally agreed when they promised to make him their chief.

The Ammonites went to war against Israel because God had given Israel their land when they entered Canaan. The Ammonites refused to allow the Jews to cross their land, so God gave the land to the Jews. Now, the Ammonites want that land back; war resulted.

Jephthah was victorious, but before the battle he promised the Lord if he was victorious the first person to come through the door of his house, upon his return, would be offered to God as a burnt offering.

His only child, a daughter, came out first and it greatly grieved him because he could not take back his vow.

His daughter made only one request, allow her two months to go down the mountain with her female companions to weep and bemoan her virginity.

It became a custom in Israel to go yearly for four days to honor Jephthah's daughter.

Now, back to the battle between the Gileadites and the men of Ephraim. The Gileadites defeated the Ephraimites at the river Jordan. Sentries were stationed along the Jordan with a password to determine if the soldier was a true Gileadite. The word was Shibboleth.

Shibboleth means a stream, as flowing, and also an ear or grain (branch) of corn. It means the same when pronounced Sibboleth by the Gibeonites.

The only difference between Shibboleth and Sibboleth is the samech is used instead of the sheen, because the Gibeonites could not pronounce the "h" sound.

A man attempted to cross, misprinted the password, and was killed by the river Jordan.

This is the "secret" Masonic word used in the "Blue Lodge" to determine if the one requesting permission to attend the Lodge meeting is a true Master Mason.

The people of Bethlehem Ephratah became identified as Ephraimite people and Bethlehem is left off the list of cities belonging to Judah.

First, know that the people of Bethlehem carry the genes of and belong to the tribes of both Judah and Ephraim, but their identity is more strongly aligned with Ephraim than with Judah.

The leading men clearly trace their heritage through the tribe of Judah but there had to be a dominant genetic contribution from the women of the tribe of Ephraim in order for the people of Bethlehem to be called Ephraimites.

The New Testament verifies that Jesus of Nazareth was actually born in Bethlehem of Judah:

"Now when Jesus was born in Bethlehem of Judea in the days of Herod the king, behold, there came wise men from the east to Jerusalem," [3]

And again we read in Luke "And Joseph also went up from Galilee, out of the city of Nazareth, into Judea, unto the city of David, which is called Bethlehem; (because he was of the house and lineage of David:) To be taxed with Mary his espoused wife, being great with child.

---

[3] Matthew 2:1

And so it was, that, while they were there, the days were accomplished that she should be delivered And she brought forth her firstborn son, and wrapped him in swaddling clothes, and laid him in a manger; because there was no room for them in the inn." [4]

A short story will help to understand how the people of Bethlehem could also identify with the Ephraimites.

Consider the story of Jim Plunkett. Plunkett is an Irish name, but Jim, who won the Heissman Trophy in 1970, played quarter back for fifteen years in the NFL, and twice won the Super Bowl with the Raiders is nearly ninety percent Mexican-American.

Jim was born in Northern California in 1947 to Mexican-American parents, both of whom were blind. His Irish great-grandfather had married a Mexican-American woman and gave his surname to her son who was fifty percent Mexican-American and fifty percent Irish. His son married a Mexican-American woman and gave their son the Irish name William Plunkett, although he was seventy five percent Mexican-American. William married a Mexican-American woman named Carmilla who gave birth to Jim, which brings Jim's Mexican-American heritage to eighty-seven and five tenths percent. Although Irish genes have been greatly depleted by the repeated pairing with Mexican-American women, the Irish heritage is easily traceable.

---

[4] Luke 2:4-7

Despite the clear Irish name and lineage, Jim identifies himself as a Chicano because of his dominant genetic Mexican-American make-up, while he rightly carries an Irish name, he is Mexican-American much more than he is Irish-American.

Thus, we understand how the people of Bethlehem can belong to both Judah and Ephraim, yet be more strongly aligned with Ephraim than with Judah.

The Scripture is correct which says that Bethlehem Ephrath is not little, because out of it would come the Messiah.

This prophecy has been faithfully fulfilled, Jesus the Messiah was born here against all odds, since Mary and Joseph lived in Nazareth.

Chapter 13
"Adored By Great Persons"

Strange as it may seem, the Messiah, who was prophesied to be despised and rejected of men [1] should also be adored by great persons. "The kings of Tarshish and of the isles shall bring presents: the kings of Sheba and Seba shall offer gifts. Yea, all kings shall fall down before him: all nations shall serve him.' [2]

We have accurate accounts of "Wise Men" coming from the East of Israel to worship the Messiah Jesus shortly after His birth. [3] These wise men were likely from the nation we know today as being Iran.

The account of the three Wise Men is difficult to elaborate with any certain facts. The thought that the three gifts prove the appearance of three wise men is without merit and is not scriptural. The number of gifts presented assumes there were three Wise Men.

The truth is that there may have been less than three, or a caravan of Magi numbering more than three. We can only take what appears to be a possible application to this event, and I do not present this as necessarily authentic.

The word 'Magi' is a Latinization of the plural Greek word magos (μαηοσ pl. μαηοι) itself from Old Persia magus. The term refers to the priestly cast of Zorastrianism.

---

[1] Isaiah 53:3
[2] Psalm 72:10, 11
[3] Matthew 2:1-11

As part of their religion, these priests paid particular attention to the stars, and gained an international reputation for astrology, which was at that time highly regarded as a science. Their religious practices and use of astrology caused derivations of the term Magi to be applied to the occult in general and led to the English term magic. The word 'Wise Men' (KJV) is also given as sorcerer and sorcery when describing 'Elymas the sorcerer' in Acts 13:16. The Greek in this verse is μαγοσ and translated: of foreign origin; a Magian, that is Oriental scientist; by implication a magician: a wise man. The same word is used in Acts 8:9-13 where the account of Simon Magus, considered a heretic by the early church is given. He is said to practice sorcery - μαγευω : to practice magic - use sorcery.

Tradition gives names to these "three" Wise Men: Caspar, Melchior, and Balthasar. These names were taken from sixth century Greek manuscripts in Alexandria.

The Persians (Iranians) give the following Persian names: Larvandad, Gushrasaph, and Hormisdas. Each name has a meaning, but upon researching these, I found the meanings to be uninteresting.

It is supposed that these Wise Men came from Persia, or even Yemen. This is based on traditions from the Jews that the Makrebs or kings of Yemen were Jews, a view held by John Chrysostom, and Byzantine art generally depict them in Persian dress. Persia had the largest number of Magi.

As usual, the Roman church with the tradition of these three wise men must make money. In the 11th century, bones of three individuals were found in the Holy Land and proclaimed to those of the three wise men. There were sufficient skeletal bones if placed in proper order would form three individuals. However, these became too important to disturb. The bones were shipped to Cologne, Germany, each in his own ship, and supposedly were buried there. From this came the Christmas song "I Saw Three Ship Asailing."

A shrine was erected, and later a Cathedral was constructed, taking 632 years to complete. The three sets of bones were supposedly placed in three separate gold-layered sarcophagus having elaborate gold sculptures of the prophets, apostles, and scenes from the life of Christ.

This shrine was completed in 1225.

These three wise men traveled much after their death. The relics originally were situated at Constantinople. They were brought to Milan by Eustorgius I, the city's bishop in 344. The Holy Roman Emperor Frederick Barbarosso took the bones from Milan and presented these to the archbishop of Cologne, Rainald of Dasssel in 1164.

The disturbing facts of all this is the description of the bones. They do not appear to be what one would consider being those of learned, "Wise Men." One set of bones was of an early youth, the next an early manhood, and the last a rather aged individual.

In the novel *Baudalino* (2000), Umberto Eco describes the relics as an elaborate hoax.

We will find our best information in the New Testament. Eyewitnesses gave these recorded events, and no definite description is available concerning the "Wise Men." What they gave as gifts is more important than who they were. It does appear likely that they came from ancient Persia, known today as Iran.

There are six notable points that need consideration to help us understand the magnitude of this visit, and to ascertain what true facts we might glean from these.

1) The Wise Men came from the east (no country mentioned) to Jerusalem, saying "Where is he that is born King of the Jews?"

It would appear that they were the first to refer to Jesus as the "King of the Jews." We see this title again as the Roman Soldiers nailed a board at the top of the crucifixion cross stating that this is the King of the Jews.

2) They told King Herod [We] "are come to worship him." They would be well known in their own country since they were learned and rich men. They now wish to worship the Christ child.

3) It is obvious they knew the prophetic Scriptures of the Old Testament. They said "Where is he that is born King of the Jews?" They must have known that the Messiah would be known also as 'the King of the Jews.'

4) The star was a guide, and they first saw this star when they were in the east. This suggests that perhaps the supposition that they were astronomers, as well as magicians. The star appears to have moved before them as they traveled from the east toward Jerusalem.

5) Once, in Jerusalem the star rested above a house in Bethlehem where Mary, Joseph and Jesus resided.

Joseph had extended family in Bethlehem and it is more than likely that he arranged with his family to reside with them for a period.

Since there was a census happening in Bethlehem, it is also likely that the eastern custom of inviting strangers into ones home would have made it impossible for Joseph to immediately find room with his family for the birth of Jesus.

When they found the home in which Jesus rested they fell down in eastern fashion to properly worship and honor King Jesus.

6) Their treasures were usual for presenting to a king.   We see symbolisms in the gifts that the Wise Men likely did not.

   a) Gold -This is an item of great value appropriate for a king. It likely became very useful to Mary and Joseph when they had to flee to Egypt to save the life of Jesus. Many traditions about the use of the gold have sometime surface, but none with any credibility. One tradition says that the gold was entrusted to Judas who kept it for himself. Another story tells of two thieves were crucified, one on either side of Him. These two reportedly stole the gold from Joseph and Mary.   Stories, such as this, do not bear repeating as being valid.

   b) Frankincense is an aromatic resin: an aromatic gum or resin used as incense, especially in religious ceremonies, and in perfumes. It is obtained from trees of the genus Boswellia, native to Africa.

This gift would relate to His priesthood, since it was placed in the censers, a container used for burning incense, especially one that is swung in the Temple representing the prayers of the priests and people.

c) Myrrh - aromatic resin: an aromatic resinous gum obtained from various trees and bushes that are native to Africa and southern Asia. Use: in perfume, incense, and medicinal preparations.

The Jews used Myrrh for burial embalming. Nicodemus provided seventy-five pounds of Myrrh for the burial of Jesus.

We can say little about these Wise Men, since the Scriptures focus on Jesus. It is important that we too focus on Jesus this Christmas rather than the "three Wise Men."

In chapter forty-five we will discover that another great person, Joseph of Arimathaea, obviously respected Jesus. His gift to Jesus was one that would come only from one who had adoration for Him.

While it is not possible to be proven as scriptural, we recognize numerous great persons of our day that truly adore Jesus. One notable personage was James Cash Penney co-founder of JCPenney Stores, Inc. Mr. Penney was known for his more than generous tithing to the Christian church. Other notables include Sir Cliff Richards, Joan of Arc, Janet Lynn (Olympic skater), Della Reese, Roy Rogers and Dale Evans, Mary Lou Retton, Fred Rogers (Mr. Rogers Show) to name but a few. Great persons are still seeking, and finding Jesus.

I insert the Christmas Song "I Saw Three Ships Asailing" only as a reminder that it was inspired by the wise men coming to Jesus. It would appear that the inspiration only produced a song, and certainly not one that has any accuracy of content.

"I Saw Three Ships Asailing"
(Author Unknown)

I saw three ships come sailing in
On Christmas Day, on Christmas Day;
I saw three ships come sailing in
On Christmas Day in the morning.

And what was in those ships all three,
On Christmas Day, on Christmas Day?
And what was in those ships all three,
On Christmas Day in the morning?

The Virgin Mary and Christ were there,
On Christmas Day, on Christmas Day;
The Virgin Mary and Christ were there,
On Christmas Day in the morning.

Pray, wither sailed those ships all three,
On Christmas Day, on Christmas Day;
Pray, wither sailed those ships all three,
On Christmas Day in the morning?

O they sailed into Bethlehem,
On Christmas Day, on Christmas Day;
O they sailed into Bethlehem,
On Christmas Day in the morning.

And all the bells on earth shall ring,
On Christmas Day, on Christmas Day;
And all the bells on earth shall ring,
On Christmas Day in the morning.

And all the Angels in Heaven shall sing,
On Christmas Day, on Christmas Day;
And all the Angels in Heaven shall sing,
On Christmas Day in the morning.

And all the souls on earth shall sing,
On Christmas Day, on Christmas Day;
And all the souls on earth shall sing,
On Christmas Day in the morning.

Then let us all rejoice again,
On Christmas Day, on Christmas Day;
Then let us all rejoice again,
On Christmas Day in the morning.

Notice that this "Christmas song" does not mention the three Wise Men. It is supposed this song was inspired by the Wise Men, but it only mentions Jesus and Mary, no mention of Joseph. Also, it speaks of "sailing" to Bethlehem, which can only be justified if they were on "ships of the desert" which we know as camels. This too is not Scriptural, as Mary rode to Bethlehem on a donkey while still pregnant. Jesus was not born during this journey. Therefore, the song makes little sense.

Chapter 14

"Have One Who Would Announce Him"

There are many important declarations made in the Old Testament that requires our attention, and the New Testament records the fulfillment of these Old Testament prophecies. The prophet Isaiah said "The voice of him that crieth in the wilderness, Prepare ye the way of the LORD, make straight in the desert a highway for our God. Every valley shall be exalted, and every mountain and hill shall be made low: and the crooked shall be made straight, and the rough places plain: And the glory of the LORD shall be revealed, and all flesh shall see it together: for the mouth of the LORD hath spoken it." [1] The prophet Malachi added his voice to this truth,

"Behold, I will send my messenger, and he shall prepare the way before me: and the LORD, whom ye seek, shall suddenly come to his temple, even the messenger of the covenant, whom ye delight in: behold, he shall come, saith the LORD of hosts"[2]

For those who will accept the truth of Scripture this is an exciting prophetic fulfillment. For those rejecting the fulfillment of the prophecies, this becomes their eternal downfall

---

[1] Isaiah 40:3-5
[2] Malachi 3:1

It was told to Zacharias, the father of John the Baptist that his barren wife would conceive and bear a child. [3] He must name the child John, even though it was not a name in their family tree. It was Jewish custom to name a child after someone within the family, such as an ancestor. Zacharias would be struck dumb until the day he wrote that "his name shall be John." for Elisabeth his wife to see. [4]

In the next chapter, Mary, the soon to be earthly mother of the Messiah went to visit her cousin Elisabeth. Mary came into the presence of Elisabeth, and as she entered, John lept in the womb of Elisabeth. Elisabeth was then made aware that Mary was the chosen virgin to give birth to Emmanuel, God with us.

The only assignment given to John, as he grew into manhood, was to "Prepare the way of the Lord."

This refers to an ancient custom of sending men before a king to make the highway passable as the King made his way to his destination. The Roman Officers would appoint a superintendent to prepare the way; the Latin called him the stratores. These were military men of a chosen body of soldiers who would explore the country to determine the proper marching route. Rocks would be cleared, bumps and craters leveled. John was to prepare the Jewish people for the coming of Messiah, no easy task.

John the Baptist came proclaiming in a loud voice for the people to be ready for the appearance of their long awaited Messiah. Malachi 3:1 said to the Jews, "whom ye seek."

---

[3] Luke 1:5-22
[4] Luke 1:63

The Jewish Church was comparable to a barren desert full of obstacles in the path of the Messiah as He journeyed to Israel. The preparations for opening up the passes to allow Him in, John called "repentance."

The words "the glory of the LORD" [salvation of the LORD] has been omitted from ancient Hebrew text prior to the Chaldee, Syriac, and Vulgate versions.

The entire sentence is missing in the older manuscripts; however, the verse is abrupt without it.

John was intent on making a highway ready for the Lord, but also for the Jews. A reference to this highway is found in "And an highway shall be there, and a way, and it shall be called The way of holiness; the unclean shall not pass over it; but it shall be for those: the wayfaring men, though fools, shall not err therein." [5]

This highway would be made available by the coming Messiah, Jesus.

2 Timothy speaks of the "righteous" judge. "Henceforth there is laid up for me a crown of righteousness, which the Lord, the righteous judge, shall give me at that day: and not to me only, but unto all them also that love his appearing" [6] We know from other Scriptures that Messiah is that righteous judge, the one being proclaimed by John the Baptist.

Isaiah continues on to prophecy that all flesh will see Messiah. In the days of His ministry on earth all flesh (Jewish) will see Him.

---

[5] Isaiah 35:8
[6] 2 Timothy 4:8

Jesus ministered to the people of Israel, mingling with them, revealing the meaning of Scriptures, etc. At His Second Coming the entire population of Planet Earth will see Him.

Some may miss the term "the glory of the LORD." This term is repeatedly used in the Exodus account when the Jews were wandering in the wilderness. We have learned through prophecy that "the glory of the LORD" as used in Genesis is a theophany, an appearance of Jesus in the Old Testament.

It was said in Malachi 3 that He would come suddenly to His Temple. Jesus entered the Temple, quite unexpectedly and drove out the moneychangers because they were making the house of prayer a den of thieves. Jesus fulfilled this prophecy more than two thousand years ago.

Malachi also refers to Jesus as the "messenger of the covenant." This refers to the covenant made with Abraham and others of his descendants. Ultimately this covenant became valid for the Israelites.

John the Baptist did not leave the Jews wondering who he was, or where he derived his authority. In Matthew 3 he plainly connects himself to the prophecy of the one who would announce Messiah's arrival. John told the people to make straight His path by way of repenting of their sins. Instead, the Jews added to their sins by not heeding the message of John. We see no outcry of protest when Herod had John beheaded for revealing the fact that he was in sin for taking his brother's wife, while his brother was still alive. The Jews remained silent at the death of John, and made much noise of approval at the crucifixion of Jesus.

Jesus spoke words of encouragement to believers by referencing John the Baptist in Matthew "Verily I say unto you, Among them that are born of women there hath not risen a greater than John the Baptist: notwithstanding he that is least in the kingdom of heaven is greater than he." [7]

This was not meant to diminish the worth of John the Baptist, but only to point out that John belonged to the era of the Old Testament, and not to the New Testament.

The old covenant was replaced at that time by the new covenant that offered eternal life, something the old covenant could not do.

John preached repentance to the Jews to prepare them for the advent of Messiah. Their repentance was not only for breaking the Law, but their total disregard for the truth of the Torah and the prophets.

The highway for Messiah was indeed filled with obstacles, and John the "harbinger" did as God instructed him, but John could not soften the stony hearts of the Jews.

Jesus met with multiple obstacles, but He navigated through Judaism without malice, deceit, or any sin.

At the end of His ministry Jesus provided for the world the sacrifice to end all sacrifices by becoming the Paschal lamb on that Passover Friday, which Christians refer to as Good Friday.

---

[7] Matthew 11:11

John the Baptist's entire life was a time of preparation for being the one who would announce the appearance of Messiah.

"And it came to pass, that, when Elisabeth heard the salutation of Mary, the babe leaped in her womb; and Elisabeth was filled with the Holy Ghost." [8]

The Holy Ghost while still in his mother's womb controlled John and He remained with John as he prepared himself for the mission before him. John lived a solitary life, devoted to discipline and without doubt searching the Scriptures regarding Messiah. By the time Messiah was born John would have known who He was and prepared himself even further.

Waiting the time when Jesus would start his earthly ministry John would have given himself to much prayer and meditation regarding the events that would encompass the life of Jesus.

John's life would not only have been a life of lonely sacrifice, but must have also been a life of weeping over the sins of Israel. This would include the time before Jesus arrived, and the events he knew would unfold at the end of the earthly life of Jesus.

Consider what Jesus said of John the Baptist. "Among them that are born of women there hath not risen a greater than John the Baptist."

Consider the works of great prophets such as Isaiah, Jeremiah, Ezekiel, Daniel, Hosea, Joel, Amos, Micah, and their beloved King David. John the Baptist was considered by Jesus as being greater than any of these.

---

[8] Luke 1:41

That is amazing, then, to know that those who put their faith in the Messiah Jesus are greater than John the Baptist.

How can that be, some may ask? Because John had periodic inspiration from the Holy Spirit, but the born again believers are filled with the Holy Spirit and are inspired by Him moment by moment to do His work and His will.

Also, John represented the Old Covenant while the Christian represents the New Covenant. The Law could only bring condemnation and death, while the Gospel provided life eternal. The born again Christian is filled with the Holy Spirit of God and moves at the impulse of His love. The Holy Spirit performs millions of great works in God's people daily as a result of the day of Pentecost when God gave the Holy Spirit to the Church.

We not only call people to "repentance", a 180 degree turn about from their sinful lives, but we introduce them to Jesus the Messiah who in turn forgives them of their sins, justifies all past sins, gives new life to their dead spiritual lives and God the Father adopts them as His children. They are now citizens of Heaven, residents of God's holy Kingdom.

As we celebrate Christmas each year we need to remember that John did what he could to call the people to repent of their sins.

He gave his life for the message he was inspired to preach. We have an even greater message because we know God's wonderful plan of salvation for mankind. To withhold such a message of life and death would be criminal. To proclaim this message is sheer joy.

There is no doubt that Messiah was prophesied to be preceded by one who would announce him. Let's follow in his steps and take up the message

Chapter 15

"Anointed With the Spirit of God"

We look to the Old Testament at the beginning
of this chapter to formulate a fact of great
importance regarding the Messiah Jesus. We find
that as the Messiah, Jesus would have the spirit of
the Lord rest upon Him and not only that, but also
wisdom, understanding, the spirit of counsel and
might, and the spirit of knowledge and of the fear
of the Lord. That is a considerable resume, but as
we delve deeper into the life of Messiah we shall
see each of these qualities in action. Isaiah wrote
"And there shall come forth a rod out of the stem
of Jesse, and a Branch shall grow out of his roots:
And the spirit of the LORD shall rest upon him,
the spirit of wisdom and understanding, the spirit
of counsel and might, the spirit of knowledge and
of the fear of the LORD; And shall make him of
quick understanding in the fear of the LORD: and
he shall not judge after the sight of his eyes,
neither reprove after the hearing of his ears:" [1]
Further, we find that the Spirit of the Lord God
was with Him, which was necessary because
Messiah was sent to do a tremendous work that no
other man could do. "The Spirit of the Lord GOD
is upon me; because the LORD hath anointed me
to preach good tidings unto the meek; he hath sent
me to bind up the brokenhearted, to proclaim
liberty to the captives, and the opening of the
prison to them that are bound;" [2]

---

[1] Isaiah 11:2,3
[2] Isaiah 61:1

Since these duties were all prophesied in the Old Testament there should be no surprise to anyone when Jesus performed each one exactly as prophesied. Again, no mortal man could perform these duties exactly as prophesied unless he was the prophesied Messiah.

I need to put to rest a question from the very onset of this subject. If Jesus is the Son of God (God the Son) why was it necessary for Him to be anointed with the Spirit of God? Jesus is Emmanuel, God with us. He is eternal in existence, and therefore possesses all the attributes of the Godhead.

My explanation may not completely cover all the theological reasoning, but since this is not a course in theology, I believe the explanation will satisfy inquiring minds.

Jesus had to fill the role of Prophet, Priest and King. All these required an anointing to verify the will of God was involved. Since Jesus came clothed in the flesh of man it would be necessary to convince the unbelieving that He was indeed the Messiah. Matthew reported, "And Jesus, when he was baptized, went up straightway out of the water: and, lo, the heavens were opened unto him, and he saw the Spirit of God descending like a dove, and lighting upon him:' [3] This was the anointing of Jesus, confirmed by the Holy Spirit.

If Jesus were to confront Satan head on, and cast out demons, He would need the power of God in His life. The New Testament records many incidents of Jesus casting out demons.

---

[3] Matthew 3:16

"How God anointed Jesus of Nazareth with the Holy Ghost and with power: who went about doing good, and healing all that were oppressed of the devil; for God was with him." [4]

Aaron and his sons were anointed into the priesthood, which involved a consecration and sanctification "And thou shalt put them upon Aaron thy brother, and his sons with him; and shalt anoint them, and consecrate them, and sanctify them, that they may minister unto me in the priest's office." [5] Jesus was conveying the message to the people that He was consecrating Himself to the Father (declaring Himself Holy before the Father) and was also sanctifying Himself for the Father's use (setting Himself apart for God's special use).

"Thou lovest righteousness, and hatest wickedness: therefore God, thy God, hath anointed thee with the oil of gladness above thy fellows.
All thy garments smell of myrrh, and aloes, and cassia, out of the ivory palaces, whereby they have made thee glad." [6]

Samuel was commanded to anoint Saul King over Israel "To morrow about this time I will send thee a man out of the land of Benjamin, and thou shalt anoint him to be captain over my people Israel, that he may save my people out of the hand of the Philistines: for I have looked upon my people, because their cry is come unto me. " [7]

---

[4] Acts 10:38
[5] Exodus 28:41
[6] Psalm 45:7,8
[7] 1 Samuel 9:16

The anointing of Saul would be verified by Samuel to assure the people that Saul was the man chosen by God for this position.

Elijah was given the command to anoint Elisha as a prophet to take his place when God would take Elijah to Himself. In 1 Kings we read: "And Jehu the son of Nimshi shalt thou anoint to be king over Israel: and Elisha the son of Shaphat of Abelmeholah shalt thou anoint to be prophet in thy room." [8]

When John the Baptist balked at baptizing Jesus, we read in Matthew "Then cometh Jesus from Galilee to Jordan unto John, to be baptized of him. But John forbad him, saying, I have need to be baptized of thee, and comest thou to me?
And Jesus answering said unto him, Suffer it to be so now: for thus it becometh us to fulfil all righteousness. Then he suffered him." [9]

Matthew 3:16, 17 record the fulfillment of the verse in Isaiah the 11th chapter regarding the Spirit of the Lord resting on Messiah. God did not intend to leave any room for doubt. In that verse we read "And Jesus, when he was baptized, went up straightway out of the water: and, lo, the heavens were opened unto him, and he saw the Spirit of God descending like a dove, and lighting upon him: And lo a voice from heaven, saying, This is my beloved Son, in whom I am well pleased." [10]

Not only did the Holy Spirit rest upon Jesus, but also He did so in a visible form, using the symbol of the dove. The dove is a symbol of peace and gentleness.

---

[8] 1 Kings 19:16
[9] Mathew 3:13-15
[10] Matthew 3:13-17

To assure there would be no misunderstanding on the part of the doubters God gave His affirmation to the anointing by declaring Jesus as His beloved Son, in whom He is well pleased.

God anointed Jesus with a full measure of the Holy Spirit, holding nothing back from Him, because His mission was of great importance. "The Father loveth the Son, and hath given all things into his hand".[11]

Isaiah the 61st chapter tells the reason for the anointing the Messiah with the Holy Spirit: "The Spirit of the Lord GOD is upon me; because the LORD hath anointed me to preach good tidings unto the meek; he hath sent me to bind up the brokenhearted, to proclaim liberty to the captives, and the opening of the prison to them that are bound; To proclaim the acceptable year of the LORD, and the day of vengeance of our God; to comfort all that mourn; to appoint unto them that mourn in Zion, to give unto them beauty for ashes, the oil of joy for mourning, the garment of praise for the spirit of heaviness; that they might be called trees of righteousness, the planting of the LORD, that he might be glorified." [12]

Before I continue with this thought it must be said that when Jesus read this portion of Scripture in the Jewish Synagogue he did not read the entire portion. Jesus stopped at a comma, not a period, because had He continued to read, being God the Son, Emmanuel, God with man, the remainder would have immediately come to pass. That included "the day of vengeance."

---

[11] John 3:35
[12] Isaiah 61:1-3

That day is yet to come, at the Second Coming of Messiah immediately after that terrible seven years of Tribulation spoken of in the Book of Revelation.

Jesus came to:

1) preach the good tidings to the meek. The good tidings are the Gospel, the "good news" that Jesus can free us from the penalty of sin and death.

2) bind up the brokenhearted.

Sin brings nothing but grief, and Jesus came to heal that wound by the wounds He would suffer, as He became our "Lamb slain from the foundation of the world."[13]

3) proclaim liberty to the captive. Not just the opening of the prisons, but every kind of liberty- complete redemption.

The "year of acceptance" is an allusion to the year of jubilee, which Jesus applies to Himself. During the year of jubilee, the Hebrew slaves were to set free and all debt canceled.

In a future time, "the day of vengeance of our God" will happen. Jesus, when offered the scroll in Luke 4:18 He stopped at the comma not the period. Had He continued by saying "the day of vengeance of our God, the time of "Jacob's Troubles" would immediately started, the day we refer to as the Great Tribulation.

When Jesus was anointed with the Holy Spirit His anointing was far more powerful than that of any Prophet, Priest or King. "For he whom God hath sent speaketh the words of God: for God giveth not the Spirit by measure unto him." [14]

---

[13] John 9:1-3
[14] Isaiah 11:2

Jesus was being endued with all the necessary power required for the Messiah. Isaiah recorded, "And the spirit of the LORD shall rest upon him, the spirit of wisdom and understanding, the spirit of counsel and might, the spirit of knowledge and of the fear of the LORD;" [15]

He would have:

1) The Spirit of Wisdom - decisions and judgments based on His Divine personal ability.

2) Understanding - the ability to perceive and explain the meaning or nature of somebody or something.

"And as Jesus passed by, he saw a man which was blind from his birth. And his disciples asked him, saying, Master, who did sin, this man, or his parents, that he was born blind?

Jesus answered, Neither hath this man sinned, nor his parents: but that the works of God should be made manifest in him."

3) Counsel - the ability to give good advice on a professional level. This Jesus did in an extremely wonderful manner in the sermon we refer to as the Beatitudes in Matthew the 5th chapter.

He first told the listeners how to be happy then went on to give good advice regarding their personal witness.

4) Might - this is not a reference to physical power, but rather to Divine power that can overcome the wicked one. Jesus will share this might with His followers that they might be free from sin.

---

[15] Isaiah 11:2

5) Knowledge - Jesus had the knowledge regarding facts, ideas, truths and principles that man did not possess. Many of these were greatly distorted and He came to help us understand.

6) The fear of the Lord - This refers to a total respect for the Almighty. Jesus went through some of the most horrible of situation against His person, yet He never sinned because of circumstances. Jesus had a total respect for the Godhead, having personal knowledge of the Trinity.

What a terrible loss it was to the Jewish population of His day to have such a one walk among them to teach them the ways of God, and yet reject Him and all He had to offer.

It becomes most apparent, as we view the life of Jesus that He was anointed with the Spirit of God.

Since the day of Pentecost God has made His Holy Spirit available to each of us if we will only ask Him to empower us with His Spirit. This would mean following the example of Jesus in consecration and sanctification and having a total respect for the Lord our God.

The Holy Spirit was prophesied to be the Spirit of Christ. All that embodied Jesus is in the Holy Spirit, and He can reside in the life of the believer to direct their spiritual path.

Why would not anyone with any degree of logical thinking request that the Heavenly Father baptize us with the Holy Spirit and power to help us be the mighty witnesses He expects us to be?

Why would anyone with a sound mind not at least give serious consideration to the possibility that all the Old Testament prophesied, and the New Testament testified to, really did happen.

If all that was prophesied up to that time was fulfilled exactly, we can be certain that the remainder of prophecy will also be fulfilled to an exacting degree. Should we not be aware of the remainder of the prophesies, and align our lives with the will of God in order to be found in His favor during the "day of wrath?"

Chapter 16

"Be A Prophet Like Moses"

Have you read Deuteronomy 18:15 & 18:18? If you have not I would encourage you to open your Bible now and read that portion. Do you understand what Moses was saying? Do you realize that Moses was prophesying the coming of the Messiah Jesus who would deliver his people from sin and death? Moses was a type of Messiah in as much as he was a deliverer from Egypt, which was a symbol of sin. Pharaoh was a type of Satan who kept the Hebrews in bondage and made them suffer tremendously. Moses was sent by God to deliver them by confronting Pharaoh (Satan) and cause him to let God's people go. When Pharaoh pursued them, God destroyed him. This is an exact scenario of what the Messiah Jesus will do in the last days as He frees humanity. Jew and Gentile alike will be freed from the clutches of Satan. Satan will be cast into the Lake that burns with fire for all eternity. He will not be destroyed; he will suffer for all eternity.

The children of faith will be free eternally.

Those who refuse to believe the Messiah will be like those of Moses day that rebelled and found themselves devoured by fire or have the earth open up to swallow them for their sin.

Further, Moses was told to construct a rod with a serpent on it. The serpent is the symbol of sin. When the poisonous serpents bit the sinning Hebrews, looking to the serpent on the pole could heal them. Strange thought, is it not?

Not so strange when one realized that Jesus took our sins upon Himself, became sin for us (like the serpent on the pole) and took our sins to the cross of Calvary where anyone who looked upon Calvary with faith would be healed of their sins. Truly, Moses was speaking of the Messiah in those verses. [1]

The prophecy given by Moses in Deuteronomy the eighteenth chapter is so explicit that no human could ever fulfill the prophecy in every respect. The 'prophet' that was promised was to be like Moses in all his positions of authority and duty.

Through this prophecy, God promised to give the Jews an infallible guide who will tell them all things for their peace, and his declarations will completely answer all knowledge that so-called prophets, false prophets, pretended to give.

The Christ was to be a man because the Jews could not endure to hear the voice of God (verse 16). To fulfill a prophecy, every high priest is taken from among men (Heb 5:1); and of his kingdom, as in Deut 17:15 "from among thy brethren". This was to be no ordinary prophet as He was to be like Moses. Consider what Deuteronomy has to say about Moses "And there arose not a prophet since in Israel like unto Moses, whom the LORD knew face to face, In all the signs and the wonders, which the LORD sent him to do in the land of Egypt to Pharaoh, and to all his servants, and to all his land, And in all that mighty hand, and in all the great terror which Moses shewed in the sight of all Israel."[2]

---

[1] Acts 3:20-22
[2] Deuteronomy 34:10-12

126

We need to examine what all this "prophet" must do to be the One Moses prophesied in order to understand that any false prophet could not counterfeit these qualifications.

Moses was a prophet, legislator, and king to his people, mediator, and the chief of the people of God. The Messiah Jesus is the very person of whom Moses was the type, and who should accomplish all the great purposes of God. No other prophet had ever existed who could equal the One promised.

Dr. Jortan, in his remarks on Ecclestical History said, "If one would search historical records to discover one like Moses in every respect, and cannot find one, then we have found Him of whom Moses in the law and prophets did write."

God never commissioned any human being to give laws to mankind but Moses and Christ.

Both gave God's laws in a faithful manner; Moses gave the law of the Old Testament (the Old Covenant) and Jesus gave us laws regarding the New Covenant between man and God in the New Testament.

Christ crucified was the person whom God had from the beginning appointed, or designated for the Jewish people.

It was not a triumphant Messiah that they were to expect but One who would suffer and die. Jesus was that person; and by believing in Him, as having suffered and dying for their sins, He would again be sent, in the power of His Spirit to justify and save them. Jesus will return at the time known as the Second Coming.

At that time there will be Jews, who having gone through the time of Jacob's Troubles, will have acknowledged Jesus as their Messiah. These will be saved from eternal damnation, but the unbelieving masses will have made that their choice by default.

It should be mentioned here that God never created Hell for man. Hell was created for Satan and the fallen angels that rebelled against Him in Heaven.

If man chooses to reject Jesus as the Messiah, Emmanuel, God with us, then he has also taken by default the pathway to Hell.

God sends no one to Hell, man, by his own decision has purchased his one-way ticket to an eternity of damnation, torment and separation from the love of God.

The verse in Acts tells us that the Heavens must receive Him until the time of restitution of all things. Jesus, after His resurrection spent time with His disciples and were seen by an additional five hundred others. After that, His disciples were present when Jesus ascended into Heaven to sit on the right hand of the Eternal Father. Again, I remind you that when one sits on the right hand of one in great authority he assumes the same power as the one sitting next to him. Jesus is truly the Son of God, or God the Son.

Again, our subject is "Messiah Must Be a Prophet like Moses. It is now easy to see that Jesus fulfilled every requirement of that prophecy. There can be no doubt in the mind of an honest inquirer for truth that Jesus is the One of whom Moses prophesied.

Jesus, according to the prophecy, would come out of His people Israel, and that means that He surpassed Moses in that regard. God did not permit Moses to enter the land of promise. Moses had disobeyed God regarding speaking to the rock, which was another prophecy of the Messiah. Instead, Moses struck the rock twice, and Messiah was to be struck only once, that is, crucified. After that, we need only to speak to Him to secure that which will sustain eternal life.

Jesus walked among His people Israel in an active ministry of three years before the prophecy of His crucifixion was fulfilled. During those three years, Jesus gave Israel, and the world, more spiritual knowledge and law for their salvation than could any other could give.

It is evident from the New Testament that Jesus fulfilled the role spoken of by Moses.

Jesus is a legislator: "A new commandment I give unto you, That ye love one another; as I have loved you, that ye also love one another." [3]

This was spoken to His disciples, but it was applicable to all Israel. During this period of Jewish history there was little love being shown to their fellow man. The Pharisees, Scribes, Levites, and even the High Priest had concern only for their own welfare, especially in the matter of extorting money from the people. The High Priest, under Roman rule, was bought and sold to the highest bidder. If the High Priest did not please the Roman rulers in Jerusalem, a new High Priest would be chosen.

---

[3] John 13:34

The apostle Paul, having been out of the city of Jerusalem for a considerable time had no idea of the fast turn over of the office of High Priest. We read in the book of Acts "And Paul, earnestly beholding the council, said, Men and brethren, I have lived in all good conscience before God until this day.

In addition, the high priest Ananias commanded them that stood by him to smite him on the mouth. Then said Paul unto him, God shall smite thee, thou whited wall: for sittest thou to judge me after the law, and commandest me to be smitten contrary to the law? And they that stood by said, Revilest thou God's high priest?

Then said Paul, I wist not, brethren, that he was the high priest: for it is written, Thou shalt not speak evil of the ruler of thy people." [4]

Paul, being a believer in obeying the law of God immediately apologized to the High Priest, explaining that he did not know him to be the High Priest. It is likely, that being outside the Temple, the High Priest was not wearing the traditional garments of the High Priest for identification purposes.

Jesus is a King: We read in the Gospel of **John** "Then Pilate entered into the judgment hall again, and called Jesus, and said unto him, Art thou the King of the Jews?

Jesus answered him, Sayest thou this thing of thyself, or did others tell it thee of me? Pilate answered, "Am I a Jew?" Thine own nation and the chief priests have delivered thee unto me: what hast thou done?

---

[4] Acts 23:1-5

Jesus answered, My kingdom is not of this world: if my kingdom were of this world, then would my servants fight, that I should not be delivered to the Jews: but now is my kingdom not from hence.

Pilate therefore said unto him, Art thou a king then? Jesus answered," Thou sayest that I am a king. to this end was I born," [5]

"And when they had crucified him, they parted his garments, casting lots upon them, what every man should take. And it was the third hour, and they crucified him.

And the superscription of his accusation was written over, THE KING OF THE JEWS." [6]

This may have been written by the Romans to upset the Jewish leaders, however, without their knowledge they had written the truth.

Jesus is the King of the Jews, and the King of kings, the King of the Universe.

Jesus like Moses was to be a 'mediator'. There are many who still pray to idols and dead humans. Their prayers are not only going unanswered, they are also an abomination to the Almighty.

It has been made amply clear to those who read and understand the New Testament that we have only one mediator, the Messiah Jesus: "For there is one God, and one mediator between God and men, the man Christ Jesus; " [7]

---

[5] John 18:33-37
[6] Mark 15:24 - 26
[7] 1 Timothy 2:5

Those who pray to any other than Jesus obviously are not well informed regarding the prophecies of the Old Testament regarding Messiah must be a prophet like Moses, and that includes being the only mediator appointed by the Lord God.

Jesus is to be the chief of the people of God. On two occasions, God made His will perfectly well known regarding Jesus being His choice as the chief of the people of God.

"And Jesus, when he was baptized, went up straightway out of the water: and, lo, the heavens were opened unto him, and he saw the Spirit of God descending like a dove, and lighting upon him: And lo a voice from heaven, saying, This is my beloved Son, in whom I am well pleased." [8]

Again in Matthew we have a "second witness" as is required by the law: "And, behold, there appeared unto them Moses and Elias talking Then answered Peter, and said unto Jesus, Lord, it is good for us to be here: if thou wilt, let us make here three tabernacles; one for thee, and one for Moses, and one for Elias.

While he yet spake, behold, a bright cloud overshadowed them: and behold a voice out of the cloud, which said, This is my beloved Son, in whom I am well pleased; hear ye him."[9]

Again, we have overpowering proof that Jesus is the long awaited Messiah. Another important prophecy regarding what the Messiah must be has been fulfilled and proven.

---

[8] Matthew 3:16 & 17
[9] Matthew 17:3-5

Yet, there will be many in our lifetime, both Jew and Gentile that will not accept the salvation He provided for the world at the expense of His suffering and death.

We cannot convince anyone regarding spiritual matters, nor convince them to make a decision in favor of Jesus and their eternal well being.

We can pray, however, and as believing, faith filled Christians hold fast to the promise that our prayer will be answered. We do need to remember, however, that man's free will cannot be violated, and the Lord God will not cause anyone to believe, He will simply present the facts and command the Holy Spirit to speak to their sprit.

Keep in mind that it is the office work of the Holy Spirit to convict man of his sins and lead him into all righteousness. This can only be accomplished if the individual is open to the Word of God and is willing to listen to the still small voice of the Holy Spirit as He speaks words of eternal salvation.

Chapter 17

"Binding Up the Broken Hearted"

Any minister of the Gospel, upon returning to his own hometown and to his own friends, neighbors and family realize that "A prophet is not without honor, save in his own country, and in his own house" [1] Jesus was well aware of this fact, yet He felt it necessary to go back to Nazareth to reveal who He is.

Jesus went to the synagogue and was invited to read from the Holy Scriptures. He was given the scroll of Isaiah and the sixty-first chapter. This was no accident or coincidence; this was a Divine appointment of God the Father. This portion contains one of the more important prophecies in the Old Testament regarding the Messiah.

We will be looking at the prophecy that tells us that the Messiah must have a ministry of binding up the broken hearted, proclaiming liberty to the captives and announcing the acceptable year of the Lord.

This prophecy is found in Isaiah "The Spirit of the Lord GOD is upon me; because the LORD hath anointed me to preach good tidings unto the meek; he hath sent me to bind up the brokenhearted, to proclaim liberty to the captives, and the opening of the prison to them that are bound; To proclaim the acceptable year of the LORD, " [2] & 3

---

[1] Matthew 13:57
[2] Isaiah 61:1-2 : [3] Luke 4:18

We find Jesus returning to His home in Galilee to proclaim that He is the one sent by the Lord God to fulfill this prophecy. From this point forward, the tension builds in the Jewish community of Nazareth.

Returning to His own home would be an act of great courage, since the stepbrothers of Jesus did not believe Him to be the Messiah. Into this semi-hostile environment, we find Jesus. We find this episode in the life of our Messiah in the New Testament, as well as prophesied in the Old Testament.

Isaiah's prophecies, as I have said previously, usually have a primary and a secondary sense, one remote, the other near at hand. The primary sense to Isaiah 61:1-2 is Isaiah preaching to the Jews regarding their deliverance from Babylonian captivity. This is constantly shown to foreshadow the salvation of humankind through Jesus Christ.

The phrase, "opening the prison" refers to a 'perfect liberty, a liberty through complete redemption. This reminds us of the year of jubilee which was announced by the sound of the trumpet. This was a year of general release of debts and obligations, freeing Hebrew slaves, lands, possessions sold from families and tribes revert to those previously owned. (Leviticus 25:5 &c.)

I have covered this previously, and it will be valuable to us to see the result of Jesus making this proclamation.

Jesus has just returned the scroll to the leader of the synagogue and He had every ones attention at that moment. Jesus told the Jews that He was the One mentioned in this prophecy.

He then evidently preached a sermon on grace, which the listeners referred to as "gracious words."

No record is given of the entire content of the sermon. It was not necessary for our salvation or it would have been recorded. It was not for general edification, but for informing the Jews that He was their Messiah.

The Jews raised the question concerning his family. Is this not this the son of Joseph? Matthew 13 reveals more information: "Is not this the carpenter's son? is not his mother called Mary? And his brethren, James, and Joses, and Simon, and Judas? And his sisters, are they not all with us? Whence then hath this man all these things? And they were offended in him. But Jesus said unto them, A prophet is not without honor, save in his own country, and in his own house." [3]

In verse 23, Jesus anticipated their thoughts and said, "And he said unto them, Ye will surely say unto me this proverb, Physician, heal thyself: whatsoever we have heard done in Capernaum, do also here in thy country."

It is as though they were saying; heal the broken hearted in your own country of Capernaum. Jesus continued by saying that they were thinking He should do in Nazareth what He had done in Capernaum. However, these Jews were not ready to receive salvation and were therefore not healed.

In verse 24, Jesus rightly told them "No prophet is accepted in his own country." [4]

---

[3] Matthew 13:55-57
[4] Luke 4:24

Jesus then put the bare truth of Judaism before those in this Nazareth synagogue. There were plenty of widows in Israel in the days of Elijah when there was a great famine, but Elijah was not sent to any of these. Instead, he was sent to Sarepta, a city of Sidon, to a widow woman.

He also said there were many lepers in Israel in the time of Elijah, but none were chosen by God to be cleansed, except Naaman the Syrian.

The Jews in the synagogue were then filled with wrath. Jesus had just told them that God by-passed the Jews to perform miracles for the Gentiles.

They pushed Jesus outside the city to the top of a high hill where they intended to throw Him headfirst. No doubt, they also intended to stone Him if the fall did not kill Him.

Luke records that Jesus passed through the midst of them and went His way. Either Jesus caused them not to be able to see Him, or He overwhelmed them by His Divine might. [5]

A family member that presents a scene something similar to what I suppose passed on this occasion presents the following fact:

A missionary, who had been sent to a strange land to proclaim the Gospel of the kingdom of God, and who had passed through many hardships, and was often in danger of losing his life, through the persecutions excited against him, came to a place where he had often before, at no small risk, preached Christ crucified.

---

[5] Luke 4:28-30

Illustration:

About fifty people, who had received good impressions from the word of God, assembled: he began his discourse and, after he had preached about thirty minutes, an outrageous mob surrounded the house, armed with different instruments of death, and breathing the most sanguinary [bloodthirsty] purposes.

Some that were within shut the door; and the missionary and his flock betook themselves to prayer. The mob assailed the house, and began to hurl stones against the walls, windows, and roof; and in a short time almost every tile was destroyed, and the roof nearly uncovered, and before they quitted the premises scarcely left one square inch of glass in the five windows, which enlightened the house. While this was going forward, a person came with a pistol to the window opposite to the place where the preacher stood, (who was then exhorting his flock to be steady, to resign themselves to God, and trust in him,) presented it at him, and snapped it; but it only flashed in the pan!

As the house was a wooden building, they began with crows and spades to undermine it, and take away its principal supports.

The preacher then addressed his little flock to this effect: "These outrageous people seek not you, but me; if I continue in the house, they will soon pull it down, and we shall be all buried in its ruins; I will therefore, in the name of God, go out to them, and you will be safe."

He then went towards the door; the poor people got round him, and entreated him not to venture out, as he might expect to be instantly massacred; he went calmly forward, opened the door, at which a whole volley of stones and dirt was that instant discharged; but he received no damage. The people were in crowds in all the space before the door, and filled the road for a considerable way, so that there was no room to pass or repass.

As soon as the preacher made his appearance, the savages became instantly as silent and as still as night: he walked forward; and they divided to the right and to the left, leaving a passage of about four feet wide for himself and a young man who followed him, to walk in. He passed on through the whole crowd, not a soul of whom either lifted a hand, or spoke one word, till he and his companion had gained the uttermost skirts of the mob!

The narrator, who was present on the occasion, goes on to say: "This was one of the most affecting spectacles I ever witnessed; an infuriated mob, without any visible cause, (for the preacher spoke not one word,) became in a moment as calm as lambs!

They seemed struck with amazement bordering on stupefaction; they stared and stood speechless; and, after they had fallen back to right and left to leave him a free passage, they were as motionless as statues!

They assembled with the full purpose to destroy the man who came to show them the way of salvation; but he, passing through the midst of them, went his way. Was not the God of missionaries in this work? The next Lord's day, the missionary went to the same place, and again proclaimed the Lamb of God, who taketh away the sin of the world!"

After leaving Nazareth Jesus returned to Capernaum where He resided most of the time when He was not traveling around Israel.

He taught the people there on the Sabbath days and they were astonished at his doctrine, because His word was powerful.

There is an old saying that familiarity breed's contempt. The Jews of Nazareth were too familiar with Jesus to see Him as being more than the son of the carpenter.

Did anyone there ever ask Him about His birth? Had they ever heard that Joseph was his stepfather? Did they really care?

The same questions might be asked today of the average person on the street.

At the conclusion of the questions, the last question must be asked, "Do they really care?"

I would suppose the lesson we glean from this, other than that Jesus fulfilled the prophecy of Isaiah, is that if those near to us, friends, neighbors, etc. will not listen to us, then we must "shake the dust off our feet" and go to those who will hear. It is still true today that the prophet is not without honor except in his own town.

While that may be true, we must never discontinue presenting the Gospel story, we simply must find those who will hear us. Those who will not listen to us must be the recipients of our prayers. They may be able to prevent us from giving them the glorious gospel of freedom, but they cannot prevent our prayers.

Chapter 18

"The Ministry of Healing"

It is obvious from the Scriptures in the Old
Testament, prophesying that the Messiah would
have a ministry of healing, and the evidence by
eyewitness in the New Testament that Jesus is the
promised Messiah. "Then the eyes of the blind shall
be opened, and the ears of the deaf shall be
unstopped. Then shall the lame man leap as an hart,
and the tongue of the dumb sing: for in the
wilderness shall waters break out, and
streams in the desert." [1] "The blind receive their
sight, and the lame walk, the lepers are cleansed,
and the deaf hear, the dead are raised up, and the
poor have the gospel preached to them." [2]

I see no need to make a more in-depth search of
prophecy or fulfillment to prove who Jesus is. Our
time will be better spent on His healing ministry.

The eyes of the blind shall be opened:

Imagine yourself as being blind, feeling the wind
against your face and hearing it rustle the leaves of
the palm trees, but never having seen a tree.
Around you are crowds of people, pushing and
shoving to see this man Jesus who is said to be a
great healer. You want desperately to have Him
touch you and give you sight, but you could not
penetrate the crowd.

---

[1] Isaiah 35:5,6 :Matthew 11:15
[2] Matthew 11:5

Jesus is approaching, you are sure of that because the crowd is calling out His name. In desperation you too call out "Jesus, thou son of David, have mercy on me." [3] Son of David? Yes, you really do believe Him to be the promised Messiah.

Those around you tell you to be quiet, but you call out even louder because your need is so great. "Jesus, son of David, have mercy on me!" [4]

Jesus was very close; you could tell by the way the crowd spoke more softly when they called to Him. Jesus stood still, not far from where you sat begging for alms.

Could it possibly be that was Jesus calling for you by name? It was at this point that blind Bartimaeus, the son of Timaeus, heard those around him saying "Be of good comfort, rise; he calleth thee."

Blind Bartimaeus cast off his dirty outer garment and went to Jesus. When Jesus asked what Bartimaeus wanted from Jesus, he answered "Lord, that I might receive my sight. Saying only a few words, Bartimaeus heard Jesus say, "Go thy way; thy faith hath made thee whole. And immediately he received his sight, and followed Jesus in the way.

Give particular attention that his faith in Jesus as being the Messiah was what Jesus was referencing. When he called out "Thou son of David", that was his faith. His desire for sight was secondary to his belief that Jesus was the promised Messiah. [5]

Here we find a man blind, unable to work for a living, and is reduced to begging in the streets of Jericho.

---

[3] Luke 18:30
[4] Luke 18:38-39
[5] Mark 10:46-52

144

Realizing that Jesus had come to Jericho, he immediately began to cry out to Him for healing. His plea was that Jesus would have mercy on him.

Using the word 'mercy' the blind man was requesting Jesus remove the distress of blindness. Mercy is that quality that Jesus, in His Divinity, may bestow on His creatures. Mercy is the unmerited favor of God, not something that is a right. The blind man cast off his garment. He realized the power of Jesus to grant mercy, but also realized he had done nothing to merit the healing, therefore, he pleaded for mercy.

A great revival of religion took place in some of the American States, about the year 1773, by the instrumentality of some itinerant preachers sent from England. Many, both whites and blacks, were brought to an acquaintance with God who bought them.

Two of these, a white man and a Negro, meeting together, began to speak concerning the goodness of God to their souls, (a custom which has ever been common among truly religious people.) Among other things they were led to inquire how long each had known the salvation of God; and how long it was, after they were convinced of their sin and danger, before each got a satisfactory evidence of pardoning mercy.

The white man said, "I was three months in deep distress of soul, before God spoke peace to my troubled, guilty conscience."

"But it was only a fortnight," replied the negro, "from the time I first heard of Jesus, and felt that I was a sinner, till I received the knowledge of salvation by the remission of sins." "But what was the reason," said the white man, "that you found salvation sooner than I did?"

"This is the reason," replied the other; "you white men have much clothing upon you, and when Christ calls, you cannot run to him; but we poor Negroes have only this, (pointing to the mat or cloth which was tied round his waist,) and when we hear the call, we throw it off instantly, and run to him."

Thus the poor son of Ham illustrated the text without intending it, as well as any doctor in the universe. People who have been educated in the principles of the Christian religion imagine themselves on this account Christians; and, when convinced of sin, they find great difficulty to come as mere sinners to God, to be saved only through the merits of Christ.

Others, such as the negro in question, have nothing to plead but this, We have never heard of thee, and could not believe in thee of whom we had not heard; but this excuse will not avail now, as the true light is come, therefore they cast off this covering, and come to Jesus.

Those in sin must first cast off that which would hinder them from coming speedily to Jesus, then when the Holy Spirit speaks, asking them to tell Jesus what they desire, they need to be specific. The blind man did not talk about his issues of being a beggar, shivering in the cold with only rags about him to keep him warm.

He wanted Jesus to remove that which most disturbed him. The sinner must do the same thing, tell Jesus the sin that is separating himself from the blessings of the Almighty, and ask that the sin(s) be removed and forgiven. The ears of the deaf shall be unstopped, the tongue of the dumb sings.

The next miracle takes a strange turn as Jesus heals a man who was deaf and had an impediment in his speech. Taking the man away from the crowd Jesus put his fingers into the man's ears, and he spit, and touched his tongue.

Looking up to heaven, Jesus sighed, and said Ephphatha, that is, Be opened. Immediately his ears were opened that he might hear, and the string of his tongue was loosed, and he spoke plainly.[6]

Jesus fulfilled two phases of prophecy concerning the Messiah: he made the deaf to hear, the dumb to speak.

There must be some significance in the fact that Jesus took this man away from the crowd before he healed him. Was this an indication that Jesus wished him to separate himself from former sinful acquaintances? Perhaps. He then put His fingers in the man's ears to indicate to him that by the power of God He would restore his hearing. Next, Jesus spit.

Now this brings a bit of a dilemma, what was the purpose of this action? After spitting on the ground, Jesus touched the man's tongue. Let's put the two acts together and see if we can make some rational sense from this.

---

[6] Mark 7:32-35

Spitting on the ground may have conveyed the idea that when his tongue was healed (Jesus did touch the man's tongue) he must rid his speech of anything unholy. Many in society today could use the touch of Jesus on their tongue. The name of God is constantly blasphemed on TV, yet censors block out words considered being sociably unacceptable during prime time.

Four letter words that are offensive, but have no blasphemy attached are censored, but not the irreverent use of the name of the Lord God of Heaven.

My explanation regarding the actions of Jesus may not be wholly accurate, but I do not believe it violates any basic truth.

The lame man leap like a deer

Near the sheep market there is a pool called Bethesda, which has five porches. God allowed a supernatural happening, at certain times of the year. An angel would come down and stir up the waters and the first person that stepped into the troubled waters would be cured of whatever disease he might have.

One man, having an infirmity for the past thirty-eight years was lying by the pool when Jesus came by. Jesus, knowing all things, nevertheless said to the man, "Would you like to be made whole?" The man told Jesus that because of his inability to move quickly someone more agile would always get into the pool before him.

It is important to realize that on this day it was a Sabbath day. It was perfectly acceptable for an angel to heal on the Sabbath, and now Jesus is about to do the same.

Jesus said to the man "Rise, take up thy bed, and walk."[7]

The Pharisees had so corrupted the Law of Moses that they proclaimed it a sin to carry anything on the Sabbath. If a man was carrying a stick, and it touched the ground, he would be guilty of plowing and condemned by the Pharisees.

Jesus knew this man had been infirm for many years and took pity on him, and He also knew that he had no one who cared that he had an infirmity and therefore no one to help him into the pool.

What a sad situation, to be so ill and have no one that cared for his infirmity.

While it is true that Jesus was fulfilling a prophecy regarding miracles the Messiah would perform, He was also teaching mankind that He is full of compassion and Divine power to assist in even the more desperate of situations

Jesus became the One who both cared and could help. While it is true that Jesus was fulfilling a prophecy regarding miracles the Messiah would perform, He was also teaching mankind that He is full of compassion and Divine power to assist in even the more desperate of situations. [8] Isn't this the kind of Messiah you desire to follow and obey?

"In the wilderness shall waters break out, and streams in the desert." [9]

Adam Clarke appears to have chosen not to attempt to make comment on verses 5 & 6. Perhaps he chose not to comment because here the prophecy changes from the healing ministry of Messiah to prophecy regarding the blooming of the desert in Israel in the end times.

---

[7] John 5:8
[8] John 5:2-9 [9] Isaiah 35:6

Perhaps adding a touch of spiritualizing this verse will allow me to include verses 5 & 6. Jesus not only came to physically heal the blind, deaf, dumb and lame, but apply those terms to ones spiritual life. There is none so blind as they who will not see. Many have been exposed to the light of the Gospel but have chosen not to see the truth found there and therefore remain spiritually blind.

Many have chosen to remain deaf to the call of God and the words of salvation found in the Gospels. Some have been unable to take the Christian walk because they are spiritually lame, they cannot take a single step without falling into sin.

Then there are those who profess to be Christians but have no power when witnessing, because they are not spiritually right their witness comes through as if they were a stammered, or one who cannot adequately speak the words of life the sinners needs to hear.

Then we come to the passage of the desert blooming in the end times. Jesus brings fruitfulness, through His gospel, to the barren souls, and they are like a dead rose bush that suddenly begins to bring forth beautiful flowers. Even the worse of sinners, that society would consider to be as unproductive as a scorching desert, can become the source through whom springs of living water flow.

That one can be a conduit for King Jesus as the Holy Spirit works through the once unproductive soul and brings lost sinners to Jesus.

Once again, let me say that it is not necessary to elaborate on the fact that Jesus, the Messiah, fulfilled the prophecy of a healing ministry. History, both past and current has proven that He has met the requirements.

The point to be made here is that Jesus is ready, and capable, of healing you of your sin sickness. Sin sickness brings both physical and spiritual death.

All humanity must die the physical life because of the original sin, but the sinner also possesses an eternal spirit that is unfit for heaven. Being unfit for heaven thee is but one place for that spirit, the place of eternal torment reserved for Satan and the fallen angels.

God did not create Hell for man, but for Satan and the rebellious angels. However, should mankind decide to reject the spiritual healing powers of Jesus, and follow Him as directed in the New Testament, they have chosen by default to join with Satan and the rebellious angels.

What a tragedy to be eternally cast into a place of utter darkness, torment and separated from the love of God.

Chapter 19

"The Ministry In Galilee"

This chapter contains an illustrious prophecy of the Messiah. He is represented under the glorious figure of the sun, or light, rising on a benighted world, and diffusing joy and gladness wherever he sheds his beams. "Now when Jesus had heard that John was cast into prison, he departed into Galilee; And leaving Nazareth, he came and dwelt in Capernaum, which is upon the sea coast, in the borders of Zabulon and Nephthalim: That it might be fulfilled which was spoken by Esaias the prophet, saying, The land of Zabulon, and the land of Nephthalim, by the way of the sea, beyond Jordan, Galilee of the Gentiles;

The people which sat in darkness saw great light; and to them which sat in the region and shadow of death light is sprung up." [1]

We will find fulfillment on this prophecy, however, by focusing our attention on the location mentioned. Our goal is to prove the prophecies as being fulfilled, and this prophecy informs us that the Messiah must have a ministry in Galilee. "And they shall look unto the earth; and behold trouble and darkness, dimness of anguish; and they shall be driven to darkness.

---

[1] Matthew 4: 16

Nevertheless, the dimness shall not be such as was in her vexation, when at the first he lightly afflicted the land of Zebulun and the land of Naphtali, and afterward did more grievously afflict her by the way of the sea, beyond Jordan, in Galilee of the nations.

The people that walked in darkness have seen a great light: they that dwell in the land of the shadow of death, upon them hath the light shined." [2]

Nephthalim [Naphtali] and Zabulon [Zebulun] are located west of the Sea of Galilee. Both are located in Galilee the scene of Jesus Christ's ministry.

Perhaps some background activity will be helpful in understanding what has transpired in Israel prior to the advent of Messiah.

Chapter eight of Isaiah tells of the fall of Damascus and Samaria. Isaiah is commanded by God to take a large brass mirror and write on it with an engraving scribe.

The words he is to write tell of the coming downfall of Damascus and Samaria. The words he writes mean, "To hasten the spoil", "to take quickly the prey". This appears to be a commission to the Assyrians to destroy and spoil the cities.

Isaiah, at the beginning of the prophecy he was to make, was to make his wife conceive and bear a son. The son's name was to be Maher-shalal-hashbaz. The name means the same as that which was written on the brass mirror for the people to read.

---

[2] Isaiah 8:22-9:1,2

It was in the form of a warning if they did not turn to God for their sufficiency.

Before the child would reach three years of age this prophecy would be fulfilled. Tiglath-pileser, king of Assyria, took Damascus and for his prey, he took Reubenites, Gadites, and the half-tribe of Manasseh with him to Assyria as slaves.

"Blow ye the trumpet in Zion, and sound an alarm in my holy mountain: let all the inhabitants of the land tremble: for the day of the LORD cometh, for it is nigh at hand; A day of darkness and of gloominess, a day of clouds and of thick darkness, as the morning spread upon the mountains: a great people and a strong; there hath not been ever the like, neither shall be any more after it, even to the years of many generation." [3]   This is another two-level prophecy since it prophesies the terrible time about to come upon these people, but it also will be fulfilled in Israel in the future, during the time of the "wrath of God."

According to this chapter, the people of Israel were in a state of spiritual darkness, in their spiritual walk they were as one who stumbled, tottered through weakness and were ready to fall. This describes Israel in their spiritual darkness at the time when Jesus made His advent as Immanuel.

It is significant to note that Isaiah 8 also refers to the son of Isaiah as "Immanuel."

---

[3] Joel 2:1,2

Note that Messiah came to bring salvation to the world, but to Israel, who rejected Him, He was much less. "And he shall be for a sanctuary; but for a stone of stumbling and for a rock of offense to both the houses of Israel, for a gin and for a snare to the inhabitants of Jerusalem." [4]

Jesus is the cornerstone of the Christian Church, but a stone of stumbling to the Jews.

As the "rock" He will not bring forth living water for them, because they reject what He came to provide. Instead, He becomes a "rock of offense."

"Jesus saith unto them, Did ye never read in the scriptures, The stone which the builders rejected, the same is become the head of the corner: this is the Lord's doing, and it is marvellous in our eyes?" [5]

Knowing the spiritual condition of Israel at this time makes it understandable why God chose this time to send Messiah. The people were sitting in great spiritual darkness and Jesus came and illuminated that darkness for those who would receive it.

The Scriptures reveal that Messiah would have a ministry in Galilee, and the New Testament confirmed that this is the scene of the ministry of Jesus, the Messiah.

Jesus was a stumbling block to the Jews, not because it was so designed, but because they would not accept Him as the corner stone of the Church that was taking them out of the Old Covenant into the New Covenant.

---

[4] Isaiah 8:14
[5] Matthew 21:42

156

The Old Covenant foretold the coming of the Messiah who would be the sacrifice for sins that would end all sacrifices. When the Temple was destroyed in 70 AD, and still not restored, it should have become evident that this marked the end of animal sacrifice for sin.

This "rock" prophesied throughout the Old Testament was capable of supplying living waters, the Gospel of Truth that would bring eternal salvation.

Instead, because Israel rejected Jesus as their Messiah this "rock" became a rock of offense. Jesus is still an offense to the Jews who have not come to realize He is their Messiah.

The prophecy is clear; the Messiah must have a ministry in the Galil. The fulfillment is also clear, and a historical fact: Jesus had a ministry in Galilee. He brought to this land the light they needed, because He is the Light of the world.

Once again, we have revealed the fulfillment of a prophecy out of the Old Testament. The prophecies are there for all to read, but so many refuse to accept the reality. Unfortunately the day of the "wrath of God" will come because there will still be Jews, and Gentiles, that have rejected the Son of God.

Chapter 20

"Tender and Compassionate"

I can almost hear the tenderness in the voice of this often stern prophet as he describes the coming Messiah. Like a shepherd, he will feed his flock. He will gather the lambs under his arm, and pulling it close to him to keep it warm, he will carry it home. Those with young that are nursing, needing to move a little more slowly to allow the lambs to suckle, he will be gentle.

Isaiah then uses the analogy of one who is weak, a bruised reed. This one he will not break, but rather he will help that one to grow strong as the cedars of Lebanon. The smoking flax represents one who is like a candle ready to go out. The person is worn and weary and Messiah will not require him to do more than he is capable of doing. Instead, he will fan the "smoking flax" until it glows red with a burning flame that sheds light around it.

The fortieth chapter of Isaiah is another two-layered prophecy, predicting the return of the Jews from the nation of Babylon to their ancestral home of Israel.

The words used by Isaiah are reminiscent of the Exodus from Egypt when God [Jesus, a theophany] guided them safely through the terrible desert and supplied their every need.

This prophecy has the tone of consolation to a people who have been enslaved and lost hope. Isaiah is telling them to prepare to leave Babylon, and we can hear the voice of a harbinger as he goes forth to declare that the Almighty God will go before them.

"Comfort ye, comfort ye my people, saith your God. Speak ye comfortably to Jerusalem, and cry unto her, that her warfare is accomplished, that her iniquity is pardoned: for she hath received of the LORD's hand double for all her sins."
The voice of him that crieth in the wilderness, Prepare ye the way of the LORD, make straight in the desert a highway for our God. Every valley shall be exalted, and every mountain and hill shall be made low: and the crooked shall be made straight, and the rough places plain:"[1]

Isaiah is telling them to prepare to cross the vast desert area between Babylon [Iraq] and Israel. Prepare the way as one would prepare the way for a great king, because the Lord God will be at the head of their column to guide them safely back to Jerusalem.

The very first verse has the tone of one who is tender and compassionate. "Comfort ye." This comforting message is carried over into the New Testament as Messiah Jesus shows Himself to be tender and compassionate.

"He shall feed his flock like a shepherd: he shall gather the lambs with his arm, and carry them in his bosom, and shall gently lead those that are with young."

---

[1] Isaiah 40:1-4

This describes the compassion of Jehovah as He releases His people from their bondage, which was the result of their own sinfulness, and now tenderly gathers them for the journey home.

The allusion of a loving shepherd is used to convey to the Jews that they will be treated with the utmost consideration. It reminds us of the words Jacob said to Esau when they met after so long a period of strained relationship.

"And he said, Let us take our journey, and let us go, and I will go before thee. And he said unto him, My Lord knoweth that the children are tender, and the flocks and herds with young are with me: and if men should overdrive them one day, all the flock will die."[2]

As anxious as Jacob was to mend the relationship with his brother he felt he must decline his offer. Esau would go before Jacob, taking his army of four hundred men to secure safe passage. Jacob, however, considered his flocks and herds, as would any good shepherd. The journey would be too difficult for the young to take, moving at the speed of Esau's army, and the movement without ample periods of stopping for the young to nurse to keep their strength.

Isaiah used the same type of comforting words to the people of the captivity "He shall feed his flock like a shepherd: he shall gather the lambs with his arm, and carry them in his bosom, and shall gently lead those that are with young."[3]

---

[2] Genesis 33:12,13
[3] Isaiah 40:11

Yes, it is a long journey and difficult, but Jehovah will care for you as a shepherd would his flock. He will treat you like a lamb needing special attention; He will gently lead you back to your homeland. It is more than likely that these Jews were born in captivity, as their parents would now be long dead.

Yet, it is probable that they had heard the horror stories from their parents about the tortuous journey from Israel to Babylon, under slave masters having no mercy. They certainly did not go to Babylon under the compassionate care of soldiers acting like loving shepherds. Now, the Jews were told they are about to make the return journey, and the first image coming into their mind would be the stories they had heard from their parents regarding the journey to Babylon.

Thus, the words come tenderly and lovingly: "Comfort ye, comfort ye my people, saith your God. Speak ye comfortably to Jerusalem, and cry unto her, that her warfare is accomplished, that her iniquity is pardoned: for she hath received of the LORD's hand double for all her sins."[4]

Can you hear the voice of the Messiah Jesus as He comforted His disciples "And straightway Jesus constrained his disciples to get into a ship, and to go before him unto the other side, while he sent the multitudes away. And when he had sent the multitudes away, he went up into a mountain apart to pray: and when the evening was come, he was there alone. But the ship was now in the midst of the sea, tossed with waves: for the wind was contrary.

---

[4] Isaiah 40:1,2

And in the fourth watch of the night Jesus went unto them, walking on the sea. And when the disciples saw him walking on the sea, they were troubled, saying, It is a spirit; and they cried out for fear. But straightway Jesus spake unto them, saying, Be of good cheer; it is I; be not afraid."[5]

The Jews leaving Babylon had every right to be as much afraid of the journey before them as did the disciples when they thought Jesus walking toward them on the Sea of Galilee was a ghost. The same comfort is offered to the Jews as was given to the disciples, perhaps the words were different, but the love behind the words was the same.

In Isaiah it says, "comfort ye", and in Matthew Jesus said "Be of good cheer …be not afraid." Why should they not be afraid, it is dark, they are in the middle of the Sea of Galilee, and they believe they are seeing a ghost? They soon had good reason not to be afraid, because Jesus said, "It is I." What more could anyone ask than to know that it is Jesus that is there where you once thought there was nothing but distress and terror.

The Jews felt the same way, but when they heard the familiar words of preparing a way through the wilderness, they realized that at the head of their column they would not find distress and terror, but Jehovah Himself.

---

[5]Matthew 14:22-27

When Jesus knew that the Pharisees were holding a council against Him which would ultimately bring about His death, He did not run and hide. Instead, Jesus simply turned His back on those who tried to fill His heart with distress and terror and went into the midst of the multitudes that were hurting in so many ways.

Those who were hurting [bruised reeds] to the extent that they felt they could no longer withstand the rigors of living, Jesus came with tenderness and compassion. "A bruised reed shall he not break, and smoking flax shall he not quench, till he send forth judgment unto victory." [6]

These may seem like strange words to us, but it was quite plain to the Jews who used oil lamps with wicks for household light. When the wick was about to burn itself out, leaving nothing but black ash, it was time to quench it and replace it with a new wick.

The multitudes gathering around Jesus were much like the wick that was about to burn out, but Jesus would not quench their desire for salvation and peace with God. Jesus came to bring them the Gospel of peace.

Now for the ultimate in tenderness and compassion. Jesus has been severely beaten, the hair of his beard pulled out, a sharp crown of thorns mockingly slammed down on His head causing terrible pain.

He is then placed on a very rough wooden cross, likely full of splinters, and nails driven through His hands and feet.

---

[6] Matthew 12:20

The cross is pulled to an upright position and it falls into the retaining hole with a terrible thud, jarring His entire body, and putting additional stress on his wounded hands and feet.

Below Him Roman soldiers are laughing and gambling for His clothing. In the crowd are Jews mocking Him, including the very Jewish leaders that had accused Him falsely before the Roman authorities.

"And they that passed by reviled him, wagging their heads, And saying, Thou that destroyest the temple, and buildest it in three days, save thyself. If thou be the Son of God, come down from the cross. Likewise also the chief priests mocking him, with the scribes and elders, said, He saved others; himself he cannot save. If he be the King of Israel, let him now come down from the cross, and we will believe him."[7]

What words of condemnation and hatred did Jesus hurl back at them? Not one word, instead He spoke to His Father in Heaven and said "Father, forgive them, for they know not what they do." [8]

That is the most tender compassion ever found on Planet Earth. There is no doubt that the Messiah Jesus was tender and compassionate.

Christians sing a chorus:

"No one ever cared for me like Jesus,
There's no other one so kind as He,
No one else could take the sin and darkness from me,
Oh how much he cares for me."

---

[7] Mathew 27:39-42   [8] Luke 23:34

Chapter 21

"Meek and Unpretentious"

Imagine a man in our modern day, having the supernatural power possessed by Jesus, without becoming brassy and drawing attention to him; it just would not happen.

Yet, this is exactly what we find prophesied concerning the Messiah Jesus.

"He shall not cry, nor lift up, nor cause his voice to be heard in the street."[1]

As a proof that Jesus, having this supernatural ability, did not draw attention to himself, we read ""But when Jesus knew it, he withdrew himself from thence: and great multitudes followed him, and he healed them all; And charged them that they should not make him known: That it might be fulfilled which was spoken by Esaias the prophet, saying,

Behold my servant, whom I have chosen; my beloved, in whom my soul is well pleased: I will put my spirit upon him, and he shall shew judgment to the Gentiles. He shall not strive, nor cry; neither shall any man hear his voice in the streets." [2]

The fortieth chapter of Isaiah tells us of God comforting His people Israel as they prepare to leave the captivity of Babylon and begin their long arduous journey back to Israel. In that account there is intimation that Jehovah was also alluding to the fact that He would lead them to perfect peace through the Messiah.

---

[1] Isaiah 42:2
[2] Matthew 12:15-19

This Messiah would be not only tender and compassionate toward them but He would also not be one to project Himself and expect them to be submissive to Him because of His power or wealth.

He would be one who came unassuming, simply presenting a Gospel of hope for all who would recognize Him as the promised Messiah.

Consider how different Jesus was when compared to the Pharisees. "And he spake this parable unto certain which trusted in themselves that they were righteous, and despised others: Two men went up into the temple to pray; the one a Pharisee, and the other a publican.

The Pharisee stood and prayed thus with himself, God, I thank thee, that I am not as other men are, extortioners, unjust, adulterers, or even as this publican.

I fast twice in the week, I give tithes of all that I possess. And the publican, standing afar off, would not lift up so much as his eyes unto heaven, but smote upon his breast, saying, God be merciful to me a sinner. I tell you, this man went down to his house justified rather than the other: for every one that exalteth himself shall be abased; and he that humbleth himself shall be exalted." [3]

We see another example of the vast difference between Jesus and the self-righteous Pharisees that went to extremes to bring attention to them.

"But all their works they do for to be seen of men: they make broad their phylacteries, and enlarge the borders of their garments, And love the uppermost rooms at feasts, and the chief seats in the synagogues,

And greetings in the markets, and to be called of men, Rabbi, Rabbi."[4]

---

[3] Luke 18:10-14
[4] Matthew 23:5-7

Jesus taught a much different philosophy of life, "But be not ye called Rabbi: for one is your Master, even Christ; and all ye are brethren. And call no man your father upon the earth: for one is your Father, which is in heaven.
Neither be ye called masters: for one is your Master, even Christ.
But he that is greatest among you shall be your servant."[5]

Why did Jesus tell His disciples not to be called Rabbi? None of the prophets ever received this title or any of the learned teachers before the time of Hillel and Shammai, which was about the time of our Lord.

The Pharisees, who always sought the honor that comes from men took to themselves the title Rabbi and told their followers they must be so addressed.

The half-brothers of Jesus tried to convince Him into proclaiming Himself as the Messiah before it was time. Their reason cannot be known; perhaps they were jealous of the attention He was getting from His disciples.

Having been raised in the home of Mary and Joseph they must have heard the account of the angel Gabriel visiting both parents to declare that Mary would be giving birth to the promised Messiah. Yet, in the Gospel of John we learn that even though they would have been taught the Scriptures of the Old Testament, they still did not believe Jesus was the Messiah.

That being the truth of the matter, it is logical to presume they were jealous of the attention Jesus was receiving from the disciples that followed Him wherever He would go.
Not only were the twelve apostles in his retinue but also many other disciples who wished to learn from Him.

---

[5] Matthew 23:8-11

"After these things Jesus walked in Galilee: for he would not walk in Jewry, because the Jews sought to kill him. Now the Jew's feast of tabernacles was at hand. His brethren therefore said unto him, Depart hence, and go into Judea, that thy disciples also may see the works that thou doest. For there is no man that doeth any thing in secret, and he himself seeketh to be known openly. If thou do these things, shew thyself to the world. For neither did his brethren believe in him. Then Jesus said unto them, My time is not yet come: but your time is alway ready. The world cannot hate you; but me it hateth, because I testify of it, that the works thereof are evil. Go ye up unto this feast: I go not up yet unto this feast: for my time is not yet full come."[6]

It may be that these half-brothers were indeed jealous of Jesus and wished to see Him publicly ridiculed and rejected as the Messiah. That would certainly discourage His following. This is pure conjecture, but based on what we read in the Gospel of John it could possibly be their reasoning.

Messiah, however, was prophesied to be meek and unostentatious. Being meek, (having mildness and a quietness of nature) Jesus did succumb to their disbelief by retaliation or strong argument.

It is true that as the Son of God, Jesus was an extraordinarily powerful individual, but meekness also means "strength under control and that clearly describes Jesus. "After these things Jesus walked in Galilee: for he would not walk in Jewry, because the Jews sought to kill him."[7] Now the Jew's feast of tabernacles was at hand. His brethren therefore said unto him, Depart hence, and go into Judea, that thy disciples also may see the works that thou doest. For there is no man that doeth any thing in secret, and he himself seeketh to be known openly.

---

[6] John 7:1-6
[7] John 7:1

170

If thou do these things, shew thyself to the world. For either did his brethren believe in him.

Then Jesus said unto them, My time is not yet come: but your time is alway ready. The world cannot hate you; but me it hateth, because I testify of it, that the works thereof are evil.

Go ye up unto this feast: I go not up yet unto this feast: for my time is not yet full come. When he had said these words, after these things Jesus walked in Galilee: for he would not walk in Jewry, because the Jews sought to kill him. His time had not yet come.

Jesus had taken His ministry to the Northern regions of Israel, into Galilee because the Jews in Jerusalem would no longer tolerate Him and it would be dangerous for Him to continue there.

It was now time for the Feast of Tabernacles and this was one of the three compulsory feasts for all men. Jesus must go back into the arena of hatred fueled by the Pharisees, Levites, Sadducees, Priests and High Priest.

To admit that Jesus was the prophesied Messiah would require them to relinquish power and authority over the people and that would mean a loss of much income. Their greed overcame their knowledge of the Old Testament and the Prophets concerning what the Messiah must do, and what He must be to prove His authenticity.

The Feast of Tabernacles was held on the fifteenth of Tisri. This month relates to our calendar during the last half and September and the first half of October.

In preparation for the Feast the men would cut branches of Palm trees, Willows, Myrtles, tying these together in a bundle with cords of gold and silver, or ribbons of these colors. These would be carried into their synagogues and kept with them during their time of prayer.

The Feast of Tabernacles lasted for eight days. During this time tents would be erected on the top of houses, in gardens, or whatever space was available.

During the celebration of the Feast the men would carry their bundle of branches into the temple and walk around the altar singing Hosanna! Save, we beseech thee-the trumpets sounding on all sides.

The crowds would be enormous and could conceal any covert activities of those Jews wishing to kill Jesus. Into this hostile situation Jesus is about to enter.

Recall what Jesus' brothers said He should do: "His brethren therefore said unto him, Depart hence, and go into Judea, that thy disciples also may see the works that thou doest. For there is no man that doeth any thing in secret, and he himself seeketh to be known openly. If thou do these things, shew thyself to the world"

There were likely many disciples (not the apostles) that believed in Jesus as the Messiah, yet had not seen the miracles He had performed. It is certain that much gossip was voiced in Jerusalem concerning what this man Jesus could do, and therefore He must be the promised Messiah.

His brothers, however, intimated that what Jesus had done was done in secret, and if He is capable of doing what was rumored, do it openly for the entire world to see it. It is as though they were saying; you do your work in the small area of Galilee, among the poor and ignorant. Why don't you go to Jerusalem where there are leaned doctors and in the sight of the entire nation of Israel; there you can get a name for yourself.

Satan had no doubt been at work in these brothers trying to bring an untimely death to Jesus, thus destroying the prophecy, which stated exactly when He was to be crucified.

The answer Jesus gave His brothers was simple, but penetrating. "My time is not yet come: but your time is always ready." He was saying, the Prophecy gives the exact time when I will be executed for the sins of the world, and I cannot allow this to happen until the time of the prophecy.

On the other hand, you have no set date in prophecy and can die at any time. My time is not yet come. Jesus refused to go with them to the Feast, knowing a trap would be planned for Him and they would watch for the entrance of His family.

Jesus stayed behind for a time, and then secretly made His way into Jerusalem by less prominent routes.

Jesus must be meek and not project Himself to the nation of Israel, which would violate the prophecy.

This urging by His brothers was not something that Jesus could lightly put aside. True, He knew the prophecy regarding Himself, but He also had a human side and could be tempted with every temptation common to man.

Hebrews remind us of the fact that Jesus was not shielded against temptation: "Wherefore in all things it behoved him to be made like unto his brethren, that he might be a merciful and faithful high priest in things pertaining to God, to make reconciliation for the sins of the people. For in that he himself hath suffered being tempted, he is able to succor them that are tempted." [8]

Perhaps this is the reason the apostle Paul wrote in his epistle to the Corinthians "There hath no temptation taken you but such as is common to man: but God is faithful, who will not suffer you to be tempted above that ye are able; but will with the temptation also make a way to escape, that ye may be able to bear it." [9]

Jesus already knew the truth of the promise recorded by the apostle Paul. Jesus refused to allow his brothers to interfere with God's plan of salvation.

Jesus attended the celebration of the Feast, and did not go into hiding, as one would be tempted to do when his life was being threatened. Instead we find Jesus in the temple teaching as He had done so many times before.

---

[8] Hebrews 2:17, 18
[9] 1 Corinthians 10:13

He even entered into intense discussion with the Jews concerning who He is and whether He was really sent from God.

On the "great day" of the Feast [The last day] Jesus made a daring appearance. This eighth day was called the "great day" because of certain traditional observances. On this day they offered sacrifices for Israel. They then went to the pool Siloam to get water to bring back to the temple.

The water was carried by a priest, the water in a gold vessel. The water was taken to the temple where the priest would pour the water at the foot of the altar. The ceremony pointed out the influence of the Holy Spirit, and Jesus called the Jews to Himself that they might receive this benefit, not symbolically, but in reality.

"In the last day, that great day of the feast, Jesus stood and cried, saying, If any man thirst, let him come unto me, and drink. He that believeth on me, as the scripture hath said, out of his belly shall flow rivers of living water. (But this spake he of the Spirit, which they that believe on him should receive; for the Holy Ghost was not yet given; because that Jesus was not yet glorified.)" [10]

It is noteworthy that Jesus was not calling the people to Himself for the sake of self-aggrandizement but for the spiritual benefit of the Jews. Come away from the dead works of Judaism, such as pouring water at the base of the altar.

Come into the New Covenant God has prepared for Israel; there you will experience the Holy Spirit in reality, not just symbolically.

Some declared that Jesus must be the promised "prophet" spoken of by Moses.

---

[10] John 7:37-39

This could have been Jesus' finest hour for promoting Himself and gaining public recognition to boost His ego. However, we read that Jesus continued to fulfill His role as Messiah by being meek and unostentatious.

Once again we have seen that Jesus has fulfilled the role of Messiah, a role that no other human being could have fulfilled.

No other human could contain all the knowledge, power, and influence with God the Father that Jesus had, and still remain humble.

Chapter 22

"Sinless and Without Guile"

Take a good look at our world today. Everywhere one may go to purchase goods, sell an item, or meet a stranger on the street looking for a hand out, how many of these can you honestly say are sinless and not attempting to "pull the wool over your eyes"? I confess I have not met any.

Consider Jesus, the Messiah, He was prophesied to have been sinless and was never deceitful "And he made his grave with the wicked, and with the rich in his death; because he had done no violence, neither was any deceit in his mouth."[1]

The Hebrew word for "violence" is chamas, which means Messiah had done nothing wrong or unrighteous. Isaiah declared him as being sinless.

The verse in Isaiah gives us quite a few contrasts to consider.

It would appear unlikely that one called a Nazarene, a word of contempt since Nazareth was considered as being of little worth, would be condemned to death, yet be buried in the tomb of a rich man.

Poor background, bad criminal record, yet somehow captured the affection of one who was wealthy. The life of Jesus is full of just such contradictory events, things that should never been possible to happen, but it did happen.

---

[1] Isaiah 53:9

Events were accomplished that no mortal should have been able to bring into being. Perhaps examining this verse in Isaiah will help us better understand how it was possible for Jesus to have such an unusual life.

Jesus had been crucified as a criminal, and as such, could not be buried in the burial tomb prepared for His family.

Consider the usual Roman crucifixion: The Romans normally would crucify a criminal, and then let the body hang on the cross, allowing birds and animals to pick apart the corpse.

Another method sometime used was to throw the body into a ditch and cover it with lime. Both would be a problem for the Jews as their law was specific. If one hung on a tree, he was considered a curse and must be buried the same day, even if at great risk.

To leave a body unburied in Israel was to defile the land according to the law. Even a criminal must be buried, and special burial places were designated for the burial of criminals. It was to this burial that "his grave was appointed with the wicked;"

Joseph of Arimathaea was a wealthy member of the Sanhedrin, and well respected in the Jewish community. He had much to lose by going to Pilate and requesting the body of Jesus that he might bury it before sunset.

"And after this Joseph of Arimathaea, being a disciple of Jesus, but secretly for fear of the Jews, besought Pilate that he might take away the body of Jesus: and Pilate gave him leave. He came therefore, and took the body of Jesus."[2]

---

[2] John 19:38

It would be obvious that Joseph was one who was waiting for, and expecting the arrival of the Kingdom of God, and firmly believed that Jesus was the Messiah.

Jews that were executed as criminals were to be buried in a special place reserved for criminals, and that is where it would appear the Jews would have to bury Him. However, Joseph was from Arimathaea and was a foreigner, and foreigners had special locations where they could prepare tombs for their own burial. It is in such a location that we find the body of Jesus being buried, not with the Jews, but with a foreigner, a Gentile by birth, a Jewish convert by choice.

Jesus was denied the right of a normal dignified Jewish funeral, and by law, His death was not even permitted to be mourned. Yet, the prophecy and the fulfillment both prove that Jesus was innocent, there was no fault in him and no deception in any thing He had spoken to the Jews, Priests, King Herod or Pilate. He was without sin and always presented the truth.

While A.B. Earle was holding meetings at Carson, Nevada, a man came one hundred and eighty miles through the terrible sand roads, from the city of Austin, bringing a written request, signed by ninety-nine of its citizens, asking me to come to their city, and preach Christ to them. These sinners had raised money, and sent this request, although they kept a dance hall on one corner of the street, and card-playing table on another corner, and a drinking establishment on another.

They sent me this word: We are not satisfied with this business, or this way of living, but do not know what else to do. But if you will come and hold a meeting with us, we will quit all this business, and attend the meeting. Why was this desire in the hearts of these men?

Why this dissatisfied feeling, when they were living wicked lives, and pursuing this wicked business? Was it not because man is a noble being, though fallen, and it may be a wreck, yet he is a wreck of dignity, a creature of great worth?

Man has a soul of vast desires; He burns within with restless fires. I thought then, and think so still, if I could be the humble instrument in saving one such soul, I could afford to die. The joy-bells of heaven would ring louder and longer over such an event than over all the victories of the battlefield, or any other earthly achievement. I suppose, out of 1,500,000,000 of our race, not one person can be found who is really happy, in the true sense, without being born again, and having the love of God shed abroad in his heart by the Holy Ghost. In view of the lofty, godlike desires found in every human bosom, and the vast capabilities of the soul, how weighty and appropriate those words of Jesus: What is a man profited if he shall gain the whole world, and lose his own soul, or what shall a man give in exchange for his soul? Oh, what worth! What vast capabilities! [3]

Jesus not only taught this precept, He lived and died by it. Man, to be happy must be free of sin, because man was first made to be perfect and without sin. Sin is an intrusion on God's plan for man's life and man is well aware of it.

---

[3] A.B. Earlle, From: Incidents used ,published 1888

The sinless Jesus came to rectify this problem, many millions have taken advantage of it, and I would hope that many more millions would do so before He returns.

In 1 Peter we find a portion of Scripture where Peter is telling slaves that if their masters for wrongdoing beat them, it is no more than what they deserve. However, if beaten without fault and they bear it patiently that is acceptable unto God. He then gives an example "For even hereunto were ye called: because Christ also suffered for us, leaving us an example, that ye should follow his steps:

Who did no sin, neither was guile found in his mouth: Who, when he was reviled, reviled not again; when he suffered, he threatened not; but committed himself to him that judgeth righteously:

Who his own self bare our sins in his own body on the tree, that we, being dead to sins, should live unto righteousness: by whose stripes ye were healed."[4]

Jesus had just rescued a woman taken in adultery. After telling the Jews that those without sins should cast the first stone, they dropped their stones. At a later time, Jesus again addressed the Jews and a lively discussion broke out as to whether He is the Messiah. They asked, "Who are you?" His answer was, "Just what I have been claiming all along." They then discussed his human lineage, especially focusing on Mary's husband Joseph, then proudly saying, Abraham is our father, we are not illegitimate!

---

[4] 1 Peter 2:21-24

Jesus said "And because I tell you the truth, ye believe me not. Which of you convinceth me of sin? And if I say the truth, why do ye not believe me?" [5] Jesus was saying, can any of you prove me guilty of sin?

Jesus then told them that their father "Abraham rejoiced at the thought of seeing my day; he saw it and was glad." (v56) The Jews then said, you aren't even 50 years old and you have seen Abraham? Jesus said, before Abraham was born, I am!

They then took up stones to kill him for blasphemy, but Jesus slipped away from them, as He had done in Nazareth.

They were blind guides of the blind, accusing Jesus of sin, but not being able to produce one incident where He had sinned. They might have considered His I AM statement as a great sin, but they could not disprove His declaration that He and the Father are one.

It is extremely important for us to believe, and know without a doubt, that Jesus is the sinless Son of God. If He were not without sin, His sacrifice for our sins would not be valid.

However, God would not have allowed Jesus to fulfill all the other prophecies pertaining to the Messiah had He not been sinless. God would have known from the foundation of the world whether Jesus could endure temptation and avoid sin.

In addition, we know that Jesus is not only the Son of God, but also God the Son, and that settles the sin problem once and for all.

---

[5] John 8:45-46

Had God sinned while in the flesh, He would no longer be a god, and the Universe would, at the moment of the first sin, begin to come apart without having the creator to continue to be the "preserver and governor of all things."

Since all is still in place there can be no doubt that God is still God, and that as Immanuel, the sinless God Son, Jesus was without sin and guile. I rest my case!

Chapter 23

"Bear the Reproach Due Others"

Perhaps one of the more familiar passages in the New Testament is the one that informs us that every person on earth has sinned, "For all have sinned, and come short of the glory of God."[1] That alone is bad enough, however we have also read "Behold, all souls are mine; as the soul of the father, so also the soul of the son is mine: the soul that sinneth, it shall die." Adam and Eve had already received this message from God. They knew that one day their body, which was created to be eternal and perfect, would begin to age and ultimately die.

Also, their immortal spirit, which can never die, was now spiritually dead. That indicated that their spirit must be "born again" by some supernatural power. If it were not, their immortal spirit, which is the essence of the person, would spend an eternity shut off from the love of God, and suffer in that terrible place created for Satan and the fallen angels. Hell loomed in their future, unless God offered them a cure.

God spoke of the Messiah He would send to affect that cure. "He shall see of the travail of his soul, and shall be satisfied: by his knowledge shall my righteous servant justify many; for he shall bear their iniquities. Therefore will I divide him a portion with the great, and he shall divide the spoil with the strong; because he hath poured out his soul unto death: and he was numbered with the transgressors; and he bare the sin of many, and made intercession for the transgressors."[2]

---

[1] Romans 3:23
[2] Isaiah 53:11,12

185

In the 53rd chapter of Isaiah the incarnation, preaching, humiliation, rejection, suffering, death, atonement, resurrection and mediation of Jesus Christ are all predicted.

Our subject at this time, however, is that the Messiah must bear the reproach due others. It is an easy task to trace this through the Old Testament and the New Testament.

Jesus never acted as one who sought wealth or ease. Instead, He endured the insults and weakness of the very one He created. [3] His creatures deserved the punishment that fell on Him, and that punishment was both vicious and extremely offensive.

If every sinner, that refused to repent of their sins and receive the salvation offered by Jesus, had to suffer the vicious and offensive punishment given to Jesus, then also spend an eternity of torment in Hell, there might be many more converts to Christianity. That was not God's plan for fallen man, as He is compassionate and full of mercy. As Immanuel God took onto Himself the punishment humanity deserves.

Jesus Himself witnessed to the fact that He would bear our sins "For the zeal of thine house hath eaten me up; and the reproaches of them that reproached thee are fallen upon me. When I wept, and chastened my soul with fasting, that was to my reproach."[4] I know, that is an Old Testament Scripture, but never forget that Jesus is God the Son, He is eternal in nature.

That is the essence of the love of God, He grants mercy, which means we do not get what we deserve, and instead He grants to us His grace, meaning we receive what we do not deserve.

---

[3] John 1:1-5   [4] Psalm 69:9-10

186

Isaiah 53:11 records that Messiah shall see of the travail of his soul, and shall be satisfied. Strange words, until we read sections found in the New Testament regarding Jesus as He fulfilled the role of Messiah. In Matthew 26:38 we hear Jesus in deep agony as He contemplates the punishment and crucifixion that is soon to be His lot. Jesus said, "My soul is exceeding sorrowful. In the language of today it would be 'my soul is grieved in every way possible; the sadness is intense beyond description. Jesus then prayer three times this prayer "O my Father, if it be possible, let this cup pass from me.' The "cup" was symbolic of the cup of poison sometimes given to condemned criminals by the Greeks. In the punishment of Jesus the punishment by drinking a cup of poison would have been far more merciful than the terrible emotional and physical abuse He sustained.

He knew exactly what to expect, as crucifixion was common in Israel in those days. Jesus could visualize the punishment to come, right down to the last ounce of pain and humiliation. The rest of that verse is also strange, as it says, "he shall be satisfied."

One definition of "satisfied" is to achieve or be of sufficient standard to meet a requirement of standard. Messiah, although being capable of visualizing the agony of His soul, and actually experiencing the agony in His human body, would come to the place where He would meet the required standard of God the Father.

That knowledge allowed Jesus to say "nevertheless, not my will but thine be done."

"He shall see of the travail of his soul, and shall be satisfied: by his knowledge shall my righteous servant justify many; for he shall bear their iniquities. Therefore will I divide him a portion with the great, and he shall divide the spoil with the strong; because he hath poured out his soul unto death: and he was numbered with the transgressors; and he bare the sin of many, and made intercession for the transgressors."

By the knowledge Jesus had of himself, he would endure the agony and pain to secure justification [provided the grace of God for the forgiveness of sins] for all who would accept Him as the Messiah, and also His plan of salvation.

The words of Isaiah, 'and made intercession for the transgressors' should cause us to say; now I understand Luke 23:34 "Then said Jesus, Father, forgive them; for they know not what they do." He was not talking about the Jewish leaders that had held an illegal trial after dark, nor the fact that they sought out two witnesses that would lie under oath, and that they took him to the Romans asking for his death.

He also was not talking about the Roman soldiers that were crucifying him or those at the foot of the cross that were gambling for his seamless robe. Jesus was talking to the Father in an intercessory prayer for the sinners of the world, both then and in the future. Father, forgive the sinners, they have been blinded by Satan and the sin Adam passed on to them. They are so spiritually blinded that they do not know the terrible effects or eternal consequences of sin.

With his death, Jesus made it possible for the Father to answer that prayer.

The New Testament offers the sinner much consolation: "Wherefore he is able also to save them to the uttermost that come unto God by him, seeing he ever liveth to make intercession for them."[5]

"And almost all things are by the law purged with blood; and without shedding of blood is no remission. It was therefore necessary that the patterns of things in the heavens should be purified with these; but the heavenly things themselves with better sacrifices than these. For Christ is not entered into the holy places made with hands, which are the figures of the true; but into heaven itself, now to appear in the presence of God for us:" [6] What a wonderful blessing is ours, knowing that King Jesus has entered into the very presence of God the Father, taking with him the result of His crucifixion, burial and resurrection.

No longer is it necessary for man to rely on the blood of animals, which had an effect only for that particular sin, but now the blood of the Messiah will permanently be sufficient for the cleansing away of our sins.

Jesus sits on the right hand of God making intercession for us and proclaiming the penitent sinner as being born again. God the Father accepts the word of the Son of God (God the Son), and the sins are forever forgotten and mercifully forgiven.

Psalm 69:9-11 provides much for thought. This is a prophecy of what Messiah would endure, and it is by no means a light affliction on his soul.

When we move it from being prophetic to the stages of fulfillment we see Jesus as he shed tears for the sins of the world.

---

[5] Hebrews 7:25   [6] Hebrews 9:22-14

How very often the New Testament records Jesus going off by himself for an all night of prayer. I can well imagine that one who would sacrifice sleep in order to pray all night had a heavy burden on his heart. He would have shed many tears of remorse for the sins of the world.

His intense prayer was a type of chastening or self-disciplining of his own body and soul in behalf of the sinners of the world. This all became his reproach, that is, his feelings of extreme disapproval for the sins of mankind. He felt shame for those who felt no shame for the sin in their lives.

The New Testament expresses this reproach in plain enough language: "The reproaches of them that reproached thee fell on me." [7] The world, then and now, should bear the reproach for the sin in their lives, yet mankind continues sinning and inventing new and abominable ways to sin even more.

As Jesus died on the cross at Calvary He took with Him all the various sins that man is capable of committing and when He died, the power of those sins died with him.

If man sins today it is because he wishes to sin, sin no longer has a hold on his life. Satan is a defeated foe and sin has lost its power over man.

The apostle John had learned this lesson well as he sat at the feet of Jesus the Messiah. He wrote in 1 John 2:16 "For all that is in the world, the lust of the flesh, and the lust of the eyes, and the pride of life, is not of the Father, but is of the world."

Note that the sin does not originate in the power of sin itself, but rather it is what the body desires, the eye covets and the pride in ones life reaches for.

The sin comes from man's own desire, and man no longer is powerless against it.

---

[7] Romans 15:3

The Bible tells it like it is "There hath no temptation taken you but such as is common to man: but God is faithful, who will not suffer you to be tempted above that ye are able; but will with the temptation also make a way to escape, that ye may be able to bear it."[8] Plainly put, we sin because we want to, not because we have no power to resist it. God provides all the power necessary for us to be victorious over sin.

This is all the result of having a Messiah that was willing to bear the reproaches due others.

---

[8] 1 Corinthians 10:13

Chapter 24
"Be A Priest"

Have you ever met a man of mystery? One, who commands the utmost respect, draws others to him, yet little is know of him? It is certain there are few such persons in our world today. Those who might have become a "man of mystery" are too quick to reveal all their good traits and stretch their pride as far as it might go.

Abraham met a man of mystery, and many today still wonder just who is this Melchizedek that so impressed Abraham that he paid tithe to him. We may not completely solve the mystery in this chapter, but we will be capable of shedding some light on Melchizedek. He is an historic figure that is worth our consideration.

The Old Testament renders a portion of Scripture regarding Abraham giving tithe to Melchizedek, a figure that has been somewhat of a mystery. Melchizedek is not so much a name as it is a title or designation of honor. A position or office has to be filled by a worthy candidate.

The term is a transliteration of two Hebrew words, melek and tsedeq. The Hebrew melek means king and tsedeq means righteous. Therefore, the term "melchizedek" means literally, "king of righteousness." Because a king is always preeminent in his jurisdiction, whoever Melchizedek was, he had to be preeminent in righteousness.

He had to be the "king" of righteousness. Melchizedek was said to be without father.

The "Sun" of Righteousness and the King of Righteousness is the same person, Jesus Christ. Malachi could not use the word 'Son' because in this verse it would have implied that the Messiah was the son of Melchizedek. [1] In Hebrews **7:3** Paul says that Melchizedek was without father or mother, i.e. He had no parents. Paul's statement should be taken literally, because he was, in fact, emphasizing the deity of Melchizedek.

God was not the father of Melchizedek. Melchizedek, like the Most High God, was without parents. Neither of them had beginning of days nor end of life.

The two of them had always lived and there had never been a time that each of them had not lived. Life was not given to Melchizedek; He was not anyone's son.

"Your throne, O God, is forever and ever, a scepter of righteousness is the scepter of your Kingdom." "The sceptre shall not depart from Judah, nor a lawgiver from between his feet, until Shiloh come; and unto him shall the gathering of the people be."[2]

Jesus proved, by the fulfilling of so many prophecies regarding the anointed One that we know He is also the One called "Shiloh." The word Shiloh comes from the verb הִשְׁתַּו שָׁלַאה translates to "sent", which also describes the Messiah who was sent to make atonement for our sins.

---

[1] Malachi 4:2
[2] Genesis 49:10

Every priest taken from among men is anointed as a priest. This signifies the consecration, that is, the willingness to be sanctified [being set apart for God's special purpose].

The anointing of Levi and his sons is well documented in the Old Testament giving specifics regarding the ceremony. Jesus too had a ceremony of being anointed. His anointing, however, was visibly by the Holy Spirit of God, followed by a verbal declaration from God Himself. Jesus was anointed as Prophet, Priest and King. The three gifts mentioned at the time of His birth, coming from the Wise Men of the East, signify the same intention.

"For this Melchizedek, king of Salem, priest of God Most High, who met Abraham returning from the slaughter of the kings and blessed him, to whom also Abraham divided a tenth part of all (being first, by interpretation, King of righteousness, and then also King of Salem, which is King of peace; without father, without mother, without genealogy,
having neither beginning of days nor end of life, but made like unto the Son of God), abideth a priest continually"[3]

Because this Melchizedek so completely describes Jesus the Christ, we can only assume that he was a theophany, an appearance of the Messiah in the Old Testament. We find many such appearances of Jesus as a theophany in the Old Testament Scriptures. Jesus is the King of kings, and He is the King of Righteousness.

---

[3] Hebrews 7:1-3

Therefore, we can safely assume that Jesus is our High Priest, sitting on the right hand of God, and before them is an altar to remind us that Jesus was our sacrifice for sin. Animal sacrifice is no longer valid, therefore we never see an animal on the altar in Heaven, and we only see the Righteous sacrifice as He sits on the throne of the King of kings.

Throughout His life, Jesus prophesied much, and His prophecies are accurate. As our High Priest He placed the supreme sacrifice on the altar, and that sacrifice ended all sacrifices forever. That sacrifice was on the altar at Calvary, and He was the sacrifice for sin.

The title of our devotional is Messiah, Our High Priest. It would be more accurate to say Messiah Must Be Our High Priest, because that is exactly what Jesus is: our High Priest.

In the Old Testament, we read of those thought to be guilty of some offence being brought to the Priest to determine guilt. In the case of a husband suspecting his wife was unfaithful, the Priest would administer the bitter water (Numbers 5th chapter). In the Book of Revelation, we see the masses of Earth being brought before King Jesus to determine guilt. "And I saw a great white throne, and him that sat on it, from whose face the earth and the heaven fled away; and there was found no place for them."[4]

John reveals that Jesus has been given the authority of judgment; therefore, it is He that is on the Great White Judgment Throne. "For as the Father hath life in himself; so hath he given to the Son to have life in himself; And hath given him authority to execute judgment also, because he is the Son of man."[5]

---

[4] Revelation 20:11
[5] John 5:26,27

If you have never before considered the role of Jesus as our High Priest, this is the portion of Scripture that should come to mind. He is not just one who officiates over spiritual sacrifices, because He Himself is the sacrifice. Much more than that, as the High Priest He will sit on the Great White Judgment Throne and will judge with Righteousness, because He is the King of Righteousness.

Many who have never given thought to what is meant by Jesus being our High Priest likely thinks this is a wonderful designation. As our High Priest He is over the Church and we go to church and sing His praises. But, how often do we really give due consideration to the in-depth meaning of High Priest? Perhaps it is time for the dedicated Christian to notify the world of the complete duties of the High Priest, Jesus the Messiah.

Chapter 25

"Enter Jerusalem On A Donkey"

This is an amazing story when examined properly. This is not simply a fulfillment of a prophecy; this is a visual sermon for sinful man. One cannot possibly fully understand what all this triumphal entry conveys to us in a spiritual manner, and then continue in the same old manner. To continue to live our lives as we did before the Holy Spirit revealed the inner meaning of this event is to be in sin, and sin brings spiritual death.

The Old Testament clearly prophesied that the Messiah would enter Jerusalem on a donkey "Rejoice greatly, O daughter of Zion; shout, O daughter of Jerusalem: behold, thy King cometh unto thee: he is just, and having salvation; lowly, and riding upon an ass, and upon a colt the foal of an ass."[1]

God had commanded Israel not to multiply horses. Solomon and other kings of Israel broke this commandment.

Jesus came to fulfill the law. Had He in his title of king rode upon a horse, it would have been a breach of a positive command of God; therefore, he rode upon an ass, and thus fulfilled the prophecy, and kept the precept unbroken. As a result, we read "And it shall come to pass in that day, saith the LORD, that I will cut off thy horses out of the midst of thee, and I will destroy thy chariots."[2]

---

1 Zechariah 9:9
[2] Micah 5:10

This is another Scripture verse brushed aside lightly because it is not properly understood.

No wars shall be employed to spread the kingdom of the Messiah, because it will be founded and established, "not by might nor by power, but by the Spirit of the Lord of hosts" [3]

This triumphal entry was the triumph of 1) humility over pride and worldly grandeur. How often we see Christians that have never prayed for humility and never received it. Because of their neglect, they retain hidden pride deep down in their heart. Worldly grandeur becomes so precious for too many modern Christians.

It is as though they are saying "look at me, I am really somebody." The fact is, that as a Christian, and therefore a child of the Lord God, we are already somebody, but it is not something to be flaunted, but something to be humbly shared.

2) It was a triumph of poverty over affluence. How modern man strives to gather in all the wealth possible, partially from greed and partially from pride. A poor man is looked down upon by those who have the wealth, but often it is the poor who are rich, that is, if they are sons of the Almighty God.

The wealthy, unsaved individual cannot take their wealth beyond the grave, but the poor child of God goes to a mansion and is an heir of God, and all that will ever be required will be supplied.

---

[3] Zechariah 4:6

It was a triumph of meekness and gentleness over rage and malice. Malice is a desire to do harm to someone, either emotionally or physically. Christians are not above this, however if they indulge in this type of behavior they are at risk of losing their eternal place in God's kingdom.

Many churches have been split because of Christians who lack meekness and gentleness. Christians inwardly filled with rage over trivial things hold a desire to do harm to another, either emotionally or physically. "Again, a new commandment I write unto you, which thing is true in him and in you: because the darkness is past, and the true light now shineth. He that saith he is in the light, and hateth his brother, is in darkness even until now. He that loveth his brother abideth in the light, and there is none occasion of stumbling in him. But he that hateth his brother is in darkness, and walketh in darkness, and knoweth not whither he goeth, because that darkness hath blinded his eyes." [4]

"Ye have heard that it was said to the ancients, Thou shalt not kill; but whosoever shall kill shall be subject to the judgment." [5]

"But I say unto you, that every one that is lightly angry with his brother shall be subject to the judgment; but whosoever shall say to his brother, Raca, shall be subject to the Sanhedrim; but whosoever shall say, Fool, shall be subject to the penalty of the hell of fire." [6][Darby Translation].

---

[4] 1 John 2:8-11   [5] Matthew 5:21,22

[6] Matthew 5:22

Almost forty years in the ministry has taught me that Christians today have a tendency to interpret Scripture in whatever manner meets their life style, but God does not play that Game "Be not deceived; God is not mocked: for whatsoever a man soweth, that shall he also reap." [7] It is a mockery of God to distort the meaning of the Scriptures. To be angry with another "without cause" translates from the Greek to mean because the other one failed in something, and the animosity toward the other is a vain thing, a matter of sinful pride and arrogance. What about the word "angry"? That translates into being exasperated with another. This exasperation makes a thing worse and brings about an unpleasant condition.

Putting this all together, we find that Jesus was protecting us when He said "A new commandment I give unto you, That ye love one another; as I have loved you, that ye also love one another." [8]

We are to love our fellow man, regardless of what he has done. Jesus was riding into Jerusalem to place Himself into the hands of the very ones that were about to kill Him. Yet Jesus had taught His disciples, and us, that we are to love, and that means without condition. His ride into Jerusalem was without malice; He felt no animosity toward the Jewish leaders that He knew would plead with the Roman officials to crucify Him.

There would be no such thing as a split in a church if every Christian would obey this commandment given by Jesus. Sinners would not be discouraged from becoming a Christian if love was the overwhelming attitude of the church members.

---

[7] Galatians 6:7
[8] John 13:34

I wonder what the gathering crowd at Jerusalem that day would have thought as they gathered up palm branches in His way, if someone had stopped them and told them Jesus was riding to His execution? Would they still have shouted Hosanna, O save us? I don't think so; I believe their accolades for Jesus were not a matter of worship but a matter of self-desire. They only wanted from Jesus what they had firmly implanted in their mind; the Messiah was coming to free them from Roman rule.

Is this all the modern Christian wants from Jesus, to supply them with what is firmly implanted in their mind? Is their desire only to secure a place in Heaven, or is the more deeply rooted desire to obey His commandments, follow His example of meekness and humility? Much of humanity today is a control freak. If you do not believe me just watch the way people drive the streets of the city. Many decide they are the only ones deserving the right of way, and the speed limit was posted for others, but not them.

Watch people in the stores when the store is extremely busy, the lines long, and moving slowly. People get exasperated because they cannot be waited on immediately.

Those who are impatient in their cars, and those impatient in the store, and those impatient with their fellow man are really saying "Don't you know who I am? Make way for me, do it my way, I am more important and deserving than you. What a sad commentary on mankind in our society.

I believe that after going deeper into the entrance of Jesus into Jerusalem on a donkey we can see that there may be times when we fall short of His expectations.

However, oh well, I am saved by the blood of Christ, and it is acceptable for me to interpret His commands to best suit my lifestyle. Unfortunately, that is not what the apostle John said, he said if we lived in that manner we are putting our eternal soul at risk. We cannot disobey the commands of Jesus and go to Heaven.

A willful act of disobedience can only be forgiven if it is acknowledged, the soul is in a state of repentance and obeying the command as Jesus intended makes restitution. I fear that once we get to Heaven we will be surprise at the absence of so many "good church members" that could talk like a Christian, but did not reflect the Christ of Christianity.

Here is what I gather from this devotional for myself. There are precious souls out there in need of salvation. I know what I must be if I am to be capable of gaining their confidence allowing me to talk with them and have some influence on their lives. I also realize that it is not enough to be saved by the precious blood of Jesus, I must obey His every command or it is the equivalent of trampling on that precious blood. Once I am saved, I must be what Jesus expects of me, not what man has taught me.

My Bible must be my only guide, as it is the only trustworthy guide I have. Therefore, I must study this manual on a daily basis, because on a daily basis I am confronted with events that might cause me to sin by disobedience.

1 John 4:19 says it all; this is a perfect wrap for our chapter, "We love him, because he first loved us." [9]

---

[9] 1 John 4:19

Chapter 26

Enter the Temple With Authority"

Malachi prophesied the coming of Messiah, and before him would come John the Baptist. John would be a corrector of civil abuses and be a preacher of righteousness. "Behold, I will send my messenger, and he shall prepare the way before me: and the LORD, whom ye seek, shall suddenly come to his temple, even the messenger of the covenant, whom ye delight in: behold, he shall come, saith the LORD of hosts." [1]

The one "whom ye seek" is the one found in Daniel 9:24. He will cleanse the Temple of all defilement and fill it with his glory. He will be coming shortly; this would be in approximately 397 years.

Jesus came into Jerusalem riding on a donkey, meek and with no bitterness toward those he knew would turn him over to the Roman authorities to be crucified.

In this narrative, Jesus is declared to come into the Temple with authority.

Just because Jesus came with authority does not mean that he was lacking in compassion or love. When He came into the Temple He had a mission on His mind. He had observed this scene far too often, and it was now time to take action. Because this was a planned event, no doubt covered with prayer, it is not to be considered an act of anger.

---

[1] Malachi 3:1

This was a pre-meditated act that must be accomplished. Anger is something that swells up inside, and erupts out of control at the most inappropriate moment. Jesus knew exactly what He must do, and in order to do it He must act with authority.

It is said that the people were proclaiming Jesus as the prophet from Nazareth, and they no doubt thought Him to be an earthly Messiah to free them from Roman rule.

Jesus went to the Temple, obvious that He was on a mission and would not be turned aside to bask in the public recognition of the masses.

Once inside the Temple Jesus found exactly what He knew would be there: people selling merchandise, a blatant sign of greed as there were markets places they could have used for selling.

However, here would be a concentration of people from many cities and towns around Israel who might not visit the market place. There were also moneychangers, exchanging currency into the Temple shekel, and at a nice profit by cheating the people; then there were those selling doves to the poor who could not afford to offer a sacrifice of a lamb. Some were too poor to provide a greater offering, but cheated when they purchased doves from these thieving Jews. There were also those who sold oxen and sheep according to John the 2nd chapter. It is interesting that Jesus only addressed the dove salesmen saying "And said unto them, It is written, My house shall be called the house of prayer; but ye have made it a den of thieves." [2]

---

[2] Matthew 21:13

Perhaps it is recorded in this manner to show Jesus' extreme displeasure with those who especially were cheating the poor.

Isaiah prophesied "Even them will I bring to my holy mountain, and make them joyful in my house of prayer: their burnt offerings and their sacrifices shall be accepted upon mine altar; for mine house shall be called an house of prayer for all people." [3] That was God's purpose for the Temple, a place to come and commune with Him.

Perhaps an illustration will help us understand this portion of Scripture.

Our Lord is represented here as purifying his temple. This we may understand he did in reference to his true temple, the Church. His action declares that nothing that was worldly or unholy should have any place among his followers. It is marvellous that these interested, vile men did not raise a mob against him: but it is probable they were overawed by the Divine power, or, seeing the multitudes on the side of Christ, they were afraid to molest him.

A case something similar to this did not succeed so well. A very pious Clergyman observed a woman keeping a public standing to sell nuts, gingerbread, etc., at the very porch of his Church, on the Lord's Day. The clergyman desired her to remove thence, and not defile the house of God, while she profaned the Sabbath of the Lord.

She paid no attention to him. He warned her the next Sabbath, but his words fell on deaf ears.

---

[3] Isaiah 56:7

Going in one Lord's Day to preach, and finding her still in the very entrance, with her stall, he overthrew the stall, and scattered the stuff into the street. He was shortly after summoned to appear before the royal court, which, to its eternal reproach, condemned the action, and fined the man of God in a considerable sum of money!

"Is this house, which is called by my name, become a den of robbers in your eyes? Behold, even I have seen it, saith the LORD." [4] God was speaking to the prophet Jeremiah and this became a prophecy for the Messiah.

A "den of thieves" refers to the many caves around Jerusalem where thieves would hide their stolen goods and money, as well as a safe place to live to keep from being discovered.

Jesus took a scourge of small cords and drove all these greedy merchants out of the Temple. Since He used only small cords to make the scourge it must have been His countenance that brought fear into their heart, not the "weapon". It is amazing that they did not attack Him, as they were greater in number than was Jesus and His disciples. Yet, the multitudes were proclaiming Him as the prophet, and the merchants were more than likely afraid of the crowd of people that followed Him into the Temple.

In John 2:13 mention is made that it was the time of the "Jews" Passover. This is significant, because we read in Exodus "And thus shall ye eat it; with your loins girded, your shoes on your feet, and your staff in your hand; and ye shall eat it in haste: it is the LORD's Passover." [5]

---

[4] Jeremiah 7:11
[5] Exodus 12:11

The shift in name is due to the fact that the Jews had become so detached from God's commandments that the apostles now refer to it as being the Jew Passover. This indicates that it is no longer recognized by God as the Passover observance He commanded in Exodus.

In the Gospel of John the 2nd chapter we once again read, "the zeal of thine house hath eaten me up." A prophecy come true; the zeal of Jesus for the things pertaining to the Father was so great that it took preference over all other desires in His life.

Immediately after this it is recorded that the lame and the blind came to Jesus and He healed them. This is the proper use of the house of God, not the wicked merchandizing. Strange that today we think of our churches as a place of prayer, but seldom as a place where physical miracles are to be performed, the blind made to see, the lame to walk.

Mark gives us some food for thought: "Take ye heed, watch and pray: for ye know not when the time is."[6]

For the Son of Man is as a man taking a far journey, who, left his house, and gave authority to his servants, and to every man his work, and commanded the porter to watch.

Watch ye therefore: for ye know not when the master of the house cometh, at even, or at midnight, or at the cockcrowing, or in the morning:" [7]

---

[6] Mark 13:33
[7] Mark 13:34-35

Two things to consider: Jesus ascended into heaven but before He departed He gave His servants (that's us) authority, and each man has been given a specific work to perform. He emphasized the necessity of using the authority granted to us, and the performance of the assigned work, because we have no idea when He will return to call us into account.

What authority did Jesus confer upon His servants? First, realize that since He was going on a long journey it is only reasonable to assume He gave us the same authority He gave the apostles. "Verily, verily, I say unto you, He that believeth on me, the works that I do shall he do also; and greater works than these shall he do; because I go unto my Father." [8]

Jesus did not say that only the apostles would do greater works than He had done. It targets those who believe on Jesus and the works that He did. The reason we are expected to do greater works is because He had but a three-year earthly ministry, and we are here for a considerably longer period. What has happened to the faith today? We can't blame it entirely on the charlatans that perform phony miracles in the name of Jesus. That is simply one of the tricks of Satan, and we should by faith prove to the world that God is still in the miracle performing business.

It is easy for us to justify ourselves by saying we were not commissioned to perform miracles, but is that being honest and does it coincide with the Scriptures we have just heard?

---

[8] John 14:12

The chief priests and Scribes were greatly displeased with the crowds proclaiming Jesus as the Messiah. Jesus answered their complaint by quoting Scripture from the Old Testament "Out of the mouth of babes and sucklings hast thou ordained strength because of thine enemies, that thou mightest still the enemy and the avenger." [9]

Children were often used by the Jews to give public acclamation to hail celebrated Rabbins. To the chief priests and scribes this would be nothing unusual, but Jesus attempted to remind them that it was prophesied. One wonders if they really understood, or were they already "dull of ears?"

Jesus entered Jerusalem meek and unpretentious, but He also entered as a priest whose zeal for the things of God allowed Him to enter the Temple with authority, and retain His sinless nature.

The topic "Messiah Must Enter the Temple With Authority" would seem to be a few simple sentences of explanation.

It is not all that simple, as the Word of God gave us so much to consider and which requires much meditation before coming to any simple conclusions.

---

[9] Psalm 8:2

Chapter 27

"Hated Without Cause"

In a Southern city a man who resided there was generally regarded and pronounced a miser, when his heart and life were diametrically opposite. He had been cast on the world as a poor ignorant boy, and had been made to know the bitterness and almost unexceptionable hopelessness of such a lot. He, however, through remarkable talent and energy, pulled through, and was known to be a maker and layer up of money.

He dressed in the seediest of clothes and lived on the plainest of fare. And yet he possessed a fortune and was acquiring more. What could all this mean, thought the world, but that he was a miser!

Do not misers all act this way? So the children threw rocks at him, and, taught by a mistaken public opinion, cried out Miser! And yet he was a philanthropist! Nor was that all. He was laying up money to educate and fit for life the children of the very city where they cast missiles at him, and called him miser!

We have seen a statue of him in the same community, with children in a marble group looking up to him and reaching to touch his outstretched hands; and as we gazed we thought of the years that this man had walked unknown, misunderstood and misjudged in this very city, while the young people used their hands then to cast stones at their benefactor, who poorly dressed walked unrecognized in their streets. (Illustration from the 19th Century)

I would imagine there are dozens of such stories that could be told of unselfish individuals that bore the brunt of ridicule and shame, and that without a murmur. As selfless as that may be, it cannot compare with our subject of the "Messiah must be hated without cause." The stories we might hear would likely not end in the death of the ones suffering ridicule or reproach. It was not just reproach Jesus had to endure; it was hatred in the vilest form.

The hatred, ridicule and reproach heaped upon Jesus would eventually end in the most wicked and tortuous death imaginable.

The Old Testament prophesied that Messiah would feel the stinging reproach is a most cruel manner: "Thus saith the LORD, the Redeemer of Israel, and his Holy One, to him whom man despiseth, to him whom the nation abhorreth, to a servant of rulers, Kings shall see and arise, princes also shall worship, because of the LORD that is faithful, and the Holy One of Israel, and he shall choose thee." [1]

Again, we read "They that hate me without a cause are more than the hairs of mine head: they that would destroy me, being mine enemies wrongfully, are mighty: then I restored that which I took not away. O God, thou knowest my foolishness; and my sins are not hid from thee." [2]

This does not describe a handful of small boys jeering and throwing rocks, this speaks of a multitude of dangerous men in positions of authority seeking a way to end the life of Messiah.

---

[1] Isaiah 49:7
[2] Psalm 69:5

The Jews of that day should have known the Scriptures regarding Messiah, and I cannot help but believe that many of the Jewish leaders were knowledgeable, but their greed for power, position and prosperity overcame their knowledge. Surely, they must have realized the truth of the words of Jesus, if not in the exact wording, at least in concept "He that hateth me hateth my Father also." [3]

Surely, the Jewish rulers had read "He that sitteth in the heavens shall laugh: the LORD shall have them in derision."[4]

Although this chapter is prophetic, the Jews should have taken a clue from it as they read, "The kings of the earth set themselves, and the rulers take counsel together, against the LORD, and against his anointed, saying, Let us break their bands asunder, and cast away their cords from us."[5]

The terrible day will come when those who resisted God and His Messiah will find that there will be no mercy extended to them.

While God may not visibly "laugh", He will hold them in scorn. His judgments against them will be what they should have expected, but thought this could never happen to them.

Jesus is saying that those who hate Him also hate the Heavenly Father says more than just what we glean from a rapid reading. Not knowing God is the basis of all religious persecution. Jesus conveyed this message to His disciples, and we see the truth of it in our world today.

---

[3] John 15:15-25
[4] Psalm 2:4
[5] Psalm 2:2-3

Consider the many Christian missionaries who, when attempting to bring the Word of Truth to idolatrous religions, suffered hardship, persecution, privations, and even death. All this is the result of not knowing the God of love whom we serve. The missionaries were attempting to put these lost ones in touch with love Personified, but they were met with the same hatred, as did Jesus.

In the Gospel of John Jesus told the disciples that the world would hate them because it hated Him. The degree of hatred they would experience would only be in proportion of their faith. That rule of thumb applies to Christians today also.

Jesus told them not to be concerned over this hatred, but rather "rejoice." Why rejoice? Because it is a proof that their faith is working and they can gauge the strength of their faith by the degree of hatred they experience.

It has been written, "The laws of Christ condemn a vicious world, and goad it to revenge! "
– Gambold- If evil men had watched Jesus for the purpose of accusing Him for something that He had said, they will be watching the disciples also past and present.

Jesus said these vicious men had nothing for which they could hide, because His works proved Him to the Messiah. Their rejection of Christ cannot be justified by any argument or excuse.

The Messiah must be hated without cause. It was true in the days of His earthly ministry and it is true today. Christians today are quick to exempt themselves from what Jesus said regarding persecution and hatred leveled at those who follow Him.

What Jesus said those many years ago are still valid as Gospel truth today. We may not have experienced the hatred spoken of by Jesus, but should it come we need not be caught off guard.

As was true of the ancient disciples, it will also be true for us; faith in God the Father will see us through anything He allows to enter our lives. "Verily, verily, I say unto you, The servant is not greater than his Lord; neither he that is sent greater than he that sent him".[6]

The following story, as terrible as it may sound, aptly describes the level of hatred the Jews had for Jesus. "One of the worst cases of hatred I have ever come across is found in a will written in 1935 by a Mr. Conohoe.

It says, 'Unto my two daughters, Francis Marie and Denise Vicoria, by reason of their unfilial attitude toward a doting father....I leave he sum of $1 to each with a father's curse. May their lives be fraught with misery, unhappiness, and poignant sorrow. May their deaths be soon and of a lingering malignant and tortuous nature.' The last line of the will is so vicious I shutter to quote it. It reads, 'May their souls rest in hell and suffer the torments of the condemned for eternity."[7]

It is unfortunate that the Jews of Jesus day did not have someone writing for a publication available to all, and containing the following words by Ann Landers. "Hatred is like acid. It can destroy the vessel in which it is stored as well as the object on which it is poured."

---

[6] John 13:16 ; [7] Our Daily Bread. February 18, 1994

While their hatred "destroyed" Messiah for that period on the cross, nothing could prevent the Messiah Jesus from resurrecting from the dead. Unfortunately, many millions since that day have continued this hatred for Messiah in order to satisfy their own way of life. That hatred will, and has, destroyed many vessels containing the acid of hatred.

Chapter 28

"Undesired and Rejected By His Own People"

Artists in Christian circles paint Jesus in a far different light than did Isaiah. It would appear that God purposefully made certain that Jesus would not be a suave, handsome Jew that would make Him popular "For he shall grow up before him as a tender plant, and as a root out of a dry ground: he hath no form nor comeliness; and when we shall see him, there is no beauty that we should desire him. He is despised and rejected of men; a man of sorrows, and acquainted with grief: and we hid as it were our faces from him; he was despised, and we esteemed him not." [1]

It was necessary that Jesus be esteemed for the truth He offered, and the salvation He provided at Calvary.

I cannot think of anything worse than to be barred from the affection of one's own family.

We can tolerate not being accepted by the strangers, and even our close acquaintances, but to lose the love and approval of one's own family because of your love for the things of God would be heart breaking.

This is exactly what was prophesied for the Messiah Jesus. His own half-brothers did not believe Jesus to be the promised Messiah. These siblings obviously did not accept what Mary and Joseph may have told them about the birth of Jesus, or they thought it to be a nice story, like a fairy tale marriage.

---

[1] Isaiah 53:2-3

The siblings, among others, found Jesus to be undesirable. The Jewish leaders also failed to recognize the fulfillment of Scripture:

"And the multitude cometh together again, so that they could not so much as eat bread. And when his friends heard of it, they went out to lay hold on him: for they said, He is beside himself. And the scribes which came down from Jerusalem said, He hath Beelzebub, and by the prince of the devils casteth he out devils." [2]

His friends though He was having psychological problems and the Jewish leader attributed to Satan that which was from God. The reproach for Jesus was great, but the punishment for attributing to Satan that which was brought about by the Lord God will be much worse.

"Now the Jew's feast of tabernacles was at hand. His brethren therefore said unto him, Depart hence, and go into Judaea, that thy disciples also may see the works that thou doest. For there is no man that doeth any thing in secret, and he himself seeketh to be known openly. If thou do these things, shew thyself to the world. For neither did his brethren believe in him." [3]

I can almost hear the scorn in the voice of the brothers as they prodded Jesus to go into Judea and perform miracles for all to see. They were also accusing Him of performing miracles before the poor and ignorant because they could easily be fooled by trickery. I would think that much of the emotional hurt for Jesus was not for Himself, but for the unbelieving brothers.

---

[2] Mark 3:20-22
[3] John 7:2-5

222

Being undesired and rejected is comparable to one inflicted with leprosy.

What a terrible future to prophesy for one who was to come to love these people. He was to have no form [bodily structure], nor any beauty to attract others to him, and his countenance [expression] was not such that any should desire him. In other words, if He was not approving of their sin He did not put on a fake smile to entice them to Himself.

Isa 63:3&5 reads, "I have trodden the winepress alone; and of the people there was none with me" - no man had any part in making the atonement; it is entirely the work of Messiah alone. "for I will tread them in mine anger, and trample them in my fury;" this speaks of the indignation [righteous anger] of Messiah at being rejected by His own creatures. "their blood shall be sprinkled upon my garments, and I will stain all my raiment." Isaiah "Who is this that cometh from Edom, with dyed garments from Bozrah? this that is glorious in his apparel, travelling in the greatness of his strength? I that speak in righteousness, mighty to save. Wherefore art thou red in thine apparel, and thy garments like him that treadeth in the winefat?"[4]

This appears to be Isaiah seeing Messiah in the last days and asked the rhetorical question for our benefit.

The answer Jesus gives cannot speak of His crucifixion as He speaks of the fact that He already is the One that is mighty to save [salvation has already been secured] but speaks of Messiah "treading the winepress", an act of smashing the 'grapes' until they release their wine.

---

[4] Isaiah 63:1-2

This obviously speaks of a time in the future when Messiah Jesus will arrive at the time known as the Second Coming. The first appearance was to bring peace between man and God; the second time is to punish those who refused this peace treaty.

"And I looked, and behold a white cloud, and upon the cloud one sat like unto the Son of man, having on his head a golden crown, and in his hand a sharp sickle. And another angel came out of the temple, crying with a loud voice to him that sat on the cloud, Thrust in thy sickle, and reap: for the time is come for thee to reap; for the harvest of the earth is ripe. And he that sat on the cloud thrust in his sickle on the earth; and the earth was reaped.

And another angel came out of the temple that is in heaven, he also having a sharp sickle.

And another angel came out from the altar, which had power over fire; and cried with a loud cry to him that had the sharp sickle, saying, Thrust in thy sharp sickle, and gather the clusters of the vine of the earth; for her grapes are fully ripe. And the angel thrust in his sickle into the earth, and gathered the vine of the earth, and cast it into the great winepress of the wrath of God. And the winepress was trodden without the city, and blood came out of the winepress, even unto the horse bridles, by the space of a thousand and six hundred furlongs" [5]

---

[5] Revelation 14:14-20

This is simple enough to understand even though it uses symbolism. The sharp sickle of Messiah will be thrust down on earth and will gather the vine "fruit" of the earth [people] and cast them into the place of the wrath of God. At the Second Coming Messiah Jesus will pour out His wrath on the sinners of earth, and especially on those attacking Israel.

The blood from the battle of Armageddon will flow starting in the valley of Megiddo and flowing for 180 English miles, or, 200 Italian miles. This matches exactly the Italian miles [curious, food for thought about Rome].

Since the blood will flow for approximately 180-200 miles, it is obvious that it will flow beyond Israel, which is only 85 miles long. Looking at the map, it would indicate the blood would flow either through Jordan into Saudi Arabia, or, into the Red Sea. Since Jordan and Saudi Arabia will both be involved in the battle of Armageddon, it suggests to me that it will flow into these countries, but that is only my opinion.

Isaiah prophesied a future event of Messiah: "their blood shall be sprinkled upon my garments, and I will stain all my raiment." [6]This term "will stain" is in the preterit form that indicates the past tense, past historic.

Their blood will be upon the garments of Messiah because they refused to accept Jesus as the Messiah and remained in the sins. Jesus here reminds us that He has stained His garments to prevent them from being cast into the winepress of God's wrath, but they refused the gift.

---

[6] Isaiah 63:3

Now His garments are not only stained from the blood of Calvary, but also with the blood of unbelieving sinners being cast into the "wrath of God", which is Hell.

"Is not this the carpenter, the son of Mary, the brother of James, and Joses, and of Juda, and Simon? and are not his sisters here with us? And they were offended at him." [7]

They did not apply the truth of Scripture regarding Jesus, they only applied what worldly knowledge they had of Him; people still do that today.

Luke tells us that at this time in Jesus life He realized He was undesirable to His own siblings and had no permanent place to call home: "And Jesus said unto him, Foxes have holes, and birds of the air have nests; but the Son of man hath not where to lay his head." [8]

"He came unto his own, and his own received him not." [9]

"His brethren therefore said unto him, Depart hence, and go into Judaea, that thy disciples also may see the works that thou doest. For there is no man that doeth any thing in secret, and he himself seeketh to be known openly. If thou do these things, shew thyself to the world. For neither did his brethren believe in him." [10]

---

[7] Mark 6:3
[8] Luke 9:58
[9] John 1:11
[10] John 7: 3- 5

226

How terrible it must have been to be the Son of God (God the Son), the promised Messiah that was expected by the Jews, yet upon His appearance to bring them the good news of salvation (the New Covenant), they rejected Him. Only a handful of disciples firmly believed in Him, even when His own brothers did not.

It should not surprise Christians today if their attempts to introduce the spiritually lost to the Messiah, only to be neglected, abused, or in some countries executed. Humanity has not changed in this regard since the days when Jesus walked the Earth to tell sinful man the way back to the Father.

One author said the Christian must Watch, Work and Wait. That speaks volumes to me. I will Watch the world events and match these to the Word of God. I will Work to convert sinners from their unbelief to that of a firm belief in the Messiah Jesus.

I will wait for the coming of the bridegroom as He comes for His Bride, the Church, those who are born again Christians.

As I Wait, I will also continue to pray for the Peace of Jerusalem as commanded in Psalms, "Pray for the peace of Jerusalem: they shall prosper that love thee." [11] In the peace and prosperity of the city, the Jews will find their prosperity.

A reminder to all: there will never be peace in Jerusalem until Messiah Jesus makes His Second Coming a reality. Ezekiel 38 must be fulfilled before the Second Coming of Jesus. Continue to pray for the Peace of Jerusalem to bring about the Second Coming of Jesus the Messiah.

---

[11] Psalm 122:6

Chapter 29

"Rejected By the Jewish Leadership"

We might well ask the question, did the Jewish leaders of Jesus' ministry know the Scriptures as well as they might? The answer must be a resounding "yes", because among them were many Scriptural scholars. Surely they had read "The stone which the builders refused is become the head stone of the corner." [1] Is it not true, however, that one might read a portion of Scripture, but if the Holy Spirit does not enlighten them regarding it, they might well misunderstand it.

David wrote this psalm intending it to point to himself, not realizing that it was also to become prophetic of the Messiah. The Jewish rulers had rejected David, but God, having chosen David, caused him to become the great ruler of his people Israel.

Consider the prophecy as it applied to the promised Messiah. The terms used by King David are those of a brick mason. A mason might find a stone needed for a particular place, but upon examination decides it is not suitable for the intended purpose. The stone is "rejected", cast aside and another one chosen to replace it.

Later, as the building progresses the mason discovers that the stone he thought unsuitable was exactly the one needed for the corner stone of the great edifice he was erecting.

---

[1] Psalm 118:22

So it was with Jesus, as He presented Himself to the "builders", the Jewish chief priests, elders and doctors of the law. Clearly, He told them He was the Messiah. Jesus used the familiar "I AM" phrase seven times in the book of John. The Jews certainly knew the Scriptures and could have verified whether Jesus was who He claimed to be. Instead, the "builders" rejected the very "stone" that after His crucifixion and resurrection became the corner stone of the Church of the New Covenant. Messiah now abolished the Old Covenant and the New Covenant replaced it.

What a terrible thing it was for God the Son, the Messiah, to be rejected by the very ones He had created for fellowship.

It would appear strange to me that the very ones who studied the Scriptures so diligently, and professed to be waiting for the promised Messiah, would be the body of men that would reject Messiah when He did appear.

How often Jesus disputed with Jewish leaders concerning the Scriptures and gave them ample Scriptural proof, that He is the expected Messiah. Unfortunately, the Scriptures were correct when it prophesied the Jews would be spiritually blind and deaf. It all started in the wilderness with Moses, "These are the words of the covenant, which the LORD commanded Moses to make with the children of Israel in the land of Moab, beside the covenant which he made with them in Horeb.

And Moses called unto all Israel, and said unto them, "Ye have seen all that the LORD did before your eyes in the land of Egypt unto Pharaoh, and unto all his servants, and unto all his land;

The great temptations which thine eyes have seen, the signs, and those great miracles: Yet the LORD hath not given you an heart to perceive, and eyes to see, and ears to hear, unto this day." [2]

Jeremiah prophesied this would continue with the Jews, "Hear now this, O foolish people, and without understanding; which have eyes, and see not; which have ears, and hear not:"[3]

Ezekiel gave the same prophecy "Son of man, thou dwellest in the midst of a rebellious house, which have eyes to see, and see not; they have ears to hear, and hear not: for they are a rebellious house." [4]

Jesus explained to His disciples why He spoke in parables that were difficult to understand until He gave the true meaning.

"And the disciples came, and said unto him, Why speakest thou unto them in parables? He answered and said unto them, Because it is given unto you to know the mysteries of the kingdom of heaven, but to them it is not given.

For whosoever hath, to him shall be given, and he shall have more abundance: but whosoever hath not, from him shall be taken away even that he hath.

Therefore speak I to them in parables: because they seeing see not; and hearing they hear not, neither do they understand.

---

[2] Deuteronomy 29:1-4
[3] Jeremiah 5:21
[4] Ezekiel 12:2

And in them is fulfilled the prophecy of Esaias, which saith, By hearing ye shall hear, and shall not understand; and seeing ye shall see, and shall not perceive: For this people's heart is waxed gross, and their ears are dull of hearing, and their eyes they have closed; lest at any time they should see with their eyes and hear with their ears, and should understand with their heart, and should be converted, and I should heal them." [5]

Is it any wonder that it was prophesied that the Jewish leadership must reject the Messiah? They were a prime example of the blind leading the blind, and the deaf preaching to the deaf.

Psalm 118:12 speaks of the "stone" that was refused by the builders became the head of the corner stone.

This is a familiar term even in modern days. The cornerstone is often laid during a ceremony and it gives the date of the building. We often use a hollow cornerstone in order to place various items in it, which in years to come will be extracted, and give further description of the building and its intended use. It is the stone that is at the corner of a building uniting two intersecting walls.

The technical term for a cornerstone is quoin, which refers to a cornerstone especially when it is different in size or material, from the other blocks in the wall.

I see here two items that catch my attention:
1) The cornerstone unites two intersecting wall in this case, the Jewish Religion and the Christian Church. Because of Christ, our cornerstone, these two will be united at His Second Coming making us one.

---

[5] Matthew 13:10-15

2) The quoin is different in size or material from the others in the wall. How descriptive of Messiah who is sinless, holy, pure, righteous, and has all the attributes of the Lord God. He is definitely different from either the Jew or the Christian.

The verse in Psalm 118 speaks of a rejected stone. David was using a stonemason term that means that during the building, a stone would be selected and an attempt made to fit it into a spot in the building that needed a stone at that time.

Often, the chosen stone would not fit into that location and would be laid aside [rejected] for the moment. However, later it may be found that this very stone was a perfect fit as a cornerstone and the "rejected" stone now takes a choice and important place in the building.

The Church is represented in Scripture under the name of the Temple and house of God in Jerusalem. "Know ye not that ye are the temple of God, and that the Spirit of God dwelleth in you?" [6] This takes on more meaning as we consider ourselves as the Church and Jesus is our cornerstone that gives definition to our lives; the date we became a Christian, important documentation" within the cornerstone regarding the intended purpose of this individual.

"And are built upon the foundation of the apostles and prophets, Jesus Christ himself being the chief corner stone; In whom all the building fitly framed together groweth unto an holy temple in the Lord." [7]

Our foundation is that which the apostles and prophets reveal to us and Jesus our Messiah brings it all together into a holy temple in the Lord.

---

[6] 1 Corinthians 3:16
[7] Ephesians 2:20-21

The builders that rejected the cornerstone were the chief priests and the elders of the people of Israel.

The 118th psalm, verse 12 was first written as a description of King David when, at first, he was rejected as king over Israel. In 2 Samuel, we read that the men of Judah, having heard that Saul and Jonathan were both dead, immediately anointed David as king over Judah. Abner, the captain of Saul's army, heard about this and took Ishbosheth and made him king over all Israel. This divided the Jews into Israel and Judah. David was "rejected" as the corner stone, but later became the one to bring the two together into one kingdom. This also is a prophecy of Messiah at the time of His rejection by the chief priests and elders of Israel.

The last part of that verse in Matthew 21:42 said that this was done by the Lord, and it is marvellous in our eyes. Jesus became the source of joy and the person of admiration for all His followers as well as the glory of man.

Coming back to our topic, Messiah must be rejected by the Jewish leaders; we go now to John the 7th chapter. The Jews were confused about Jesus, saying we know where this man comes from, but no one will know where the Messiah is from when He appears. Finally, on the last day of the Great Feast Jesus called the Jews to Himself as the "living water." Some Jews said surely this is the prophet.

The Temple guards had been sent out to capture Jesus and bring him back to the Jewish Leaders. Upon their return to the leaders, being empty handed, they were asked "Why didn't your bring him in?" Their answer was simple, "No one ever spoke the way this man does." The leaders shouted, "You mean he has deceived you also?" The Pharisees spit out the words "Has any of the rulers or of the Pharisees believed on him, No!
But this mob that knows nothing of the law-there is a curse on them."

It could not be plainer than that; the Jewish leader and Pharisees agreed that none of them had ever believed on him. They were, of course, not completely correct, because Joseph of Arimathaea was a member of the Sanhedrin and he was a believer. There is no doubt, though; that this Scripture fulfills the prophecy found in the Old Testament that the Jewish leadership would reject Messiah.

We read in John 8:36 that Jesus was telling the Jewish leaders that if He, the Messiah, would make them free they would be free indeed. Jesus also acknowledged their statement that they were Abraham's seed. He then added that they intended to kill him. He also said if they were truly Abraham's children they would do the works of Abraham.

Jesus then told them that their father was the devil and you will do the lusts of your father. Satan was a murderer from the beginning and had no truth in him; he is a liar and the father of it.

Their answer was an accusation, saying that Jesus was a Samaritan [terrible slander to a Jew] and He was possessed of a devil.

When Jesus finally told them that before Abraham was, I AM, they picked up stones to kill Him. Jesus then "hid" Himself, going through the midst of them leaving the Temple.

There is no doubt that Jesus fulfilled the prophecy concerning the Messiah that said He must be rejected by Jewish leadership. There can be no doubt that Jesus, the Messiah, fulfilled the titled prophecy.

Chapter 30

"Plotted Against By Jew and Gentile"

There are some religious groups that would try to convince us that it is the Jew that crucified king Jesus. While the Jewish leaders did take a prominent role in the death and crucifixion, both the Jew and Gentile plotted against Him to bring him to Mt. Calvary.

The truth is, it was not any one group that crucified Jesus, it was every person who has ever sinned. Jesus came to bring salvation to the entire world, Jew and Gentile alike. The bit players only represented sinful man, regardless of his ethnic background.

We have read much about the hatred of the Jewish leaders for Jesus, yet here we find prophesied that it is not only the Jews but also the Gentiles. Of all people, the Gentiles should receive Jesus with open arms. The promises of the Lord God were given to the Jews through Abraham and his descendants.

It was also prophesied in that promise that, although the Jews would be God's chosen people, all the nations of earth would be grafted into the promise. Just as a wild olive branch is grafted into the domestic olive tree, so are the Gentiles grafted into Judaism. That being a fact, the Gentiles are recipients of both the blessings and the curses pronounce upon the Jews.

In this prophecy regarding what Messiah must face in His earthly ministry we find both Jew and Gentile working against Messiah Jesus.

In the 2nd Psalm we find no reference to Judaism, but that fact has already been more than amply proven. Here, we find the "heathen", the "nations" that are "imagining a vain thing." "Why do the heathen rage, and the people imagine a vain thing?

The kings of the earth set themselves, and the rulers take counsel together, against the LORD, and against his anointed, saying, Let us break their bands asunder, and cast away their cords from us."[1]

This Psalm first refers to King David, and secondly to Jesus Messiah. David had just taken Jerusalem from the Jebusites, and made it the capitol city of the kingdom "Nevertheless David took the strong hold of Zion: the same is the city of David. And David said on that day, Whosoever getteth up to the gutter, and smiteth the Jebusites, and the lame, and the blind that are hated of David's soul, he shall be chief and captain. Wherefore they said, the blind and the lame shall not come into the house. So David dwelt in the fort, and called it the city of David, and David built round about from Millo and inward."[2]

The Philistines hearing this encamped in the valley of Rephaim, close to Jerusalem. Josephus Antiq. lib 7c.4, says all Syria, Phoenicia, and the other adjacent nations, all warlike people, united their armies with the Philistines, in order to destroy David before he had time to strengthen himself in the new kingdom. David, realizing he was being confronted with armies that were too great for him to defeat on his own consulted the Lord.

---

[1] Psalm 2:1,2
[2] 2 Samuel 5:5-9

The Scriptures reveal, "But when the Philistines heard that they had anointed David king over Israel, all the Philistines came up to seek David; and David heard of it, and went down to the hold. The Philistines also came and spread themselves in the valley of Rephaim. And David enquired of the LORD, saying, Shall I go up to the Philistines? wilt thou deliver them into mine hand? And the LORD said unto David, Go up: for I will doubtless deliver the Philistines into thine hand."[3]

The Lord gave David the victory as he totally overthrew the combined armies of his enemies.

This Psalm first celebrates the taking of Jerusalem and the overthrow of all the kings and chiefs of the neighboring nations.

The word "heathen" (goyim), and the "nations", is commonly called the Gentiles.

The word "rage" denotes the gnashing of teeth and the impulsively rushing together of those indigent and cruel warriors, is well expressed by the sound as well as the meaning of the original word.

A vain thing: Vain indeed to prevent the spread of the Gospel in the world. To prevent Jesus Messiah the King of kings, and the Lord of lords, from having the empire of His own Hearth. So vain were their endeavors that every effort throughout history tended to open and enlarge the way for the all-conquering sway of the scepter of righteousness.

In verse 2 of this Psalm, it said this rage is against the Messiah. The verse says it is against his "anointed." This signifies the anointed person of David first and secondly to Jesus.

---

[3] 2 Samuel 5:17-19

v3 "Let us break their bands" - These are the words spoken by the combined forces of the heathen armies, as well as the combined heathen forces and powers of this day.

Bishop Horn has said it better than I, and though his wording is archaic, it well expresses this verse. "We may see the ground of opposition, namely the unwillingness of rebellious nature to submit to the obligations of Divine laws, which cross the interests, and lay a restraint on the desires of men.

Corrupt affections are the most inveterate [habitual] enemies of Christ, and their language is, We will not have this man to reign over us.

Doctrine would be readily believed if they involved in them no precepts [guiding principles]; and the Church may be tolerated in the world if she will only give up her discipline."

This reminds me of a parable Jesus spoke regarding the Jewish leaders, but could also be applied to the present day rebellion in the world against Jesus and His kingdom rule. "And he began to speak unto them by parables.

"A certain man planted a vineyard, and set an hedge about it, and digged a place for the winefat, and built a tower, and let it out to husbandmen, and went into a far country. And at the season he sent to the husbandmen a servant, that he might receive from the husbandmen of the fruit of the vineyard. And they caught him, and beat him, and sent him away empty. And again he sent unto them another servant; and at him they cast stones, and wounded him in the head, and sent him away shamefully handled.

And again he sent another; and him they killed, and many others; beating some, and killing some. Having yet therefore one son, his well beloved, he sent him also last unto them, saying,

They will reverence my son. But those husbandmen said among themselves, This is the heir; come, let us kill him, and the inheritance shall be our's. And they took him, and killed him, and cast him out of the vineyard."[4]

Although it is not possible for the modern rebellious ones to kill the Son of God their animosity is strong enough to suggest they would do so, if it were possible. Since they cannot kill the Son, they satisfy themselves with killing His missionaries and witnesses.

A reminder of the words of the apostle Paul in the fourth chapter of the book of Acts will reveal the truth concerning the fulfillment of this prophecy in the New Testament "For of a truth against thy holy child Jesus, whom thou hast anointed, both Herod, and Pontius Pilate, with the Gentiles, and the people of Israel, were gathered together," [5]

Paul speaks of Jesus as being the anointed One, and Herod and Pontius Pilate (both Gentiles) and the people of Israel were gathered together against Jesus.

Today the "rage", and "gnashing of teeth" against Jesus is hidden behind hypocrisy, or perhaps "political correctness." Hidden or not, the animosity against Jesus and His followers is very real. If the believers are not physically persecuted in this country, they are ridiculed.

---

[4] Mark 12: 1-8
[5] Acts 4:27

The media attempts to give the impression that all Christians are either mentally deranged or simply brainwashed by slick speaking ministers. The Church is often viewed as being greedy for money, and the pastors only wish to fill their church for the sake of the tithe they will receive.

True believers understand that as Jesus was detested and hated, so will His followers in this world be. It is the attitude of the true believer to say, "So be it, nevertheless, come Lord Jesus."

We end this chapter with a definite statement that Jesus was plotted against by both the Jews and the Gentiles. No one group need take the blame for the death of Jesus. Jesus died for all who had sinned, and the Scriptures remind us that we each have sinned and come short of the expectations of God.

"For of a truth against thy holy child Jesus, whom thou hast anointed, both Herod, and Pontius Pilate, with the Gentiles, and the people of Israel, were gathered together," [6]

---

[6] Acts 4: 27

Chapter 31

"Betrayed By A Friend"

Imagine being in the inner circle with the Disciples as they learned from Jesus that He is God the Son, Emmanuel, God with man. Many proofs have been given by fulfilling the prophecies of healing the sick, raising the dead, etc. And yet find an inner greed that would take money from the Jews to betray this very one you had pretended to be a close friend. That is exactly what Judas did as he betrayed the Messiah Jesus.

In view of verses in the Old Testament and the New Testament we can determine that Jesus was to be betrayed by one who was an acquaintance, and one who had entered into close conversation with Him 'we took sweet counsel together.'

When Jesus said "that a man lay down his life for his friends," he was not speaking of a man that would die for a mere clansman, but rather one whom he considered actively fond of and held dear. Judas had a great privilege by being held in confidence of the twelve and being a part of their private conversations.

In the eyes of Jesus, Judas was one who was familiar, or known to Him. Judas did show himself to be more than a person who was an acquaintance that was permitted into the inner circle of teaching and conversation. Had he been sincere in his belief in Jesus he would have been known as a φιλοσ, a person considered actively fond and dear to Jesus.

I offer this from the very beginning to settle any question about the loyalty of Judas, especially in view of the fact that Jesus knew who would betray Him when it was the appropriate time. Jesus allowed Judas into the inner circle because prophecy demanded it, and Jesus came to fulfill all righteousness, that is, the Word of God.

Acts the first chapter speaks of Judas as being the one that actually betrayed Jesus. It gives further detail, which I will reserve for the future.

Judas has been 'justified' by some in past years by claiming he only intended to force Jesus to proclaim Himself as the Messiah. A church was also built in his memory and a congregation formed as a 'Christian' church.

There is little doubt that Judas was what the Scriptures proclaim him to be; he was a traitor, the one who betrayed Jesus bringing about His arrest when Judas kissed Him and said shalom lecha - peace be to thee! That was the signal that here is the man you seek, arrest him.

"And while he yet spake, lo, Judas, one of the twelve, came, and with him a great multitude with swords and staves, from the chief priests and elders of the people. Now he that betrayed him gave them a sign, saying, whomsoever I shall kiss, that same is he: hold him fast. And forthwith he came to Jesus, and said, Hail, master; and kissed him. And Jesus said unto him, Friend, wherefore art thou come? Then came they, and laid hands on Jesus and took him."[1]

Many questions arise concerning Judas, which we will ultimately address, and the answers will not be the opinions of man, but the facts of Scripture.

---

[1] Matthew 26:47-50

We can understand how committed Jesus was to fulfilling the Father's will, when at the Last Supper He told Judas to go complete his act of treachery. He knew what was to happen and made no effort to prevent it. Indeed, a friend, one taken into close communion with them, although only considered by Jesus as a clansman, and not one who deserved to be considered as a fond or dear friend.

"Now when the even was come, he sat down with the twelve. And as they did eat, he said, Verily I say unto you, that one of you shall betray me. And they were exceeding sorrowful, and began every one of them to say unto him, Lord, is it I? And he answered and said, He that dippeth his hand with me in the dish, the same shall betray me. The Son of man goeth as it is written of him: but woe unto that man by whom the Son of man is betrayed! it had been good for that man if he had not been born. Then Judas, which betrayed him, answered and said, Master, is it I? He said unto him, Thou hast said."[2]

We must remember that the Lord God does not cause, or provoke mankind into such sinful acts. He knows all things and before the world was formed. It was known to Him that Judas would be the one to betray the Messiah, and He would not interfere because it would be one piece of the scenario that would ultimately bring Salvation to the entire world.

"For it was not an enemy that reproached me; then I could have born it: neither was it he that hated me that did magnify himself against me; then I would have hid myself from him: But it was thou, a man mine equal, my guide, and mine acquaintance.

---

[2] Matthew 26:20-25

245

We took sweet counsel together, and walked unto the house of God in company. Let death seize upon them, and let them go down quick into hell: for wickedness is in their dwellings, and among them."[3]

In Psalm 41 it was prophesied that the betrayer would know that he was the one to make a profit by the betrayal, and even went so far as to violate a precious Jewish custom.

To break bread with another [to eat a meal with him] was an indication that both were in agreement. In this, Judas was in no way in agreement with Jesus or he would not have been so ready to allow his greed to overcome his supposed friendship. On the part of Jesus, there was an agreement of fellowship. He was willing to allow this traitor to be a part of the inner circle, hypocritically breaking bread with them, and ultimately become the traitor prophesied in Scripture. This was not done for the sake of Judas, but for the sake of the sinful world needing a means of reconciling themselves to God.

"And almost all things are by the law purged with blood; and without shedding of blood is no remission. It was therefore necessary that the patterns of things in the heavens should be purified with these; but the heavenly things themselves with better sacrifices than these.

For Christ is not entered into the holy places made with hands, which are the figures of the true; but into heaven itself, now to appear in the presence of God for us:"[4]

---

[3] Psalm 55:12:-15
[4] Hebrews 9:22-24

Jesus, our Savior, is now in His rightful place having taken again the glory that was His from all eternity. He presides in Heaven as our High Priest, and by His personal sacrifice on the altar of the crucifixion cross, we may be reconciled to the Heavenly Father. "For scarcely for a righteous man will one die: yet peradventure for a good man some would even dare to die. But God commendeth his love toward us, in that, while we were yet sinners, Christ died for us. Much more then, being now justified by his blood, we shall be saved from wrath through him. For if, when we were enemies, we were reconciled to God by the death of his Son, much more, being reconciled, we shall be saved by his life."[5]

Jesus died for our sins; they were nailed to the cross with Him and became powerless when He died. His resurrection was the miracle that made possible our justification [being absolved from all guilt].

He now makes intercession before the Throne of God in our behalf, witnessing that we are His by right of the 'new birth' He provided for the world.

There can be no doubt that it was prophesied, and fulfilled, that Messiah must be betrayed by a 'friend.' Scripture proves both the prophecy and the fulfillment.

---

[5] Romans 5:7-10

Chapter 32

"Sold For 30 Pieces of Silver"

In the Old Testament, we read of a similar story of a young man by the name of Joseph, his father's favorite son, sold as a slave. It was not a close associate that sold Joseph, but rather his own brothers. Yet, in this story, we can see a similarity between Joseph and Jesus. Both were innocent of any crime, yet their perpetrators thought nothing of disposing of them in a most crude manner.

The main difference in these two events is that the brothers of Joseph did not sell him to be sentenced to death, only to a life of misery. Jesus was sold by a close associate knowing that Jesus would be put to death.

It would appear that over the centuries humanity has changed little. Evil, from the original sin, has increased in its effect on man. There is no evil on earth that the imagination of man cannot conjure up.

We know little about Judas except what we learned in the last chapter that dealt with Jesus betrayed by a close associate.

It is noteworthy that the evil transactions took place at night, which seems an easier time to do evil. The shroud of darkness, covering facial features, leaves only the light gleam of the eye and the inflection in the voice. It would appear that the inflection in the voice of Judas told the priest with whom he made the deal that here was a man of true greed. No need to offer him more than thirty pieces of silver that would be sufficient to satisfy this man's greed.

This account of Judas selling Jesus for thirty pieces of silver is well known, but further in-depth information may be helpful for some.

Israel had been guilty of gross idolatry, as revealed in the 10th chapter. In the 11th chapter, the first captivity of the Jews by Nebuchadnezzar is prophesied. The prophet does it in the usual Eastern manner by giving a visual demonstration.[1]

The prophet took two shepherd crooks, naming one "Beauty" and the other "Bands."

The first crook would be the one by which the shepherd would mark every 10th sheep as it came through the chute. This sheep would be the tithe required by God.

The second crook would be the one with a crook on the end for pulling the sheep into the arms of the shepherd. The two crooks together represent the beauty and union of Israel when they were under God as their Shepherd.

Now these crooks are broken by the prophet to inform the Jews that no longer will God instruct them as their shepherd. Instead, three shepherds will be cut off in one month: 1) Priests, 2) Scribes and Pharisees, 3) the Sanhedrin and the smaller councils.

In verse 12, the prophet tells the Jews to give him his hire as a prophet, but they consider him of little value and gave him the price of a slave. [2]

We can easily see that we are now entering into that portion that deals with the coming Messiah and how He will be sold for 30 pieces of silver: The prophet is then instructed not to accept the thirty pieces of silver, but rather give it to the potter.

---

[1] Zechariah 11:12
[2] Exodus 21:32

This likely referred to giving it to the poorest of the Levites who worked as potters to make vessels for the Temple. It is also prophetic concerning the thirty pieces of silver received by Judas.

In verse fifteen, the Jewish priests are compared to a shepherd that has only that which is useless: a bag without bread, money of no value, and a shepherds crook with no crook on the end to bring the sheep to themselves.

Messiah has now been in His earthly ministry for over three years and as we learned earlier a "friend" betrayed him. In this account, we find He is prophesied to be sold for the price of a slave. This seems like an unlikely prophecy that could not possibly come true. How would one sell the Messiah? Why was He to be sold for such a small price, a price that would label Him to be practically worthless? Why would one sell a slave if that slave had any value to his household? Yet, Judas did sell Messiah for the price of a slave because Satan entered into Judas prompting him to make a bargain with the Jewish priests and leaders.

"When Jesus had thus said, he was troubled in spirit, and testified, and said, Verily, verily, I say unto you, that one of you shall betray me. Then the disciples looked one on another, doubting of whom he spake.

Now there was leaning on Jesus' bosom one of his disciples, whom Jesus loved. Simon Peter therefore beckoned to him, that he should ask who it should be of whom he spake. He then lying on Jesus' breast saith unto him, Lord, who is it? Jesus answered, He it is, to whom I shall give a sop, when I have dipped it.

And when he had dipped the sop, he gave it to Judas Iscariot, the son of Simon. And after the sop Satan entered into him. Then said Jesus unto him, That thou doest, do quickly."[3]

Judas was likely a man naturally given to greed. Perhaps he thought that if this man Jesus had performed miracles showing Himself to be very powerful, He could escape. Perhaps he would get a choice place in His kingdom rule, once He declared Himself king over Israel. Judas, like many other Jews likely thought Jesus would be the one to break the Roman rule and re-establish Jewish law.

That alone would seem to be sufficient reason to loose his greed, especially if he began to doubt that Jesus would ever become Israel's king. The deciding factor came when Satan entered into Judas. This is the root cause for anyone denying that Jesus is the Messiah; Satan has entered into him or her.

It is noteworthy that the chief priests had not taken notice of Judas and secretly contacted him, and made a monetary offer if he would betray Jesus.[4] They had met to discuss capturing Jesus, but since it was the time of the Passover, and there would be many in the city, they feared a riot. Instead, we see Judas going purposefully to the chief priests, at the urging of Satan, and asking them what they would pay him to betray Jesus. This was an offer too good to pass by, so the chief priests devised a plan, which was illegal, and that was to meet after dark. They would then go to the predetermined place given by Judas and capture Jesus.

---

[3] John 13:21-27
[4] Matthew 26:14,15

The trial, being held after sundown would also be illegal, but that was no concern to the chief priests. Hatred and fear of loss of prestige and monetary gain will overcome their religious thinking.

This erases all doubt from my mind that Judas had some more lofty reason in mind for betraying Jesus. It was not to force His hand, making Him publicly announce He is the Messiah and forcefully taking the rule of Israel out of the hands of the Roman government. Judas sold Jesus out of greed and the prompting of Satan. Thirty pieces of silver was not only the price of a slave, but also the price of the most worthless slave! What gall we see in Judas who did not even try to barter with the chief priests for a more reasonable sum. After all, they desperately wanted to arrest Jesus, why would they not agree to a handsome betrayal sum.

For me, the answer is simple. It was not only greed, but it was prophesied that Messiah would be sold for this amount. Satan, likely thought himself quite clever by helping Judas make this bargain, but he literally fell into the hands of God. The Lord God ordered every movement made by Jesus, and even Satan helped fulfill the prophecies.

We could try to imagine what the chief priest were thinking, or how Judas felt about the betrayal as he received the money, but that is not our subject.

The Old Testament has faithfully prophesied the betrayal of the Son of God for thirty pieces of silver, and the New Testament has amply confirmed the fulfillment.

He who was sold for the price of the least valuable of slaves is the One who created the Heaven and the Earth, and everything in them.

The ill-gotten gain became of little value to Judas as he realized what a terrible thing he had done. He returned the coins, but because it was "blood money" it could not be used in the Temple treasury. The treasury was the place where people brought gifts to God, and this would be too close to the Holy One.

Instead, it was used to purchase the potter's field, as prophesied, and use as a burial ground: "And they took counsel, and bought with them the potter's field, to bury strangers in. [5]

---

[5] Matthew 27:6-7

Chapter 33
"His Price Thrown On the Temple Floor"

Imagine the emotion that filled the Temple on the day Judas re-visited the conniving Jewish leaders. Judas had repented of his deed and was filled with guilt and remorse. That alone is a terrible emotion to carry around. On the part of the Jewish leaders the emotions would have been contempt for this little man of greed. They had no sympathy for his emotions, or for the fact that he had repented and wanted forgiveness. Instead of ministering to his spiritual needs, they simply said, that is your problem, what is that to us.

Had emotions been flammable I would think that the Temple on that day would have burned to the ground. Instead, it was business as usual, and it was not necessarily God's business.

How very accurate we find the Old Testament account of Messiah being betrayed. The account goes so far as to tell us that the thirty pieces of silver given to Judas was returned to the Temple and thrown on the floor.

Judas had realized his sin and wanted no part of this blood money. The Jews would not take the money back so Judas threw it on the Temple floor and left.

"And the LORD said unto me, Cast it unto the potter: a goodly price that I was prised [prized] at of them. And I took the thirty pieces of silver, and cast them to the potter in the house of the LORD."[1]

---

[1] Zechariah 11:13

In the scripture reading in Zechariah the Lord calls the price of the betrayal His own price. "give me my price". Give Judas whatever you have agreed to give him for he can neither betray nor crucify me, except I grant permission. Just remember, although I give my permission it does not mean you have to do it. Even without you playing a part in this treachery and murder, the salvation of the world will still be established by Messiah.

The reading of this portion is sometimes attributed to Jeremiah, but that is only because the scriptures of the Old Testament were divided into three portions; the first into the Law, the five books of Moses.

The second portion is the Psalms and consists of the Psalms. The third portion is the prophets beginning with Jeremiah: thus, then, the writings of Zechariah and the other prophets being included in that division, beginning with Jeremiah, all quotations from Zechariah go under the writings of Jeremiah.

I offer this only in the event a question might be raised concerning the accuracy of the location of this portion of Scripture.

The prophet Zechariah records that the thirty pieces of silver were not retained by the one to whom it was given, but rather it was cast into the treasury in the house of the Lord. The money was returned to the house of the Lord.

" Judas, realizing what a terrible thing he had done returned to the Temple and attempted to give it back to the chief priests. They refused to take back the money and he threw the money on the floor and left:" [2]

Casting the money to the potter in the house of the Lord refers to the fact that some of the Levites were assigned to a very poor occupation linked to the Temple. They were potters, making vessels for the Temple use. The money could not be kept because "it was the price of blood." What hypocrites these Jewish leaders were, to judge an innocent man as being worthy of the death sentence, yet be so careful about ceremonial directions from the Law of Moses. Satan even had these religious leaders deluded with spiritual superstitions supposedly based on conscience.

Dr. Lightfoot, normally a reliable source by the Church of England, gives a strange story about the death of Judas, which has no scriptural verification. Dr. Lightfoot said he is of the opinion "that the devil caught him up into the air, strangled him, and threw him down on the ground with violence, so that his body burst, and his guts shed out! This was an ancient tradition.

It should be noted that Bishop John Lightfoot (1601-1675) was an English scholar partially responsible for the Westminster Confession. However, the Bishop had some rather strange interpretation of the New Testament, especially Matthew the 24th chapter.

---

[2] Matthew 27:3-5

He said he could see that this chapter was fulfilled in the first century of Christianity. Because we can see prophecy unfolding daily before our eyes, we know the good Bishop was mistaken. He was also sadly mistaken about the death of Judas.

One thing is certain; Judas was instrumental in the fulfillment of prophecy concerning the fact that Messiah must have His price thrown onto the Temple floor. True, it did not go into the collection box for the operation of the Temple, but it was expended by the Temple treasurer for the purchase of the potter's field. Once again, the New Testament proves the Old Testament to be a reliable source of prophecy regarding the Messiah.

A few facts regarding Judas for information sake. Judas was the only one of the twelve disciples to come from Judea.

His name indicates he came from Kerioth, which is situated about 10 miles south of Hebron, but is no longer a city but rather a ruin. Judas, in Hebrew, means "God is praised." Some claim he was a member of an Israeli terrorist group with the name Sicarii, but this is not possible because this group existed from 40's-50's CE before the destruction of Jerusalem in 70CE.

John 12:6 describes Judas, the one carrying the disciples money bag, was a thief. His unbridled sin was evidently greed for monetary gain.

Chapter 34

"Forsaken By His Disciples"

This chapter is one of deep, dark emotions. Jesus is not only being arrested after being betrayed by an associate, but He watches as His disciples, like sheep, are scattered.

Before the battle, it is an easy thing to expound on the courage the warrior will exhibit in the face of danger, but when the battle starts, that is an entirely different story.

The disciple, after forsaking Jesus must have been full of emotions that ran the gamut. They would feel fear, shame guilt and self-condemnation for their cowardice.

The Old Testament prophesied that the Messiah's disciples would all be scattered like sheep because the shepherd appears helpless to come to their aid.

They must have felt a measure of confusion also, having seen all His mighty miracles, and yet on this night they had serious doubts about whom He really is. All very human, and all very understandable.

"Awake, O sword, against my shepherd, and against the man that is my fellow, saith the LORD of hosts: smite the shepherd, and the sheep shall be scattered: and I will turn mine hand upon the little ones."[1]

To understand this verse in Zechariah we must know that the "sword" is Diving Justice, the "shepherd" is the Messiah Jesus, "the man that is my fellow" is also Jesus, the "sheep" are the disciples, and the one speaking is the Lord God.

In this verse, the Lord God is speaking to the sword of Divine Judgment. The sword has been "sleeping" or inactive for a considerable time. Man has been in a state of sin and the penalty for sin is death.

---

[1] Zechariah 13:7

The sword of Divine Justice is now commanded to strike down either the sinful man or his substituted; the time had come and can no longer be delayed. Man did not become the object of the Divine Justice because Messiah has already volunteered to be the substitute in the death penalty for sinful man.

The command is now specific, "smite the shepherd." Then the Lord God promises that the disciples will be cared for, against Jewish malice and Gentile persecution.

To "turn His hand upon the little ones" is equivalent to saying I will place My protective hand over the disciples and no one will be able to harm them as long as My hand is over them.

I would imagine that even if the learned priests and scribes understood the general meaning of this prophecy they likely did not connect it to Jesus and His disciples. This is a case of being so close to the forest that they could not see the trees. It was all there in the Scriptures for them to read and understand, but they had eyes to see and could not see. Their minds were clouded against a clear understanding of Scripture. The clouded mind with these Jewish leaders during the day of Messiah was no different than it is today. Man's understanding of the Divine Word could not be understood by the Jews, and the same is true of modern man.

The reason is clear, and recorded in the New Testament. "Now we have received, not the spirit of the world, but the spirit which is of God; that we might know the things that are freely given to us of God. Which things also we speak, not in the words which man's wisdom teacheth, but which the Holy Ghost teacheth, comparing spiritual things with spiritual.

But the natural man receiveth not the things of the Spirit of God: for they are foolishness unto him: neither can he know them, because they are spiritually discerned."[2]

We have watched the Jewish leadership as they operated in a state of malice, plotting against Jesus, and we question why they did not understand the prophecies about the Messiah. The apostle Paul wrote the reason that we should have known by the words of Jesus.

He answered His disciples when they asked why He taught the Jews by way of parables. They said to Jesus that the Jews could not understand the parables, and thereby implied that Jesus should have used a more easily understood language in His teachings.

Jesus said the Jews had eyes to see but see not, and ears to hear and hear not. This also was a fulfillment of prophecy concerning Messiah. Paul, taking what Jesus said put it into language his converts could understand. To understand Scripture one must be born again of the Spirit of God. A dead spirit within man is incapable of seeing or hearing, it must be regenerated by the Holy Spirit, and He will not do that until the sinner has been born again by the sacrifice of Jesus for their sins.

Matthew explains much concerning the actions of the disciples at the time of the arrest. "Then saith Jesus unto them, All ye shall be offended because of me this night: for it is written, I will smite the shepherd, and the sheep of the flock shall be scattered abroad."[3] Jesus told them they would, this very night, be offended because of me. He was saying they would all "forsake me', the Greek παντεσ υμεισ σκανδαλισθησεθε gives the sense that they would lose a great measure of their confidence in Him.

---

[2] 1 Corinthians 2 :12 - 14
[3] Matthew 26:31

Peter told Jesus that he would stand by Him even unto death. He started out to prove his intent by using a sword to cut off the ear of Malchus, the servant of the High Priest at the time of the arrest.

Unfortunately, Peter was doing what many do today in a crisis; they rely on their own ability and strength instead of His. Peter had seen Jesus heal the sick, give sight to the blind, enable the dumb to speak, raise the dead, cast out demons and even walk on water. All this is evidently forgotten in the heat of battle and Peter resorts to human devices rather than asking Jesus what He wanted him to do to assist him. When one is our leader we do not prepare and carry out a battle plan, we wait for the leader to give orders.

Peter soon was awakened, once again, to the power of Jesus as he picked up the severed ear and reattached it as though it had never been severed.

Later that night we watch Peter as he follows Jesus from a safe distance, and then fulfill the prediction Jesus gave him, that before the cock crowed Peter would betray Him three times (John 13:38).

In Mark we see the "sheep" scattering and one in particular is mentioned, but not by name. "And they all forsook him, and fled. And there followed him a certain young man, having a linen cloth cast about his naked body; and the young men laid hold on him: And he left the linen cloth, and fled from them naked."[4]

Matthew gave us further details that prove the fulfillment of the prophecy of the prophet Zechariah "Thinkest thou that I cannot now pray to my Father, and he shall presently give me more than twelve legions of angels?

---

[4] Mark 14:51 - 52

But how then shall the scriptures be fulfilled, that thus it must be? In that same hour said Jesus to the multitudes, Are ye come out as against a thief with swords and staves for to take me? I sat daily with you teaching in the temple, and ye laid no hold on me. But all this was done, that the scriptures of the prophets might be fulfilled. Then all the disciples forsook him, and fled." [5]

The night arrest scene must have been a time of real terror for the disciples. Jesus had just told them He had the power to call for 1200 angels.

If He could do that, certainly He could protect His disciples against this murderous mob.

Standing before them, holding Jesus as their prisoner, was a mob of Jewish leaders and their servants, all with the look of murder on their faces. Torches were flaring in the night and reflected off the drawn swords of the servants. The disciples were outnumbered, and they did not see 1200 angels to protect them, so they did what most would do in such a situation, they ran for their lives.

Once again, the prophecy of the Old Testament has been revealed to us and the fulfillment in the New Testament proved the accuracy of the prophet. Jesus could have called down twelve legions of angels to protect Him, but He, as a lamb before the slaughter is dumb, so did Messiah refrain from defending Himself. Isaiah 53:7 "He was oppressed, and he was afflicted, yet he opened not his mouth: he is brought as a lamb to the slaughter, and as a sheep before her shearers is dumb, so he openeth not his mouth."

This was also true during His trial, but it is equally true at His arrest in reference to His ability to call down an angel army to His defense.

---

[5] Matthew 26:56

Our subject topic in this study has now been proven accurate. The Messiah must be forsaken by his disciples. The night and next day of terror and excruciating pain has begun, and it was all for you, and for me.

Chapter 35

"Struck On the Cheek"

"When thou walkest through the fire thou shalt not be burned, neither shall the flame kindle upon thee." But few if any of us have read them with the delight of the martyr, Bilney, to whom this passage was a stay while he was in prison, awaiting his execution at the stake. His Bible, still preserved in the library of Corpus Christi College, Cambridge, has the passage marked with a pen in the margin. Perhaps, if all were known, every promise in the Bible has borne a special message to some one saint; and so the whole volume might be scored in the margin with mementos of Christian experience, every one appropriate to the very letter. - SPURGEON-

Jesus was being engulfed in a blazing fire of hatred that would lead to a cruel cross and a painful death beyond description.

Perhaps the example of Jesus, as He was tortured, beaten, humiliated, and crucified was the example that gave Bilney the courage to face the flames of his execution.

He knew that Jesus had died from his severe affliction, but He had also risen victoriously from death and the grave. Because Jesus our Messiah lives, we too shall be resurrected and live eternally with him. With that wonderful hope many martyrs have faced death with bravery.

We know from prophecy that the Messiah would be brutally mistreated; however the question that comes to mind is who would dare to even think of raising a hand to strike God?

Who would be so foolish to strike the Messiah who came to save mankind from the penalty of sin?

Messiah shall be struck on the cheek? Emmanuel, God with us, the Son of God, God the Son, He who created the Heavens and He is stuck on the cheek by mere man? "Now gather thyself in troops, O daughter of troops: he hath laid siege against us: they shall smite the judge of Israel with a rod upon the cheek. But thou, Bethlehem Ephratah, though thou be little among the thousands of Judah, yet out of thee shall he come forth unto me that is to be ruler in Israel; whose goings forth have been from of old, from everlasting."[1]

The apostle Paul was struck on the cheek by order of the High Priest, and see what was Paul's reaction, an apology, Acts 23:1-5 "And Paul, earnestly beholding the council, said, Men and brethren, I have lived in all good conscience before God until this day. And the high priest Ananias commanded them that stood by him to smite him on the mouth. Then said Paul unto him, God shall smite thee, thou whited wall: for sittest thou to judge me after the law, and commandest me to be smitten contrary to the law? And they that stood by said, Revilest thou God's high priest? Then said Paul, I wist not, brethren, that he was the high priest: for it is written, Thou shalt not speak evil of the ruler of thy people."

Paul did not realize that Ananias was the high priest at that time. Under the Roman occupation the high priest was changed often, the office secured through bribery.

---

[1] Micah 5:1-2

Paul was obviously not in the area of Jerusalem when this change was made, and when Ananias commanded him to be struck on the mouth, Paul made a response such as we might expect.

Upon discovering whom Ananias was Paul explained he did not know he was the high priest and quoted the law regarding this manner. This was Paul's way of making a public apology for speaking in such a manner to the high priest. Jesus is our High Priest, but the Jews did not recognize Him as such because their eyes were blinded to Scriptures and could not discern the fulfillment when He was standing before them.

It is true that Jesus was not struck on the cheek by a Jew, but He would not have been subjected to such punishment had the Jews not turned Him over to them for execution. The Jews were as guilty of striking the King of kings on the cheek, as were the Roman soldiers, who did not have Scriptural knowledge.

Micah prophesied that the Messiah would be struck on the cheek. A careful reading is necessary to understand this second layer of prophetic fulfillment.

The first fulfillment was centered on Zedekiah the king and the brutal treatment he received at the hands of the army of Nebuchadnezzar when Jerusalem was taken. Micah wrote, "they shall smite the judge of Israel with a rod upon the cheek."

How do we know that this prophecy is about Messiah Jesus? Verse 2 informs us who is intended in this prophecy.

Israel is going into captivity under Nebuchadnezzar, but a promise is given that a ruler over Israel will be coming out of Beth-lehem Ephratah. This is very specific, since there were two Beth-lehem cities in Israel at the time of the birth of Messiah. Nothing was left to doubt here, it is definite that Jesus is being referenced here.

Matthew in the New Testament is the fulfillment of that part of the prophecy, "When Herod the king had heard these things, he was troubled, and all Jerusalem with him. And when he had gathered all the chief priests and scribes of the people together, he demanded of them where Christ should be born. And they said unto him, In Bethlehem of Judaea: for thus it is written by the prophet, And thou Bethlehem, in the land of Juda, art not the least among the princes of Juda: for out of thee shall come a Governor, that shall rule my people Israel." [2]

There was no doubt on the part of the chief priests, scribes, or Herod, which Beth-lehem Jesus would be born. Troops were given orders to go to that exact city and kill every male child under the age of two years, because by the time the Wise Men arrived in Jerusalem it was two years after the birth of Messiah.

Since we have historical and Scriptural proof that the prophet Micah was speaking of Jesus, we can easily see why this study has the title Messiah must be struck on the cheek.

Micah further continued in verse two to verify the Divinity of Jesus by saying, "whose going forth have been from old."

---

[2] Matthew 2:1-6

He was promised from the very foundation of the world, and promised again to Adam in the Garden of Eden. He is "from everlasting" wrote Micah. 'my emey olam' "From the days of all time." Since time came out of eternity, there has been no time in which He was not forth coming to save men from their sins.

He is the Creator of all things, so He is Eternal, and Jesus was no part of what was created. All beings except God have been created, and Jesus is Emmanuel, God in the flesh. God came down in the form of man to become mankind's redeemer, their substitute in the death penalty proclaimed by law for committing sin against the Holy God.

The account in Matthew the twenty-seventh chapter reveals the humiliation and physical mistreatment provided by the Roman soldiers. They removed His outer garment giving him a kingly robe in its place, and placed a crown on His head and a reed in His hand for a sceptre. Next, they bowed their knee before Him to mock Him, proclaiming, "Hail, King of the Jews."

Not satisfied that they had sufficiently humiliated their prisoner they then spit on him, which to a Jew was the ultimate insult. Taking the reed (rod) sceptre from His hand, they smote Him on the "head", or cheek, thus fulfilling the scripture.

Just a side thought here to clear up a common misinterpretation. The crown of thorns they placed on His head was not the common variety in Israel that has the long sharp spikes.

When we read this passage from the Greek, we read στεφηθυσ ακανθινον which translates Stephanos (crown) of acanthus, a plant of the herb family acanthus that is a prickly plant, and would still be most uncomfortable and likely to pierce the skin. Painters for centuries have depicted the crown as being the common thorn bush.

Once again, we have proven the authenticity and accuracy of the Old Testament by the historical and Biblical proof of the New Testament. Messiah was to be struck on the cheek.

Chapter 36

"Be Spit On"

A preacher, wearing common street clothing went to the University of Western Kentucky during an outdoor Campus Festival to preach the Gospel. He had the permission of the Dean of Students to preach, telling him that the whole area was given to freedom of speech.

He was preaching against unrighteousness: fornication, adultery, idolatry such as promoted by the Muslims, Buddhists, Hindu, Mormon's and Jehovah's Witnesses.

The crowd began to get a bit unruly and the Campus Police tried to make him leave, but the preacher refused and won the argument.

When he mentioned homosexuality as a sin, a young lady became very vocal and stood immediately in front of him shouting objections. Another student claimed that it is impossible not to sin and that started other student shouting remarks. They began calling the preacher names such as hypocrite, sinner, etc.

After about forty minutes of preaching the Gospel, without error, a student approached him and spit on him. The preacher's response was "God bless you demon."

We find many references in the Scriptures of a person being spit upon. The commentators tell us that this was the mark of the most profound contempt.

Job said they abhor [loathe, despise] me, as they spit upon him.

"I gave my back to the smiters, and my cheeks to them that plucked off the hair: I hid not my face from shame and spitting" [1]

Jesus told the multitudes: "Blessed are ye, when men shall hate you, and when they shall separate you from their company, and shall reproach you, and cast out your name as evil, for the Son of man's sake." [2]

In John He also said, "If the world hate you, ye know that it hated me before it hated you." [3]

This Kentucky preacher experienced both scriptures. The crowd became belligerent and tried to shout down the preacher. Some were quoting Scripture out of context to justify their own lifestyle.

Clothing became a real issue when he told them if the ladies wore clothing that was revealing and seductive they were in sin, and if he men lusted after such a one they had already committed adultery in their heart and it was the same as committing the actual act.

This man said nothing worthy of condemnation and ridicule, yet the student spit on him.

Consider now Jesus and the situation in which He found Himself when He was spit upon. Jesus was taken before the High Priest for questioning. When asked to answer the two false witnesses Jesus did not answer. The High Priest then asked, "Answerest thou nothing? He then asked Jesus if He was the Christ, the Son of God.

---

[1] Isaiah 50:6
[2] Luke 6:22
[3] John 15:18

272

Jesus said "Thou hast said: Nevertheless I say unto you, Hereafter shall ye see the Son of man sitting on the right hand of power, and coming in the clouds of heaven" [4]

That is when the High Priest declared they needed no more evidence of His guilt. Those standing around spit on Him, hit Him with their fist, and slapped Him with their open hand.

Both the preacher mentioned above, and Jesus was guilty of the same "crime", they both told the truth. Sinful man cannot bear the truth unless he is convicted in his own soul to the point of true repentance. Either man can repent of their sin, or they can go deeper into rebellion.

In the response of the Jewish leaders, we find they chose to go deeper into rebellion. They turned Jesus the Messiah over to the Romans to be crucified.

As Jesus was pushed and jostled down the streets of Jerusalem, carrying the instrument of His death on His shoulders, the crowds lined the streets shouting and cursing Him. It was customary for them to throw rocks at the condemned, hit him with their fists, and many would have spit on Him. To the Jewish population, a man condemned to be crucified was under the curse of God and he certainly deserved nothing but detestation.

Jesus was well aware of the treatment He would be receiving because He knew the Scriptures of the Old Testament. He realized that He would be severely beaten, they would pull the beard off His face, and He would be spit upon.

The beatings and beard pulling were extremely painful, but the people wished to give Jesus more than physical pain, they desired to humiliate him.

---

[4] Matthew 26:64

The Roman soldiers had their turn at humiliating Jesus by mocking Him as the King of the Jews, but the people desired their turn.

Spitting on a Jew was done as a mark of the most profound contempt. "They abhor me, they flee far from me, and spare not to spit in my face." [5] This was a form of the most intense rejection given to a person in the day of Jesus, and obviously in the day of Job.

The amazing thing is that the Scriptures tell us that Jesus did not attempt to avoid their humiliation and their spitting on Him. Jesus went through the pain and humiliation of the entire situation in a spirit of meekness. Meekness has been defined as showing mildness or quietness of nature.

A better definition is having strength under control. Recall what Jesus had earlier said to Peter when he tried to defend Jesus with a sword, at the time of His arrest:

"Thinkest thou that I cannot now pray to my Father, and he shall presently give me more than twelve legions of angels?" [6]

This is the same Jesus standing before the High Priest as those standing nearby spit on Him. This is the same Jesus on the way to Calvary when the crowd spit on Him, time after time. He could have, at any moment, called on the Father and He would have sent 12,000 angels to His rescue. That was not in the plan for Jesus. His plan was to die for the sins of the world, even those who had hit him with their fist, slapped him with their open hand, pulled whiskers from His beard causing His face to bleed, and even those who spit on Him.

---

[5] Job 30:10
[6] Matthew 26:53

These are the kinds of insults that a sinful man would not forget, and would definitely wish to have revenge if it was possible. Jesus had no such thoughts of revenge, His only thought was "Father, forgive them, for they know not what they do."[7]

There are many today, like those college students at the University of West Kentucky that still spit on the Messiah.

Their only motivation is to hide their sin, deny their sin, and indulge in their sinful lifestyle. To deny that Jesus is the Messiah is to say that the Old Testament is full of error and that history and the New Testament are wrong, even though verified by multiple trustworthy witnesses to the fact that Jesus fulfilled all the prophecies of the Old Testament perfectly. Dependable witnesses, the Disciples and more than five hundred others saw Jesus alive after His death, burial and resurrection. To deny this is to spit on Messiah, yet millions today are guilty of this shameful denial.

To those who would continue to spit on Messiah I remind them of the words of Jesus as He stood before the High Priest "I say unto you, Hereafter shall ye see the Son of man sitting on the right hand of power, and coming in the clouds of heaven."

---

[7] Luke 23:34

Chapter 37

"Mocked"

The subject of this study is "Messiah must be mocked." We have already proven that Jesus is the promised Messiah on numerous occasions. Unfortunately His enemies did not believe what He had told them, but had they believed they should have also known a truth as spoken by the apostle Paul to the Galatians "Be not deceived; God is not mocked: for whatsoever a man soweth, that shall he also reap."[1]

King David prophesied this very event "All they that see me laugh me to scorn: they shoot out the lip, they shake the head, saying, He trusted on the LORD that he would deliver him: let him deliver him, seeing he delighted in him." [2]

Before we begin to feel too self-righteous as a nation we need to realize that countless thousands today are doing the same as the Jews had done. Many are saying there is no God.

Others say [theisist] that a supreme being created the earth and all on it and then said, "You're now on your own. Good luck!" Doubtless there are many others who have been brought us in the strict Christian way of worship but have decided to follow their master Satan. They do this by rejecting the Word of God and living their lives to satisfy their creature comforts and lusts.

---

[1] Galatians 6:7
[2] Psalm 22:7-8

These individuals are all in the same condemnation as are the Jews of old who mocked Emmanuel.

The enemies of Jesus thought it great sport to mock Him, and they did so in numerous behavior. To strike Him, spit on Him, put royal garbs on Him and place a reed for a sceptre and prickly crown on His head was only part of the mockery. Consider the full implication of that verse in Galatians regarding the many persons involved in mocking Messiah..

In Matthew we read that they said "Then did they spit in his face, and buffeted him; and others smote him with the palms of their hands, Saying, Prophesy unto us, thou Christ, Who is he that smote thee?" [3]

And again in Matthew we read the fulfillment of King David's prophecy "And they stripped him, and put on him a scarlet robe. And when they had platted a crown of thorns, they put it upon his head, and a reed in his right hand: and they bowed the knee before him, and mocked him, saying, Hail, King of the Jews! And they spit upon him, and took the reed, and smote him on the head. And after that they had mocked him, they took the robe off from him, and put his own raiment on him, and led him away to crucify him." [4] At this point they had blindfolded Him before striking Him, and then demanded He "prophesy" as to whom it was that struck Him. He claimed to be the Son of God, the promised Messiah, and therefore should be able to tell them who it was that had struck Him.

---

[3] Matthew 26:67-68
[4] Matthew 27-28-31

What they did not realize is that one cannot mock God, Jesus knew who it was and they will reap what they had sown. I cannot even begin to imagine what sort of harvest these foolish ones might someday reap for striking the very God of the universe.

A verse in the Old Testament would be most appropriate here "Because I have called, and ye refused; I have stretched out my hand, and no man regarded; But ye have set at nought all my counsel, and would none of my reproof: I also will laugh at your calamity; I will mock when your fear cometh;" [5]

These self-important Jews remind me of one of Aesop's Fables called the Pomegranate, Apple-Tree, and Bramble. Since all three are found in Israel perhaps this is appropriate for the subject matter at hand.

The Pomegranate and the Apple-Tree disputed as to which was the most beautiful. When their strife was at its height, a Bramble from the neighboring hedge lifted up its voice and said in a boastful tone: "pray, my dear friends, in my presence at least cease from such vain disputing."

The arrogant crowd that chose to mock Messiah was much like the undesirable little bramble, a prickly little bush that insinuates that he is the most beautiful of the three. Those gathered around Jesus to mock Him were saying much the same thing,

"Who do you think you are? Prophesy you false prophet. You can't do any better than we. At least *we* know who it was that struck you."

---

[5] Proverbs 1:25-26

The "bramble" was mocking that which had real beauty to display. The beauty of holiness was in the Messiah, but the "bramble" Jews could only see their own point of view and became conceited in their opinions.

How terrible to mock the very one that created everything that was created. "In the beginning was the Word, and the Word was with God, and the Word was God. The same was in the beginning with God. All things were made by him; and without him was not any thing made that was made." [6]

The proof that this refers to Jesus is found in verses 10-14 "He was in the world, and the world was made by him, and the world knew him not. He came unto his own, and his own received him not. But as many as received him, to them gave he power to become the sons of God, even to them that believe on his name: Which were born, not of blood, nor of the will of the flesh, nor of the will of man, but of God. And the Word was made flesh, and dwelt among us, (and we beheld his glory, the glory as of the only begotten of the Father,) full of grace and truth." [7]

He came unto His own, the Jews, and the Jews did not know Him. Who was He? Emmanuel, "the Word was made flesh, and dwelt among us," Jesus is the Word of God in the flesh; He embodies all that God is and says.

---

[6] John 1:1-3
[7] John 1:10-14

Considering all this, how terrible it was that sinful man, ignorant of the Scriptures, or purposefully putting the Scriptures aside for personal reason, did not know the King of kings when He came to them. For centuries the Jews had looked for Messiah, but when He came it was not in the role the Jews wanted. They wanted an earthly king that would rule from an earthly throne and make Israel independent once again. They could not understand that the Lord God had promised that a root would come out of Jesse for the purpose of bringing them forgiveness of sins by becoming their substitute in death.

Before some raise the objection that it was only a handful of ignorant people that brought about the death of Messiah, and mocked Him before delivering Him up for crucifixion, I urge you to re-read Psalm 22:7-8, because it tells us that "all" who saw Him laughed at Him and mocked Him. This refers to the crucifixion, and on this occasion the multitudes were in Jerusalem for the Passover, and seeking entertainment would have gone to Calvary to witness the crucifixion of these three men. Hatred was so pervasive in Israel during the time of Jesus that their emotions ran the gamut from adoration to hatred in but a matter of hours. They proclaimed Him as the promised anointed One singing Hosanna as He entered Jerusalem on a donkey and in a matter of hours was shouting with the crowd, "Crucify Him!"

Can you imagine the effect it may have had on the ones who had spit on Him, struck Him with their fists, slapped Him with their open hands, pulled whiskers from His beard, only to see Him three days later as He walked the streets of Jerusalem with His disciples?

Jesus was alive, and He was obviously who He had tried to tell the people who He is; from days of old, He is the eternal One. Recall what the people had said? "And they that passed by reviled him, wagging their heads, And saying, Thou that destroyest the temple, and buildest it in three days, save thyself. If thou be the Son of God, come down from the cross.

Likewise also the chief priests mocking him, with the scribes and elders, said, He saved others; himself he cannot save. If he be the King of Israel, let him now come down from the cross, and we will believe him. He trusted in God; let him deliver him now, if he will have him: for he said, I am the Son of God. The thieves also, which were crucified with him, cast the same in his teeth." [8]

I can imagine that depression was more common in Jerusalem at that time than elation over the fact that the "trouble maker" was crucified. This is the penalty one pays when the Word of God is ignored, whether it is the written Word of God, or the God incarnate.

The Old Testament once again has been proven to be accurate as it proclaimed that Messiah must be mocked.

---

[8] Matthew 27:39-44

Chapter 38

"Beaten"

This is a subject difficult for any true Christian believer to discuss in-depth. The reality of the beating taken by Jesus is recorded not only in the New Testament, and prophesied in the Old Testament, but Josephus, Eusubous, Cicero and likely many others, wrote records.

The description given in this study is intended only to show how terrible it was for Messiah to endure this beating, which sinful man deserved. This part of His punishment by the Roman lictors (soldiers) was something no sane individual would wish to witness.

The prophet Isaiah informed us that this would be, in part, the punishment The Messiah must endure for our sins: "I gave my back to the smiters, and my cheeks to them that plucked off the hair: I hid not my face from shame and spitting." [1]

The New Testament has given us an account of the terrible punishment Messiah received at the hands of the Roman soldiers "And when they had platted a crown of thorns, they put it upon his head, and a reed in his right hand: and they bowed the knee before him, and mocked him, saying, Hail, King of the Jews! And they spit upon him, and took the reed, and smote him on the head. And after that they had mocked him, they took the robe off from him, and put his own raiment on him, and led him away to crucify him.

---

[1] Isaiah 50:6

And as they came out, they found a man of Cyrene, Simon by name: him they compelled to bear his cross."[2]

The scourge had many various styles, ranging from three to twelve leather straps tied to a wood handle. The best authorities seem to favor a scourge with nine leather straps, knotted at intervals, with the knots holding pieces of lead, zinc, iron, bone or bronze. One special scourge had a hook at the end of the leather strap, and the scourging instrument named the 'scorpion.'

The victim was placed in a bent over position for the purpose of stretching the flesh on the back, making it more susceptible to deeper wounds with each lash.

To best understand the Roman mind concerning the pain inflicted on another we need but look to a sentence penned by king Servian Tullus, the sixth king of ancient Rome. He was a successful military leader as well as a civil leader. King Servian, as he was called, wrote, "We do not feel three hundred lashes on another's back."

A Roman coin has been found bearing the figure of a Roman god, Sol, holding a Flagum in his left hand.

The Romans used the flagum as an instrument of torture to gain information from captured slaves, or to torture condemned criminals. Scripture tells us this beating was so severe that Jesus required assistance to carry His cross.

The beating would sever veins and arteries, causing severe blood loss and producing a state of shock, and in some cases, death.

---

[2] Matthew 27:29-32

Josephus (Wars I-III, Antiquities Book IX-XI) "certain rebel Jews were torn to pieces by the scourge before being crucified. Eusubous wrote, "their bodies were frightfully lacerated. Christian martyrs in Smyrna were so torn by the scourges that their veins were laid bare and the inner muscles, sinews, even entrails, were exposed.

Two lictors would administer the beating, one on either side of the victim. They would take turns administering a stripe, often pulling hard on the whip after it had embedded itself in the flesh of the victim. This would tear out large pieces of flesh, and cause severe bleeding.

Just as Isa 53:5 records, these whips produced literal 'stripes' on the body of Jesus.

Is it any wonder the Roman soldiers had no pity on Jesus as they severely beat him? After reading the thoughts of King Servian and understanding that this psychology was passed down through the ages, we no longer wonder how they could be so cruel.

A vast majority of Christians today have no clue what King Jesus suffered during the Roman scourging.

If God allowed the Messiah to endure such punishment, this should tell us something regarding how God feels about sin, since Jesus was taking the punishment the sinner deserved.

After reading Isaiah 50:6, and now having a better understanding of what was prophesied for Jesus, we see each step in his humiliation and torment moving to a higher level of suffering. Giving His back to the 'smiters', hardly describes what that entailed.

The hatred of the Jews toward Jesus was so intense, and that without legitimate cause, that they preferred to release a murderous zealot by the name of Barabbas and cried out for the crucifixion death of Jesus.

Cicero called crucifixion the "cruelest and most disgusting penalty." Josephus said that it was "the most pitiable of deaths." (Jewish Wars 7:203). It was not just the crucifixion process that made it so terrible; it was the preliminary torture that added to the cruelty of the crucifixion.

Jesus was obviously in a state of shock, which would cause far too little blood to supply the brain; this would bring on a sense of imbalance.

He had also lost so much blood that His body strength was depleted, and the New Testament reveals that a man of Cyrene, Simon by name, was commandeered to assist Him in carrying the cross.

Isaiah prophesied that Messiah would willingly give his back to the Roman soldiers as they lashed him with that terrible weapon of torture. The New Testament confirms the accuracy of the prophet Isaiah, as Jesus took the punishment deserved by His sinful creation.

Chapter 39

"His Hands and Feet Pierced"

In the twentieth chapter of the Gospel of John we find the disciples locked securely in a room fearing for their lives. Jesus had been crucified and their faith had taken a steep decline. In the gospel of John, Jesus had said in a commanding voice to the priest, and angry arresting mob, "Let these go away." [1] It becomes evident that the Jews had no plan to search for the disciples with malice intent. The disciples had no way of knowing what the Jews had planed, concerning them, and they were taking no chances. They needed time to "wait and see", and while waiting, to decide on their next plan of action.

With the door likely being barricaded against any angry mob, Jesus approached the room, and without using the door, appeared before the disciples.

"Then the same day at evening, being the first day of the week, when the doors were shut where the disciples were assembled for fear of the Jews, came Jesus and stood in the midst, and saith unto them, Peace be unto you. And when he had so said, he shewed unto them his hands and his side. Then were the disciples glad, when they saw the LORD. Then said Jesus to them again, Peace be unto you: as my Father hath sent me, even so send I you. And when he had said this, he breathed on them, and saith unto them, Receive ye the Holy Ghost: Whose soever sins ye remit, they are remitted unto them; and whose soever sins ye retain, they are retained.

---

[1] John 18:8

But Thomas, one of the twelve, called Didymus, was not with them when Jesus came. The other disciples therefore said unto him, We have seen the LORD. But he said unto them, Except I shall see in his hands the print of the nails, and put my finger into the print of the nails, and thrust my hand into his side, I will not believe.

And after eight days again his disciples were within, and Thomas with them: then came Jesus, the doors being shut, and stood in the midst, and said, Peace be unto you. Then saith he to Thomas, Reach hither thy finger, and behold my hands; and reach hither thy hand, and thrust it into my side: and be not faithless, but believing. And Thomas answered and said unto him, My LORD and my God." [2]

They were, no doubt, frightened at His sudden appearance, especially since His entrance was not one any normal human could perform. They may have thought Him to be a ghost, but Jesus calmed their fears by using a phrase familiar to them, "Peace be unto you."

Jesus then showed them His pierced hands and his pierced side, which had been preserved for proof that it was He who spoke peace to them. The miraculous resurrection could have easily also given Jesus a body that was perfect in every way, including no marks of the crucifixion episode, but these marks were preserved as a reminder of the accuracy of the Old Testament account of the Messiah, they must see where He had been pierced.

---

[2] John 20:19-28

The verse in Psalm 22 is prophesied without, "political correctness", which the present society appears to hold dear: "For dogs have compassed me: the assembly of the wicked have inclosed me: they pierced my hands and my feet." [3]

Those who took Jesus into captivity, tortured Him and murdered Him by way of crucifixion are not given polite titles. They are called "dogs" and the "assembly of the wicked." The reference to "dogs" is a very derogatory term in Judaism. In Revelation 22:15 dogs are spoken as a human with the dog-like characteristic, which is one of a contemptuous character. The dogs in that verse are in company with humans: sorcerers, whoremongers, murderers, idolaters, and liars. I believe this justifies the statement Adam Clarke wrote concerning this verse, that the dogs were intended to indicate the Gentile Roman Soldiers. The assembly of the wicked is a terrible indictment against the Jewish rulers and their angry followers.

The words dogs and wicked are the words of the Lord God against those who crucified the Messiah. If He calls these people dogs and wicked, they must be dogs and wicked in His Holy opinion.

In Zechariah the 12th chapter the prophet is speaking of the inhabitants of Jerusalem and the house of David. "And I will pour upon the house of David, and upon the inhabitants of Jerusalem, the spirit of grace and of supplications: and they shall look upon me whom they have pierced, and they shall mourn for him, as one mourneth for his only son, and shall be in bitterness for him, as one that is in bitterness for his firstborn." [4]

---

[3] Psalm 16:17
[4] Zechariah 12:10

He prophesied that the Jews will look upon "me" (the Lord God) whom they have pierced. Then the pronoun changes to "him", God in the flesh, and they will mourn for the death of Messiah as much as they would mourn for their only son who had been killed. In the end time the Jews will visibly see Messiah and will be filled with bitterness for what was done to Him and feel a personal responsibility, as though He had been their only male child.

At that time the Lord God will pour upon Israel a spirit of grace and supplication.

The description regarding the Gentile Roman soldiers require no further comment, but since Zechariah was instructed by the Lord God to be so specific about Israel we need to take a closer look at what was written.

He will pour out the spirit of grace and supplication. This is the way in which the Jews themselves shall be brought into the Christian Church.

1. They will have a spirit of grace. Grace is the undeserved favor of God. When one is filled with grace they extend underserved favor instead of harboring personal and false opinions.

2. They shall be excited to fervent and continual prayer for the restoration of Divine favor. This will likely be in a time period after Ezekiel the 38th chapter in which many Arab and Russian soldiers will have attacked Jerusalem. At that time an earthquake of great magnitude will kill many Jews in Jerusalem. Is it any wonder that Zechariah was instructed to promise the Jews of this day that the time would come when a spirit of supplication will come upon them and they will plead for the restoration of Divine favor?

3. Christ shall be preached to them and they shall look upon and believe in him whim they pierced, whom they crucified in Jerusalem. No longer will the Jews refuse to hear the Gospel of Jesus, nor will they continue to uphold the ethnic lie that the Jews had no part in His crucifixion. What they hear shall produce deep and sincere repentance; they shall mourn and be in bitterness of soul to think they had crucified the Lord of life and glory. They will hear, they will listen attentively, and they will receive the truth of the Gospel bringing Christian and Jew together into one Church, the Church with Jesus as the Head.

Any person believing that the Old Testament was inspired by the Holy Spirit to write the prophecies of the Lord God must also believe that Zechariah 12:10 means exactly what it says.

Then, any intelligent persons, capable of thinking for themselves instead of parroting what man has taught, will also realize the fulfillment recorded in the New Testament is also the Word of God.

The world is speedily coming to an end time climax; the words written in prophecy are being fulfilled before our very eyes each evening as we watch the evening world news. How can anyone deny that the Scriptures will not be fulfilled as written, and that they will be fulfilled in the lives of the majority of mankind living today?

Chapter 40

"Thirty During His Execution"

The Old Testament reveals the age of one entering the priesthood and the New Testament records that Jesus began His pubic ministry according to Levitical Law.

The Gospel of Luke confirms that Jesus began His public ministry when He was thirty years of age "Now when all the people were baptized, it came to pass, that Jesus also being baptized, and praying, the heaven was opened, And the Holy Ghost descended in a bodily shape like a dove upon him, and a voice came from heaven, which said, Thou art my beloved Son; in thee I am well pleased. And Jesus himself began to be about thirty years of age, being (as was supposed) the son of Joseph, which was the son of Heli," [1]

The Book of Hebrews speaks of the priesthood of Jesus "Seeing then that we have a great high priest, that is passed into the heavens, Jesus the Son of God, let us hold fast our profession." [2]

There has been much controversy over the age of Jesus when He was crucified, because of the controversy over the year in which He was born. The best dates are secured by noting the dates the various high officials were in office during the years of Jesus.

The Rabbins have not been helpful in this study since they have obviously entered false information to prevent the Jews from believing that Jesus is the Messiah.

---

[1] Luke 3:21-23
[2] Hebrews 4:14

One such account we read: In A Rabbinic view of Jesus' Execution, It **is** taught: They hanged Jesus [*Yeshu*] on the eve of Passover. Now a crier went forth for forty days before this (saying): --"He goes forth to be stoned because he practiced magic and stirred up Israel to apostasy. Let anyone who knows anything in his favor come forward and speak up for him!" But they found nothing in his favor and they hanged him on the eve of Passover.

[The New Testament proves that no crier ever went before Jesus seeking a witness in His favor.]

Ulla said: --"Do you suppose a revolutionary had anything in his favor!" He was an instigator [mesit[h]] (to apostasy) and the Merciful has said: --'You shall not spare or conceal him!' (Deut 13:8)" But it was different with (Jesus), for he was near to the kingdom! [3]   This is not the only time a Jewish Rabbi has attempted to contradict verifiable historic events regarding the Messiah Jesus.   The Old Testament warns that the Jews would not be capable of understanding their own Scriptures because they were spiritually blind and deaf. This "blind and deaf" Rabbi became the leader of the "blind and deaf" and unfortunately too many have believed him to the damnation of their own soul.

The question now arises, how do we verify the age of Messiah at the time of His death?

---

[3] Babylonian Talmud Sanhedrin 43a

Luke, a first person witness to the life and death of Jesus. wrote in the Gospel of Luke "Now when all the people were baptized, it came to pass, that Jesus also being baptized, and praying, the heaven was opened, And the Holy Ghost descended in a bodily shape like a dove upon him, and a voice came from heaven, which said, Thou art my beloved Son; in thee I am well pleased. And Jesus himself began to be about thirty years of age, being (as was supposed) the son of Joseph, which was the son of Heli," [4]

Doctor Luke had two things on his side as he wrote the Gospel of Luke. First, he was a Jew, and the Jews are known for their meticulous recording of genealogy. Secondly, as a physician Luke was known for being precise in his writings. He records that just as Jesus was to begin His ministry it was very close to His thirtieth birthday.

Pontius Pilate ruled from 26-36 AD. There were only three times in that period when the 14th of Nisan fell on a Friday, the years 27, 30 & 33 AD. We can judge from this, and what Doctor Luke has said, that Jesus must have died in the year 33AD.

Allow me to give you another phony attempt at setting the date of the death of Jesus by the Rabbins.

A heretic [min] said to Rabbi Hanina (bar Hama): "Have you heard how old Balaam was (when he died)?

(Hanina) said to him:

-"The record does not record (it).

But (I would say) he was 33 or 34 years from the text:

---

[4] Luke 3:23

'Men of blood and frauds shall not live out half their days' (Ps 55:23) (The heretic) said to him:
-"What you say is right!
I myself have examined the account of Balaam and it is written:
-"Balaam the lame was 33 years old, when he was killed by Phineas the Robber. [5]

Balaam" the false prophet; a frequent epithet for Jesus by later rabbis to avoid Christian censorship.

The calculation of Jesus' age was 33 at the crucifixion based on the Gospel of Luke "And Jesus himself began to be about thirty years of age, being (as was supposed) the son of Joseph, which was the son of Heli,[6]" plus the Fourth Gospel's account of a public career spanning three Passovers.

"Phineas the Robber" is probably a code name for Pontius Pilate, who confiscated temple funds.
The above was taken from "Jesus & Christians in non-Christian sources."

A later Rabbi, not a contemporary of Jesus, wrote this "story". Throughout the years, the Jewish Rabbins have changed history, and even some wording in the Old Testament, to cover up the guilt of killing the Messiah.

There are far too many scriptures in the Old Testament that have been verified in the New Testament, for any thinking person to deny the truth found there. It is far more productive, spiritually, to rely on the Word of God rather than the words of man.

The scripture verses listed above verify the act of crucifixion as prophesied. History itself, as verified by the date of rulers in Jesus day verifies His age.

---

[5] Babylonian Talmud Sanhedrin 106b
[6] Luke 3:23

It is eternally dangerous for an atheist to argue against the existence of the Lord God. Is it not more threatening for a Jew to deny the Messiah when their own Scriptures give absolute prophecies that were fulfilled exactly?   Before believing what religious leaders say a person is well advised to go to the Scriptures daily and see if these things are so.

Chapter 41

"Given Vinegar To Quench His Thirst"

To understand this prophecy and its fulfillment we need to take a step backward and remember what punishment Jesus had suffered prior to being nailed to the cross.

Recall the unnecessary cruelty inflicted upon Jesus after His arrest. His jail "cell" was a deep, narrow pit in which countless prisoners had been held prior to their execution. The bottom would have been filled with excrements, and urine and possibly blood. He was then mocked, having His beard pulled out by the roots, beaten repeatedly over the head with a reed. There was then that terrible beating with the whip laden with sharp pieces of various descriptions.

They hit Him with their fists and open hand on several occasions, and on the way to Calvary the people likely threw stones at him, hit Him when He was close enough to them, and spit on Him.

Now Jesus has been nailed through both hands and both feet. Is it any wonder that, after all this torture and loss of blood that Jesus said, "I thirst?" [1]

In a Psalm we read "Thou hast known my reproach, and my shame, and my dishonor: mine adversaries are all before thee." [2] Jesus is saying, 'you have known the brutal punishment I have suffered, now all I ask is some water to drink.'

---

[1] Psalm 69:21
[2] Psalm 69:19

Instead of water, He was offered vinegar that had been mixed with intoxicating herbs. I will describe that in more detail in a moment.

When the Psalmist wrote this Psalm, which is also a prophecy, He was referring to the treatment endured by the Jews in captivity. David may not have known that his Psalm would be prophetic of Messiah.

While the Jews were in captivity, their food was mingled with vinegar. As slaves, their food was not of the best quality and the vinegar would help preserve it. The vinegar would also make the food unpleasant and even disgusting to eat, but it would be wholesome. Instead of being given wine to drink with their meals, they were given 'sour small wines', which we term as vinegar.

David wrote "Let their table become a snare before them: and that which should have been for their welfare, let it become a trap." [3] This verse is written in the future tense and it became a prophecy, both for the captors of the Jews at that time, and for those Jews that maltreated Messiah.

The simple translation of this verse could be 'thy wrathful anger SHALL take hold of them! The evils that were inflicted on the Israelites by their captors would be visited upon themselves. God will judge them in like manner regarding their food, drink, labor and suffering. This also would become the lot of the Jews as they mistreated Messiah in such a cruel manner.

We have seen a partial fulfillment of this prophecy during the Second World War, and the complete fulfillment will occur during the fulfillment of Ezekiel the 38th and 39th chapters.

---

[3] Psalm 69:22

We now go to the scripture portions we read at the beginning of this study. We read in the New Testament the fulfillment of the Old Testament, which told us they gave Messiah gall instead of food. In the original language, the word 'gall' is ξολη, which means bitters of any kind.

It was customary to put a stupefying potion compounded of sour wine [vinegar], myrrh and frankincense to a condemned person to help alleviate the suffering, or to dull their mind so they would not be so aware of the pain.

This is based on a Proverb "Give strong drink unto him that is ready to perish, and wine unto those that be of heavy hearts." [4]

The one offering this potion to Jesus would have been someone acting out of human kindness toward Jesus. We do not know who that person might have been, but it is reasonable to assume it to have been perhaps the disciple John, or one of the women standing watch at the foot of His cross.

Jesus tasted the mixture pressed to His lips, but realizing its content, He refused to drink. Had it been only water or vinegar, or perhaps even table quality wine, He would have accepted it. The very fact that He tasted it proves that He was in a state of mind to drink.

Our Savior preferred to 'tread the winepress alone' [Isaiah 63:3], enduring the fullness of pain for our sins.

Once again, we have witnessed the accuracy of the Old Testament prophecies regarding the Messiah, being fulfilled exactly in the New Testament.

---

[4] Proverbs 31:6

The more we witness the fulfillments of these prophecies the more we become aware of:

1) God's repulsion of sin and the necessity of disposing of all sin

2) God's method of disposing of sin is by remission [the act of making the sin disappear from His Holy presence].

3) His method is, and will always be Hebrews 9:22 "And almost all things are by the law purged with blood; and without shedding of blood is no remission."

4) Simply put, either the sinner must die for his sins, or he must have a suitable substitute. That substitute cannot die for our sins if he is not sinless. If the substitute has sinned, he must die for his own sins.

5) The terrible punishment God allowed Emmanuel [God with us] to endure proves beyond any doubt that sin is abhorrent in the sight of God. If one refuses to accept the sacrifice of Jesus as being our substitute in death for our sins, an equal punishment will be theirs for all eternity. That is what Hell is all about sinners choosing an eternity of torment rather than accepting Jesus as their substitute in death for sin.

6) This act of God proves the fact that "God is love", and it is not His will that any should perish, but that all should come to salvation through Jesus the Messiah.

Chapter 42

"Executed Without
A Bone Broken"

To understand why Messiah must be executed without having a bone broken we first must understand the Passover. The Passover was instituted to prevent the death angel from harming the Jews, while at the same time bringing death to every home in Egypt, by killing the firstborn of that family. The firstborn was the heir to the power and wealth of the father, and the Egyptians represented that which is evil. The Passover struck a blow at the very heart of Egyptian idolatry and its posterity.

I will allow scripture to speak for itself: "Your lamb shall be without blemish, a male of the first year: ye shall take it out from the sheep, or from the goats": [1]

"And ye shall keep it up until the fourteenth day of the same month: and the whole assembly of the congregation of Israel shall kill it in the evening. And they shall take of the blood, and strike it on the two side posts and on the upper doorpost of the houses, wherein they shall eat it. And they shall eat the flesh in that night, roast with fire, and unleavened bread; and with bitter herbs they shall eat it. Eat not of it raw, nor sodden at all with water, but roast with fire; his head with his legs, and with the purtenance thereof. And ye shall let nothing of it remain until the morning; and that which remaineth of it until the morning ye shall burn with fire.

---

[1] Exodus 12:5

And thus shall ye eat it; with your loins girded, your shoes on your feet, and your staff in your hand; and ye shall eat it in haste: it is the LORD's passover. For I will pass through the land of Egypt this night, and will smite all the firstborn in the land of Egypt, both man and beast; and against all the gods of Egypt I will execute judgment: I am the LORD. And the blood shall be to you for a token upon the houses where ye are: and when I see the blood, I will pass over you, and the plague shall not be upon you to destroy you, when I smite the land of Egypt." [2]

Every element of the Passover is prophetic of Jesus the Messiah. He is the Passover Lamb that prevents one from the plague [penalty of death] of sin. When God sees that the believer has accepted Jesus as their Savior from sin it is His blood, shed on the cross of Calvary that protects that person from eternal damnation.

When Jesus was crucified on that Passover Friday, the priests were killing the Passover lambs below in the Temple. Little did they know that the chief priests and the Roman soldiers were killing the "Lamb slain from the foundation of the world." "And all that dwell upon the earth shall worship him, whose names are not written in the book of life of the Lamb slain from the foundation of the world." [3]

This verse in the book of Revelation informs us that Jesus [the Son of God, God the Son] was in agreement with God the Father before the Earth was even formed.

---

[2] Exodus 12:6-13
[3] Revelation 13:8

His agreement was that He would be the sinless Lamb of God that would die as the substitute sacrifice for sinful mankind. All that was necessary would be that which was similar to the first Passover. The blood must be applied to prevent the "plague".

This is accomplished by heeding the words of Jesus as He spoke to Nicodemus, a ruler of the Jews. Jesus told Nicodemus that he could not go to Heaven unless he was "born again." See this discussion in John 3:1-21, and if you do not understand what this discussion meant feel free to ask me for a clear explanation.

There are some key phrases in the account of that first Passover. These need further serious thought regarding the prophetic meanings.

1) "Take the blood"-The blood [sacrifice of Christ in place of the sinner] is made available, but until one appropriates it personally, it will not protect them.

2) "Strike it on the door posts" - It was to be on either doorpost, and on the upper doorpost. This was likely done hastily and the upper doorpost would receive a strike with the hyssop filled with blood by reaching upward and striking it with a downward blow. The two side posts would be struck, likely starting at one side and going horizontal to the other side. It is easy to imagine the sign of the cross being made at this time.

3) "Roast with fire" - the Jews did not eat roasted meat, but rather boiled meat. This instruction indicates a complete destruction of the lamb, first being roasted, secondly by being ingested by the Jew, and finally any remains must be consumed by fire.

The Messiah must be completely consumed, that is, He must be positively dead. The Jewish law, which would come later, demanded that the sin offering be completely consumed "outside the camp", even as Messiah was offered as our sacrifice outside the city of Jerusalem.

4) "Eat in haste" - The matter of being protected from eternal damnation is no small matter. We must "take the blood" in haste because we do not know when the Messiah will return to make an accounting of our life actions.

5) "First born killed" - Egypt was to become synonymous sin, because of their worship of idols. This indicates that the Messiah would take our sins to the cross with Him, and those sins would be destroyed as He died. Those sins will never be held against us as proclaiming us guilty of sin.

6) When God saw the blood that had been applied He by-passed that home and the firstborn in it. At the time of judgment, God will be looking to see if we have appropriated the blood of the Lamb; accepted the sacrifice of Christ as being our substitute in death for our sins.

We must be careful to note that the lamb was to be without spot and blameless [Messiah was sinless], "and no sacrifice is accepted if it has any defect, such as a broken bone. "He keepeth all his bones: not one of them is broken. Evil shall slay the wicked: and they that hate the righteous shall be desolate." [4]

The Passover lamb must not have a broken bone, and the fulfillment was when Jesus died His legs were not broken.

---

[4] Psalm 34:20-21

The Sabbath was about to start with the going down of the sun. The Jews would not allow a Jew to remain on a cross after sundown on the Sabbath; this was a "Holy Sabbath" because the Sabbath and the Passover were on the same day.

To make certain that the condemned were dead before sunset the Roman soldiers were instructed to use a large wood mallet to break the legs of those crucified.

Because of the method of crucifixion, it was necessary for the condemned to use their legs to raise their body in order to allow air to flow into their lungs. If their legs had been broken, they could not raise their body and would consequently suffocate very quickly.

When the soldier came to Jesus, he found that Jesus was already dead, and breaking the legs was unnecessary, therefore, the prophecy that Messiah must be executed without having a bone broken was fulfilled. "When Jesus therefore had received the vinegar, he said, It is finished: and he bowed his head, and gave up the ghost.

The Jews therefore, because it was the preparation, that the bodies should not remain upon the cross on the Sabbath day, (for that Sabbath day was an high day,) besought Pilate that their legs might be broken, and that they might be taken away. Then came the soldiers, and brake the legs of the first, and of the other which was crucified with him. But when they came to Jesus, and saw that he was dead already, they brake not his legs: But one of the soldiers with a spear pierced his side, and forthwith came there out blood and water.

And he that saw it bare record, and his record is true: and he knoweth that he saith true, that ye might believe. For these things were done, that the scripture should be fulfilled, "A bone of him shall not be broken." [5]

All these prophesies regarding Messiah have been faithfully fulfilled in an exact manner. How can we doubt that the remainder of the unfulfilled prophecies of the Bible will also be fulfilled?

Jesus promised to return again, "In my Father's house are many mansions: if it were not so, I would have told you. I go to prepare a place for you. And if I go and prepare a place for you, I will come again, and receive you unto myself; that where I am, there ye may be also." [6] This is good reason to make certain the blood shed at Calvary is appropriated in haste.

---

[5] John 19:29-36
[6] John 14:2-3

Chapter 43

"Considered A Transgressor"

It is difficult to understand how Jesus could be condemned to death, convicted as a common criminal. The attitude of the High Priest gives a good clue as to how this condemnation could come about. Consider what the apostle John wrote concerning this: "Then gathered the chief priests and the Pharisees a council, and said, What do we? for this man doeth many miracles. If we let him thus alone, all men will believe on him: and the Romans shall come and take away both our place and nation. And one of them, named Caiaphas, being the high priest that same year, said unto them, Ye know nothing at all, Nor consider that it is expedient for us, that one man should die for the people, and that the whole nation perish not. And this spake he not of himself: but being high priest that year, he prophesied that Jesus should die for that nation;" [1]

The deception of the Jewish leaders was simple but effective. They called for a council of the scribes and elders, along with Annas and the High Priest, Caiaphas. Their question was what do we do with this man Jesus? He has raised Lazarus from the dead, and if we allow Him to continue to perform miracles, the people will accept Him as the Messiah. If they choose to proclaim Him as their king, the Romans will come and destroy our Temple, and remove our civil and ecclesiastic government privileges.

---

[1] John 11:47-51

Under the pretence of good, these evil men hid their true hatred and plotted the death of Jesus. To get the people on their side the rulers simply spread the word that this Jesus will incite the Roman soldiers to destroy our nation.

This was prophesied in the Old Testament: "Therefore will I divide him a portion with the great, and he shall divide the spoil with the strong; because he hath poured out his soul unto death: and he was numbered with the transgressors; and he bare the sin of many, and made intercession for the transgressors." [2]

That is when the High Priest prophesied about Jesus, probably not realizing the full impact of what He had said. Being the High Priest it is more than likely that the Holy Spirit put the words in the mind of the priest and he spoke that which came into his mind, even though not realizing it was a prophecy.

God is a jealous God, and highly resents everything that is done and said against the eternal truth that came through Jesus Christ, by the Holy Spirit. What this council decided on that night will one day come back to haunt them in ways they could never dream.

Even though the sinless Jesus had committed no transgression, He was condemned to die with those who were transgressors.

That placed Him in the category of a criminal in the eyes of the people. Dying of crucifixion, were two criminals fastened to their own cross, one on either side of Jesus.

---

[2] Isaiah 53:12

He is condemned to die between two men that were known criminals, and one even reminded the other that they were receiving what they deserved, but Jesus had done nothing wrong.

"And one of the malefactors which were hanged railed on him, saying, If thou be Christ, save thyself and us. However, the other answering rebuked him, saying, Dost not thou fear God, seeing thou art in the same condemnation? And we indeed justly; for we receive the due reward of our deeds: but this man hath done nothing amiss." [3]

Obviously, it had become difficult for one of the thieves to believe that Jesus could be condemned to die by crucifixion. He acknowledged Jesus as "Lord", and asked that when He came into His kingdom He would remember the penitent thief.

When the word "Lord" is used in a respectful manner the Greek translation for it is God, denoting the thief recognized Jesus as being Divine and supreme in power.

The scripture verse in Isaiah reminds us that Jesus bore the sin of many. Note that the word "sin" is singular, not plural. Sin causes us to commit sins, and this reference is to the original sin. Jesus took that original sin with Him to the cross, and at the time of His death sin lost its power over man.

If we sin it is because we have chosen to sin, because sin no longer has a hold on us.

---

[3] Luke 23:39-41

That same verse says Jesus made "intercession for the transgressors." This definitely speaks of all humanity, since all have sinned and come short of the glory of God. Before Jesus released His spirit to return unto the Father, He said "Father forgive them..."

Before Jesus allowed Himself to be taken prisoner, He knelt before the Heavenly Father in the Garden of Gethsemane and prayed for His disciples. Then those marvelous words that every Christian holds dear, "Neither pray I for these alone, but for them also which shall believe on me through their word;" [4]

On the cross Jesus made intercession for the entire sinful world, but in the Garden He specifically mentioned those who would become His followers in the Christian faith.

Mankind could learn much about prayer from our Savior, Jesus. The following illustration proves that not all prayers are prayers.

In a recent meeting held by the writer a series of prayer, services had taken place beforehand asking for the outpouring of the Spirit. Two of the brethren who supplicated most vociferously for an old-time revival were the first to leave, or rather run, when the Gospel battle opened. All of this convinces us that there is a lot of praying done on earth where not only the heart is not involved but the head is also unemployed. Sentences are uttered memoriter. They have been spoken many times before.

---

[4] John 17:20

The brother praying heard somebody else use the words and adopted them. And now it is a memorized speech to the Almighty from the knees.

The man going through the motions of this means of grace is saying his prayers. Who wonders when the genuine work begins; when the Holy Ghost convicts; and the power of God falls upon mind, heart, and conscience, that such puppet figures of real soldiers of the cross go down before the roar of the first Gospel gun, or tumble over each other in their flight from the battle field. The same cannon, however, that makes some run brings a lot more to the front, and the ranks of Gods army are not weakened, but sifted and strengthened by the two movements of the goers and the comers.

It so proved in this meeting, and every other meeting that we held since we have been an evangelist. [5]

I cannot finish this study of the Messiah on a negative note, and therefore offer a final illustration regarding the power of prayer when uttered by those who are truly sincere and full of faith.

We were in the midst of an interesting series of meetings in New York.

Among those attending from no promising motives was Mr. Olin, a lawyer of marked ability and influence in the town.

One evening, at the close of the sermon, when an opportunity was given for remarks, Mr. Olin rose, and, in a bold and defiant tone, said: Mr. Earle, I have heard you speak repeatedly in these meetings of the power of prayer, and I don't believe a word of it; but if you want to try a hard case, take me.

---

[5] Living Illustrations by B. Carradine

I said, Mr. Olin, if you will come to the front seat, we will pray for you now.

He replied, I will do nothing of the kind; but if you have power in prayer, try it on me.

Before closing the meeting, I requested all who were willing, to go to their closets at a given hour, and pray earnestly for Mr. Olin; and I requested him to remember at that hour that we were praying for him.

The second or third evening after this, Mr. Olin rose in our meeting, and urged us to pray for him. I asked him if he would come forward and let us pray with him. He said: Yes, anywhere, if God will only have mercy on so great a sinner.

In a few days he was a rejoicing Christian, and soon after sold his law books, and became a preacher of the gospel. He is now a presiding elder in the Methodist church.[6]

The power of prayer, in the hands of mortal Christians, began when Jesus prayed for future Christians, as He prayed in the garden.

Then, Jesus put power into prayer for the unsaved as He prayed for the forgiveness of sinners just before He gave His spirit over to the Heavenly Father.

While it is true, that Messiah must be considered a transgressor that was only among those who perish. Those of us who have chosen eternal life see Him as the sinless Son of God, and the hope of our salvation.

---

[6] A.B. Earle, from incidents used...1888

Chapter 44

"His Death Atoned for the Sins of Mankind"

It was necessary that God send His Son (God the Son) to become the substitute in God's law of sin and death. Man had sinned from the very beginning, and from the beginning God had love and mercy for His creation. Therefore, the prophet Isaiah was given words to speak that are prophetic of Jesus the Messiah. "But he was wounded for our transgressions, he was bruised for our iniquities: the chastisement of our peace was upon him; and with his stripes we are healed. All we like sheep have gone astray; we have turned every one to his own way; and the LORD hath laid on him the iniquity of us all. He was oppressed, and he was afflicted, yet he opened not his mouth: he is brought as a lamb to the slaughter, and as a sheep before her shearers is dumb, so he openeth not his mouth." [1]

The New Testament gives eyewitness verification of the sacrifice for sin being paid by Jesus of Nazareth, God the Son. "For even the Son of man came not to be ministered unto, but to minister, and to give his life a ransom for many." [2]

The writer of the Gospel of John was intimately associated with Jesus and knew beyond a shadow of a doubt that He is the promised Messiah. John wrote, "For God so loved the world, that he gave his only begotten Son, that whosoever believeth in him should not perish, but have everlasting life." [3]

---

[1] Isaiah 53:5-7
[2] Mark 10:45   [3] John 3:16

Throughout the Old Testament God is warning us about His anger toward sin. Repeatedly Israel sinned against God, who had rescued them from their bondage in Egypt. Egypt is the symbol for sin in Scripture, and the Holy God rescued the Hebrews out of sinful Egypt. Time after time, the Hebrews displayed their ingratitude for God's love and kindness by rebelling against His commandments.

II Kings is one such example of God telling mankind that He will not tolerate sin. "And she said unto Elijah, What have I to do with thee, O thou man of God? art thou come unto me to call my sin to remembrance, and to slay my son? " [4] Some background facts will help to understand the anger of God toward Israel.

Hoshea was king over Israel in Samaria. He was one of many evil kings. Shalmaneser, king of Assyria brought his army to Samaria to attack Israel, but Hoshea surrendered to him and gave him tribute.

Hoshea then sent messengers to Egypt for help [that place of sin from which God rescued Israel] and at the same time stopped paying tribute to Assyria.

Shalmaneser put Hoshea in prison and besieged Samaria for three years. The king of Assyria then removed the Israelites from their land and dispersed them in several lands.

God brought this about because the Israelites were living the life of a heathen. They built high places to worship idols and built groves for their adulterous worship rites. The land of Samaria was filled with such high places and groves.

---

4   1 Kings 17:18

The Israelites began to mimic the heathens in their sacrificial practices of offering their children up as a burnt sacrifice to idols. The Bible tells us they "wrought wicked things to provoke the LORD to anger."

God sent warnings to them by His messenger but they would not listen. They rejected His statutes and covenants made with the Patriarchs and followed their own vanity.

They made molten calf images and worshiped the hosts of heaven, and served Baal. "Therefore the LORD was very angry with Israel, and removed them out of his sight: there was none left but the tribe of Judah only."[5] Judah was in Jerusalem, not Samaria, and God spared that tribe.

This should tell us something about how God feels about sinning against Him. In many respects modern man is little different from the Israelites in Samaria who opted to "provoke the LORD to anger."

These individuals are reminiscent of the following illustration.

"I Will Have My Way Or Die"

In the town of our childhood and boyhood, a great muscular man of thirty or forty, became offended with a silversmith about a trifle. Wrought into a kind of frenzy he walked into the jewelry store and slapped the face of the gentleman referred to.

---

[5] 2 Kings 17:18

He had been begged by friends beforehand not to do so. Men knew that the silversmith, although a small and frail looking person, had the heart of a lion as to courage. But the enraged man was bent on having his way. In fact he said he would have his way or die.

The silversmith, realizing that he had no chance in a fisticuff, deliberately armed himself, and sending word to his insulter and attacker to prepare to meet him, as deliberately set his own feet in the same fatal road in which his antagonist had entered. In thirty minutes they were both dead men. Each had received from four to five pistol balls in their bodies before falling lifeless on the brick pavement of Yazoo City. We saw the ghastly sight when a lad, and have never and can never forget it. Each one had his way and died. We have known so many distressing occurrences to take place on this melancholy thoroughfare of which we are writing, that we actually get sick and faint at heart when we hear a person saying, I am determined to have my way or die. We know in the double light of revelation and history that the speech really means, I am resolved to have my way and die!

Who can doubt this a moment who credits the statements of the Word of God, and studies certain biographies in the same sacred volume? Scores of lives held up in the Scripture can be perfectly covered and described by the sentence as amended. And Absalom had his way and died. Samson had his way and died. Baalam had his way and died. Judas had his way and died. All died while in the midst of their own way. And the death was peculiar in being premature, calamitous, tragical, dreadful and hopeless.

If we come to history it reads the same. It matters not what age or country the individual lives in; if his way is not Gods way, but is a life contrary to the Word of God, and to the Spirit of Christ, there is nothing but death in a disastrous sense to be looked for. Then there are deaths resultants from this course, which are more heartbreaking and calamitous than a mere, dissolution of soul and body.

The self-willed, perverse course often means the destruction of happiness to other people. It is a dreadful thing to behold the light and joy go out of the eyes of innocent members of a household through the selfishness and obstinacy of a single individual in that same family circle. So the course of self-will not only ends the peace of the home, but effects finally the ruin of the home itself. Who wonders that such a person is finally left to rule over a desert; or to sit as king on a throne of straw with a crown of straw in a life dungeon whose walls are loneliness, and whose atmosphere is one of unbroken silence.

The burial ground or lot of such home destroyers could very properly and suggestively be ornamented, with such shrubbery as flame scorched trees, and such monuments as a group of fire-blackened chimneys standing like ghastly sentinels in the midst of twisted rusty iron, charred beams and piles of gray ashes." [6]

---

[6] Living Illustrations By B. Carradine

Isaiah the 53rd chapter informs us that the Messiah was to become our "pacification" [a peacemaker that makes peace between two opposing parties]; that which brings us into a state of peace and favor with God. There are those, much like ancient Israel, that ignore the warnings from God and prefer to do as they please.

This chapter reminds us that Jesus became the focal point on which all the iniquity of the world fell. These rays of God's wrath should have fallen on all mankind, but Jesus deflected these and took them unto Himself. Considering the terrible penalty Jesus paid in our behalf we should realize what is stored up for those who refuse to repent of their sins and live holy lives before God.

Chapter 45

"Buried With the Rich"

Previous chapters in this book have painted a gloomy, terrifying and painful picture of the treatment afforded Jesus. All these terrible happenings were prophesied in the Old Testament.

How impossible would this prophecy seem to anyone having only the account in the Old Testament! The narrative in Isaiah paints a gloomy picture of humiliation, torture, hatred, and execution of the Messiah. Now we read an amazing verse that says "And he made his grave with the wicked, and with the rich in his death; because he had done no violence, neither was any deceit in his mouth." [1] It is believable, after reading this chapter, that Messiah would make his grave with the wicked, but how can he do that and still make his grave with the rich? It is unlikely that the rich, in the days of Jesus, would be found to be wicked and for some reason be buried at the same time as Jesus.

As usual, there are many legends surrounding Joseph, but since these are grossly overstated and unverified, I will curb the urge to elaborate on these.

---

[1] Isaiah 53:9

What we do know about Joseph of Arimathaea is that he was apparently a wealthy and honorable "counselor" which is translated into a member of the Sanhedrin. We learn from John 19:38 that he was a secret disciple of Jesus, as was Nicodemus.

Before moving to Arimathaea, he lived in Marmorica in Egypt. He moved to Arimathaea, which is in Judea and generally known by the name of Ramieh or Ramathaim-Zophim.

This is the place where David came to Samuel: "So David fled, and escaped, and came to Samuel to Ramah, and told him all that Saul had done to him." And he and Samuel went and dwelt in Naioth." [2]

Even though Joseph was a secret disciple of Jesus, he boldly went to Pilate and asked permission to claim the body of Jesus.

This could have caused suspicion that Joseph was also a disciple and caused him arrest or expulsion from the Sanhedrin.

Although being a voting member of the Council, it is unlikely that Joseph cast a ballot to crucify Jesus. It may be that when the council met at night, being illegal, Joseph refrained from attending. Only those with great hatred for Jesus would dare to violate the law concerning the operation of the Sanhedrin.

"When the even was come, there came a rich man of Arimathaea, named Joseph, who also Jesus' disciple: He went to Pilate, and begged the body of Jesus.

---

[2] 1 Samuel 19:18

Pilate commanded the body of Jesus to be released to Joseph, once he had heard his plea.

And when Joseph had taken the body, he wrapped it in a clean linen cloth, And laid it in his own new tomb, which he had hewn out in the rock: and he rolled a great stone to the door of the sepulchre, and departed." [3]

Jesus did not actually make His grave with the wicked; He was assigned a grave with the wicked. In the sense that, as a condemned criminal Jesus would not be allowed to be buried in a sacred place, it is logical to say that He "made" His grave with the wicked.

The grave was assigned to Him, was "made" for Him, but He never occupied the grave of a transgressor.

Since Jesus could not be buried on sacred Jewish burial land, it is likely that the grave of Joseph would not have been in that area. Since he was from Egypt originally, he would be considered a "stranger" and not allowed to have a burial location on the usual Jewish sites.

His tomb was a cave, carved out of stone buried under the soil of a hill not far from Calvary. An entrance door was carved out of the rock. This led into a small area facing into the raised slab on which the body would be laid. The labor of such a tomb would be expensive and it is obvious that Joseph had the wealth to provide himself with such a tomb.

Who would have guessed, by reading Isaiah, that Jesus would have such influence with a rich man at the time of the crucifixion?

---

[3] Matthew 27:57-60

It is miraculous that such a man would have the faith and courage to beg for the body of Jesus and place Him in his own tomb.

Once Joseph had placed the body of Jesus in the tomb, he departed, as it was likely close to sunset and his work at the tomb must be finished for now.

Nicodemus assisted Joseph in the preparation of the body, but it is reasonable to assume that Joseph, being a rich man, did not personally handle the body of Jesus. It would have been discrete on his part to send his servants to take down the body and carry it to the tomb. The manner of speaking in scripture would allow this action to be attributed to Joseph as though he personally had performed the labor.

An explanation of a common practice when burying the dead will be helpful in making a point in a few moments.

Because there were limited numbers of caves, when the bodies had decomposed the bones were removed and put into stone jars called ossuaries.

This is the meaning of "gathered to their fathers"

"And they buried him in the border of his inheritance in Timnathheres, in the mount of Ephraim, on the north side of the hill Gaash. And also all that generation were gathered unto their fathers: and there arose another generation after them, which knew not the LORD, nor yet the works which he had done for Israel." [4]

---

[4] Judges 2:9-10

These jars were stored in a corner, and the niches made available for further burials. The mouth of the tomb was sealed either with a disc-shaped stone that ran in an inclined groove in front of the cave or with a boulder that fell into the access hole beneath it. Either way, the stone was extremely difficult to move once it was in place.

Burial caves and sepulchres were painted white as a warning to the living that the dead were there "Woe unto you, scribes and Pharisees, hypocrites! for ye are like unto whited sepulchres, which indeed appear beautiful outward, but are within full of dead men's bones, and of all uncleanness." [5] A living person could not worship God after having had contact with the dead.

"And he took it down, and wrapped it in linen, and laid it in a sepulchre that was hewn in stone, wherein never man before was laid." [6]

Jesus was buried in the personal tomb of Joseph of Arimathaea, in a tomb that no other had ever been buried. There would have been no ossuaries sitting in the corner, as it would be unfitting for the King of kings to be buried in a used tomb.

When Joseph and Nicodemus prepared Jesus for burial they covered His body with the expensive embalming spices provided by Nicodemus.

---

[5] Matthew 23:27
[6] Luke 23:53

"And there came also Nicodemus, which at the first came to Jesus by night, and brought a mixture of myrrh and aloes, about an hundred pound weight." [7]

These spices would be applied as a paste, and were tied to the body by layers of white bandages." The paste hardened and impregnated the bandages until a hard preservative mould or cocoon was formed about the body. As one reads the account of the resurrection of Jesus we will see that the "cocoon" was undisturbed, not broken open. Over His head was placed a napkin serving as the "cap." This is contrary to the account and photos of the cloth of Turin.

An interesting feature concerning this napkin being placed over the face of Jesus is worth a second mention.

If the master of the house left the supper table for any reason, he would either wad the napkin up and place it on the table, or, neatly fold it. The neatly folded napkin was a signal to the servant that the master would be coming back.

In the account of Jesus raising Lazarus from the dead we see mention made of the burial napkin: "And when he thus had spoken, he cried with a loud voice, Lazarus, come forth. And he that was dead came forth, bound hand and foot with grave clothes: and his face was bound about with a napkin. Jesus saith unto them, Loose him, and let him go." [8]

---

[7] John 19:39
[8] John 11:43,44

The resurrection scene of Jesus indicates the napkin was given careful attention: "And the napkin, that was about his head, not lying with the linen clothes, but wrapped together in a place by itself." [9] It was "wrapped together", not wadded up and loosely thrown down. Jesus is coming back!

---

[9] John 20:7

Chapter 46

"Raised From the Dead"

Try to imagine yourself as being the prophet Isaiah and you are inspired by the Holy Spirit to write the words "He made his grave with the wicked," and "he shall see his seed, [True converts, genuine Christians] he shall prolong his days, [Christianity shall endure to the end of time.]" That is, after being crucified and declared dead the Messiah will once again live. Carefully read what Isaiah was told to write "And he made his grave with the wicked, and with the rich in his death; because he had done no violence, neither was any deceit in his mouth. Yet it pleased the LORD to bruise him; he hath put him to grief: when thou shalt make his soul an offering for sin, he shall see his seed, he shall prolong his days, and the pleasure of the LORD shall prosper in his hand."[1]

King David was given a similar prophecy, and I doubt that he understood the full impact of what the Holy Spirit had dictated for him to write. David wrote "I have set the LORD always before me: because he is at my right hand, I shall not be moved. Therefore my heart is glad, and my glory rejoiceth: my flesh also shall rest in hope. For thou wilt not leave my soul in hell; neither wilt thou suffer thine Holy One to see corruption."[2]

Might one not think that if He made his grave with the wicked he must be dead?

---

[1] Isaiah 53:9-10
[2] Psalm 16:8-10

Did David understand what God meant when he was told to write that "neither wilt thou suffer thine Holy One to see corruption"? How then, will Messiah literally see His true converts and how will his days be prolonged to the point that Christianity will endure until the end of time? How will Messiah be murdered and yet His body will never be corrupted by the process of death? A prophet of God must be obedient to the inspiration of the Holy Spirit and record that which he cannot understand.

The Christian must take the example of the prophets of old and apply that to their own life situation. If God the Holy Spirit inspires us to do something that we do not fully understand we should be obedient and then wait to see the joy that results from submission.

How many more true miracles would we see in our world today if we had the kind of unquestioning obedience that did Isaiah, Ezekiel, Daniel, and John the Revelator!

The Psalmist David wrote prophetically, but likely did not realize the full implication of what he was writing. Perhaps he was thinking about the fact that there is life after death, and was meditating on the words of Job as he commented on the future of man after death. Job said "But man dieth, and wasteth away: yea, man giveth up the ghost, and where is he?" [3] Then a question he desperately wanted answered, "If a man die, shall he live again? [4]

---

[3] Job 14:10
[4] Job 14:14

Finally, after much deliberation Job came to the conclusion that all is not doom and gloom as he said "For I know that my redeemer liveth, and that he shall stand at the latter day upon the earth: And though after my skin worms destroy this body, yet in my flesh shall I see God: Whom I shall see for myself, and mine eyes shall behold, and not another; though my reins be consumed within me." [5]

David wrote that God would not leave his soul in Hell. The Hebrew word used here was not Hell, but rather Sheol, and in this verse refers to the grave. Messiah would not remain in the grave, nor would His body decay.

Was David thinking of himself at this point, not knowing that God was referring to the coming Messiah? These are questions we cannot answer, but only wonder at what David was thinking.

Because Jesus was wrapped in a cocoon, one can understand why it was that the disciples saw and then believed in the resurrection, and why it was that the body had not been stolen. Jesus' body had passed through the cocoon of spice-impregnated bandages, just as it did through the door of the upper room.

Looking quickly through the doorway of the tomb, John thought that the body was still there because he could see the cocoon, and therefore he would not enter.

Only when John and Peter went in and saw that there was a gap where the face should have been (the cap was separated) did they realize what had happened. The napkin was folded separately.

---

5 Job 19:25-27

331

Just a reminder:

The "cap" was actually a napkin placed over the face. An interesting aspect of this is that in Jewish culture, if the master of the house were to leave the table at mealtime, he would do one of two things. If he were finished eating the napkin would have been wadded up and tossed on the table as an indication that the table can now be cleared. If the napkin was neatly folded, it meant, "I will return." The napkin in the tomb of Jesus was neatly folded as if to say, "I will return."

A few facts catch my attention as I consider the resurrection of Jesus. God was ever near during the entire episode of the arrest, torment, crucifixion and resurrection. Not only did Jesus cry out to God Eli, Eli, [ay-lee] my God, but God responded at the point of Jesus' death by causing an earthquake, among other natural phenomena. Then, when God raised Jesus from the dead, He sent a mighty angel to the tomb to roll away the large heavy stone sealing the entrance. Upon the angel obeying the command of God to go down to earth to move the stone, God sent another earthquake. An earthquake often signals the presence of God. "And Mount Sinai was altogether on a smoke, because the LORD descended upon it in fire: and the smoke thereof ascended as the smoke of a furnace, and the whole mount quaked greatly." [6]

These verses cause one to wonder if Jesus was telling us something we often miss, when he said in "For nation shall rise against nation, and kingdom against kingdom: and there shall be famines, and pestilences, and earthquakes, in divers places." [7]

---

[6] Exodus 19:18
[7] Matthew 24:7

332

Could it be that the earthquakes we are seeing on television is signaling to us that God is either doing something special on Planet Earth, or perhaps He is trumpeting His soon return as the God Son, [Son of God]?

Something we might consider regarding the fact that Messiah must be raised from the dead. It was prophesied that He must be in the grave for three days, which would be Friday just before sunset, all day on the Sabbath day and likely just a few minutes on that first Easter Sunday. In Jewish thinking, if something is involved in any part of the day it is considered as having been in that day. Therefore, Jesus was in the grave at least a part of the day on Friday, Saturday and Sunday, but that qualifies for three days.

Let's go one step "deeper", and consider that the body of Jesus was in the tomb during those three days, but His Spirit was about His Father's business as usual; you just can't keep a good man down!

"For Christ also hath once suffered for sins, the just for the unjust, that he might bring us to God, being put to death in the flesh, but quickened by the Spirit: By which also he went and preached unto the spirits in prison; Which sometime were disobedient, when once the longsuffering of God waited in the days of Noah, while the ark was a preparing, wherein few, that is, eight souls were saved by water." [8]

---

[8] 1 Peter 3:18-20

We read in Ephesians "Wherefore he saith, When he ascended up on high, he led captivity captive, and gave gifts unto men. (Now that he ascended, what is it but that he also descended first into the lower parts of the earth? He that descended is the same also that ascended up far above all heavens, that he might fill all things.)" [9]

These verses have been used to justify the word of the Apostles Creed, which states in part, "He descended into Hell, the third day He rose from the dead."

Three Greek words in Ephesians 4:9 may assist us in deciding if Jesus did preach salvation to the "saints" of the days of Noah. In fairness, it must be stated that some Biblical scholars debunk this idea, saying that when Jesus died He said, "It is finished." However, the Greek word τετελεσται, "Paid in Full". Jesus was not saying that all that needed to be done had been done. He was saying that He had paid the penalty for sin, Satan was a defeated foe, and having paid the debt completely He was now free to take again the glory He had left in Heaven.

I will give you the privilege to decide for yourself if you believe Jesus preached to the "saints" in Hades.

Peter gave us more scripture to digest as we decide on this issue. "quickened by the Spirit: By which also he went and preached unto the spirits in prison; Which sometime were disobedient, when once the longsuffering of God waited in the days of Noah, while the ark was a preparing, wherein few, that is, eight souls were saved by water." [10]

---

[9] Ephesians 4:18-19
[10] 1 Peter 3:18

334

The apostle Peter records specifically that Jesus, while His body was in the grave, went to preach to those in Hades, those who were the anti-diluvium persons never having heard the commandments of God and were completely ignorant of the Messiah to come.

Again, we turn to the original Greek to determine if what Peter appears to be saying is what the Greek tells us. "Preached", some say Jesus, if He did go down to Hades did not preach the gospel to them but rather announced His victory over Satan.

The Greek word for preached is κηρυσσα which means to preach, especially divine truth. The next word "prison" is φυκακη. this means the place where one is held. "disobedient: ουτειθεω [ap-I-theh-o], which means unbelieving.

It would seem that Peter was saying that those persons who had been unbelieving [didn't heed Noah's words] were under the patience of God and Jesus went into that part of Hades not reserved for those awaiting punishment, and literally preached divine truth.

It seems clear to me that Jesus' body laid in the tomb for three days, because the body of sin is dead and Jesus had taken upon Himself the sins of mankind, and therefore their penalty. His body was dead, and it lay in the grave during a part of each of the three days. However, during that time His sinless spirit was very much alive and He knew the patience God had with the unbelieving souls of Noah's day and He gave them opportunity to hear divine truth. We have no indication as to the result of His evangelistic tour into Hades.

Since this is all the scriptures clearly reveal, you must decide for yourself, which line of reasoning is factual.

This much we know for certain, Messiah was prophesied to be resurrected, and that the resurrection has become the anchor for the faith of countless Christians over the centuries.

Rise, heart; thy Lord is risen.
Sing His praise Without delays,
Who takes thee by the hand that thou likewise
With Him mayst rise.
- George Herbert -

Chapter 47

"Ascend To God"

The prophecy of Messiah in Psalm 16 speaks of the fact that Jesus will find His way out of the region of death, to die no more. David spoke of the "presence" of God, and in 1 John we read "Beloved, now are we the sons of God, and it doth not yet appear what we shall be: but we know that, when he shall appear, we shall be like him; for we shall see him as he is." [1]

It is interesting to note here that we shall see God as He is, and not as He displays Himself as the Son of God, God in the flesh.

David also said, "there are pleasures for evermore". Think of duration in the most extended and unlimited manner, and still there is more, and it is all pleasure!

Kind David prophesied that Jesus would sit on the right hand of God. This is the place of honor & dignity. In order to do this, Jesus must first ascend to Heaven to be with God.

We need verification that this actually happened, because this is a miraculous feat. "The LORD said unto my Lord, Sit thou at my right hand, until I make thine enemies thy footstool." [2]

The Gospel of Luke tells us that Jesus led the apostles and disciples in the direction of Bethany and there He ascended up into heaven. On the Mount of Olives, there is a tract of land that borders on Bethany, which is two miles from Jerusalem.

---

[1] 1 John 3:2
[2] Psalm 110:1

This tract of land, also known as Bethany, is only one mile from Jerusalem. Jesus "lifted up His hands", that is, He likely placed them on the heads of the apostles in a paternal blessing. It was then that Jesus ascended into heaven. King David was inspired to write of this event in the Psalms "Thou hast ascended on high, thou hast led captivity captive: thou hast received gifts for men; yea, for the rebellious also, that the LORD God might dwell among them. Blessed be the Lord, who daily loadeth us with benefits, even the God of our salvation. Selah." [3]

And again David was inspired to write, "The LORD said unto my Lord, Sit thou at my right hand, until I make thine enemies thy footstool." [4]

The disciples were led up the Mount of Olives and it was recorded that Jesus was taken up into heaven: "And he led them out as far as to Bethany, and he lifted up his hands, and blessed them. And it came to pass, while he blessed them, he was parted from them, and carried up into heaven."

Just as angels proclaimed His birth, and two angels attended His resurrection, we see an angel in attendance at His ascension. "Two men stood by them in white apparel; which also said, "Ye men of Galilee, why stand ye gazing up into heaven? this same Jesus, which is taken up from you into heaven, shall so come in like manner as ye have seen him go into heaven." [5] Not only did the angels proclaim His birth, they also proclaimed His return to Earth. Jesus will come again!

---

[3] Psalm 68:18-19
[4] Psalm 110:1
[5] Acts 1:9-11

In the book of Acts Stephen is about to be stoned for preaching Jesus and the fact that the Jews rejected Him and killed Him.

Stephen was praying and looking heavenward and told those standing nearby that he could see Jesus standing on the right hand of God. [6]

Jesus also had conversation with the apostles and gave them some instruction. Read Acts 1:4-12 for this interesting conversation.

It is noted in these verses that the angels told the apostles that Jesus would come in the same manner as they saw Him leave. This tells us that when Jesus returns we will see Him coming in the clouds. Only the Christian Church will see Him at the time of the Rapture, because this is a private event. At His Second Coming He will also descend from the clouds, but this will be a public event that will be observed worldwide.

When Jesus came to earth at His incarnation, He left His glory behind.

"Father, I will that they also, whom thou hast given me, be with me where I am; that they may behold my glory, which thou hast given me: for thou lovedst me before the foundation of the world." [7]

This is indicative of the fact that Jesus intends for us to enjoy eternal bliss with Him in the kingdom. It is His purpose to have us eternally united to Him, in the kingdom of glory.

In a strange verse, we read that Jesus gave His glory [being one with God] to the apostles,

"And the glory which thou gavest me I have given them; that they may be one, even as we are one:" [8]

---

[6] Acts 7:55
[7] John 17:24
[8] John 17:22

Jesus is speaking of those who will believe on Him through the Gospel preached by the apostles. The glory He is giving us is the privilege of being in glory for all eternity because we have believed in the salvation He provided. We too, as born again Christians become one with God. His will is our will.

When Jesus returns at His Second Coming we will see the glory He has had from all eternity, "For the Son of man shall come in the glory of his Father with his angels; and then he shall reward every man according to his works."[9]

The ascension of Jesus is a wonder for the apostles to behold, but as they were told, there is yet another wonder awaiting the world. Jesus will return and that has become the hope of untold millions of Christians. It is not His desire that anyone be left behind at the time of the Rapture, but we can be certain that unbelievers will not be taken up with Him.

The prophecy is verified, Messiah must ascend to the right hand of God. He is there at this very moment, but He is not simply sitting back on His throne taking His rest.

We who are Christian have much for which to thank Jesus, the least not being the promise recorded in Romans 8:33-34

"Who shall lay any thing to the charge of God's elect? It is God that justifieth. Who is he that condemneth? It is Christ that died, yea rather, that is risen again, who is even at the right hand of God, who also maketh intercession for us."[10]

How comforting it is to know that Jesus ascended to the right hand of God.

---

[9] Matthew 16:27 [10] Romans 8:33 & 34

Chapter 48

"Exercise His Priestly Office
In Heaven"

The Old Testament prophesied that Jesus the Messiah would be our High Priest in Heaven: "And speak unto him, saying, Thus speaketh the LORD of hosts, saying, Behold the man whose name is The BRANCH; and he shall grow up out of his place, and he shall build the temple of the LORD: Even he shall build the temple of the LORD; and he shall bear the glory, and shall sit and rule upon his throne; and he shall be a priest upon his throne: and the counsel of peace shall be between them both." [1]

The New Testament confirmed that Jesus is our High Priest: "Who is he that condemneth? It is Christ that died, yea rather, that is risen again, who is even at the right hand of God, who also maketh intercession for us." [2]

It will be beneficial to examine an illustration concerning intercessory prayer. In the book of Genesis, we find Jacob has spent the night wrestling with Jesus, here called an angel.

This is a theophany, an Old Testament appearance of the Messiah. Jacob's name means Supplanter [to take the place of another by plotting] but his name was changed to Israel. "And he said unto him, What is thy name? And he said, Jacob. And he said, Thy name shall be called no more Jacob, but Israel: for as a prince hast thou power with God and with men, and hast prevailed." [3]

---

[1] Zechariah 6:12-13
[2] Romans 8:34
[3] Genesis 32:27-28

To "wrestle" with God is to be persistent and in earnest as we pray to Him.

Jacob had wrestled with God (God the Son) not letting Him go until He blessed him; Jacob had prevailed. Because of not giving in to the urge to quit, he received a blessing; he would now be Israel, a "prince of God." This is the essence of prevailing intercessory prayer. Too often the one praying gives in to weariness or mental distraction just when God is about to answer the prayer. To get the answer requested one must prevail. Perhaps an illustration will help us understand this somewhat better.

Thou hast power with God and with men, and hast prevailed. There is an old translation that gives this passage a beautiful rendering, *because* thou hast power with God, *thou hast with men.*

An incident occurred in Wales, which illustrates this passage. At the close of an evening meeting, the Welsh pastor requested all Christians who were willing, to name some person they would go home and pray for as much of the night as they chose. After each one had named the person they would go home and pray for, the meeting was dismissed. When a pious hired girl came down the aisle weeping, saying: Pastor, you haven't given me any one to pray for; I want some one. He asked her whom she was acquainted with that she might take. She was living with a wealthy, unconverted husband and wife. The pastor asked how she would like to take her mistress. She replied, that will do. She is very kind to me, I will take her.

She returned home, and instead of going to her room, she went to a small room in the chamber, and closing the door, kneeled down, and hour after hour continued to offer just this prayer: O God, my mistress is very kind, have mercy on her soul.

The husband and wife had retired and were asleep. But about midnight the wife waked up in great distress about her soul. Said to her husband: I never saw myself such a sinner before. O I am such a sinner. I must have some one pray for me; you will have to go out and get a Christian to pray for me. The husband said, My wife, it is midnight, cant you wait until morning? But she was in such distress she could not wait. The husband perfectly kind and willing to go, said: Where shall I go to find a Christian at this hour? It finally occurred to him that some one had said their hired girl was a Christian. The wife said: Yes, she is a good Christian. I had not thought of her, we will go to her room. They went to her room but she wasn't there and the bed had not been touched. He inquired if she might not be in another room in the house. The wife said: She has occasionally slept in a room in the chamber, we will go and see. They went to this room and before they opened the door they heard her say: O God, my mistress is very kind to me, have mercy on her soul. The wife said, Here is the reason I could not sleep; here is the reason I felt I was such a sinner.

They opened the door and the wife threw herself in on her knees, by the side of her hired girl. She had power over her mistress when she had power with God.

So it will be with all Christians. They will have power over wicked men, to lead them to Christ, if they first have power to move God.[4]

That is the role of an intercessor and that is the kind of result an intercessor has a right to expect, if they prevail.

The role of the Old Testament priest was that of an intercessor. As the sacrifices were placed on the altar, it was a prayer for the forgiveness of sin.

The censors were filled with incense and God's fire was taken from the altar and place on the incense. As the smoke rose up the Priest would walk around in the tabernacle allowing the incense smoke to fill the tabernacle and ascend to God. The smoke of the incense was, to God, the prayers of the people. God was pleased with this, as this was according to His command. The sins were forgiven and the mercy of God was upon the Israelites.

The day came when the Messiah became the sacrifice offered on the altar of the cross of Calvary. The Old Testament Priesthood was no longer valid and humanity needed a High Priest to make intercession.

"And no man taketh this honor unto himself, but he that is called of God, as was Aaron. So also Christ glorified not himself to be made an high priest; but he that said unto him, Thou art my Son, to day have I begotten thee. As he saith also in another place, Thou art a priest for ever after the order of Melchisedec."[5]

---

[4] A.B. Earale, In his meetings, published in 1888
[5] Hebrews 5:4-6

Melchisedec had no mother and no father, and therefore must have been eternal in nature. Jesus was a priest forever after the order of Melchisedec. In fact, this Melchisedec could only have been another theophany, and Old Testament appearance of the Messiah Jesus.

Jesus ascended to the right hand of the Father where He continually makes intercession for us, claiming us as His own. His intercession in our behalf is perpetual, a prevailing kind of protection for our spiritual welfare.

When a sinner becomes repentant and pleads to God for mercy it is our High Priest Jesus that "stands in the gap." It is He who vouches for the sincerity of the penitent and by His continual intercession; the Holy Spirit is granted permission by the Father to regenerate the dead spirit of the penitent. It is then that the "born again" experience becomes a reality, and "old things are passed away, behold, all things are become new." [6]

This is the reason that Messiah must exercise His priestly office in Heaven.

---

[6] 2 Corinthians 5:17

Chapter 49

"Sought After By Gentiles and Jews"

Does it not seem strange that the Messiah was hated by the Jews and put to death by the Gentiles, and yet our topic is that Gentiles as well as Jews must seek after Messiah? How can it be that the Jewish community fostered such hatred toward Jesus, yet it is prophesied that the Jews would seek after Him? Similarly we find the Gentiles, largely heathens, without a sound knowledge of God would be seeking Jesus the Messiah. Both groups, being prophesied to seek after Jesus, appear to be a colossal mistake on the part of the prophets.

Isaiah tells us that the Messiah Jesus will be an ensign for the Jews, **"And in that day there shall be a root of Jesse, which shall stand for an ensign of the people; to it shall the Gentiles seek: and his rest shall be glorious."** [1]

In the Old Testament, the armies of Israel would form their fighting groups behind an ensign to which they swore allegiance, and even a family tie.

Here we are told they will one-day form up behind the ensign [banner] of King Jesus. As we observe the past, and attempt to peer into the future, one might wonder how this can ever be. What will King Jesus do to entice the Jews to join ranks under His banner?

---

[1] Isaiah 11:10

The time will come when the Gentiles, under the inspiration of God, will assist Israel in returning to their homeland and to their God. "Listen, O isles, unto me; and hearken, ye people, from far; The LORD hath called me from the womb; from the bowels of my mother hath he made mention of my name. And he hath made my mouth like a sharp sword; in the shadow of his hand hath he hid me, and made me a polished shaft; in his quiver hath he hid me; And said unto me, Thou art my servant, O Israel, in whom I will be glorified. Then I said, I have labored in vain, I have spent my strength for nought, and in vain: yet surely my judgment is with the LORD, and my work with my God. And now, saith the LORD that formed me from the womb to be his servant, to bring Jacob again to him, Though Israel be not gathered, yet shall I be glorious in the eyes of the LORD, and my God shall be my strength. And he said, It is a light thing that thou shouldest be my servant to raise up the tribes of Jacob, and to restore the preserved of Israel: I will also give thee for a light to the Gentiles, that thou mayest be my salvation unto the end of the earth." [2]

Messiah is also prophesied to be a "light" to the Gentiles. This speaks of a spiritual light, bringing them out of spiritual darkness that surrounds their heathen belief system. Observing the world today, we are surrounded by heathens.

---

[2] Isaiah 49:1-6

348

Consider the nations of this world and we see more idol worshipping nations than we can number. There are few nations in the world that can claim to be truly Christian, and the United Nations no longer lists our own country as a Christian nation; we are listed as a pagan country.

Judging from all this it would appear that only a miracle wrought by the Messiah Jesus will ever bring these prophesies to fulfillment. Before we become doubtful though, we need to remember what we have learned thus far concerning the prophecies of the Old Testament and the Fulfillment in the New Testament. Each prophecy required a miracle of God to be fulfilled exactly, yet we have absolute proof that God performed those amazing feats.

"Behold my servant, whom I have chosen; my beloved, in whom my soul is well pleased: I will put my spirit upon him, and he shall shew judgment to the Gentiles." [3] Jesus is spoken of as the "servant" of God. We see Jesus, during the years of His ministry taking upon Himself the role of the obedient servant. The Gospel of Mark especially depicts Jesus as a servant, and shows no genealogy because a servant has no genealogy.

The Jews will not immediately be pleased when the apostles preach that God has included the Gentiles in the promises made to Israel: "While Peter yet spake these words, the Holy Ghost fell on all them which heard the word. And they of the circumcision which believed were astonished, as many as came with Peter, because that on the Gentiles also was poured out the gift of the Holy Ghost.

---

[3] Mathew 12:18

For they heard them speak with tongues, and magnify God. Then answered Peter, Can any man forbid water, that these should not be baptized, which have received the Holy Ghost as well as we?" [4]

Isaiah 42:1 speaks of Messiah of the "servant" whom God will uphold. "Behold my servant, whom I uphold; mine elect, in whom my soul delighteth; I have put my spirit upon him: he shall bring forth judgment to the Gentiles." This alludes to the custom of kings leaning on the arm of their most beloved and faithful servant. This prophecy belongs to Messiah, not Cyrus.

God required an acceptable and perfect service from man; but man, being sinful, could not perform it. Jesus, taking upon him the nature of man, fully performed the whole will of God, and communicates grace to all his followers, to enable them perfectly to love and worthily to magnify the maker.

" A Fountain Run Dry"

On the main avenue is a kind of stone pagoda covering a fountain; the pretty construction being the gift of a gentleman in the West to this city. His name is carved in large letters, with an added sentence that he gave this water supply to the community. The four sides of the granite structure bear the words, Faith Hope Charity Temperance. It all looks well; but the trouble is that something is the matter with the fountain. It has quit flowing. It is about the driest looking object and place on the avenue.

---

[4] Acts 10:45-47

So in spite of the doctors self-laudatory inscription of 'This is the gift of Dr. So-and-So;' and in face of the beautiful words, Faith, Hope, Charity, Temperance, the spring itself is dry.

We at once thought of religious denominations which have arisen in the world and announced themselves and their creed as a great gift to a famishing world, and yet have run perfectly dry. They had inscriptions of panels of faith and doctrine that were higher sounding than the four words we have cited attention to; have announced a fourfold, and a forty fold Gospel, but after that ran dry.

The doctors four words are really best understood, and generally experienced and practically lived, when the Fountain Christ Jesus is opened up in the heart. What a Faith we have now! What Hope for people and the cause of Truth! What Temperance in the very best and fullest sense of the word, in spirit, speech, conduct, as well as life habits!

And what Charity that is not puffed up, is not easily provoked, thinketh no evil, but beareth all things, endureth all things and never faileth! It takes the Living Water, Christ Himself, to bring the genuine experience and character into the life covered by the words Faith, Hope, Temperance and Charity.

So as we studied the four high-sounding phrases carved on the walls of the little stone pagoda or pavilion, and observed the dried-up water supply, we had to do some smiling.

It was all so suggestive, so mutely eloquent, so much like a first-class arable, that there was nothing that anyone could do but smile, unless it should be the doctor when he hears his spring has ceased to flow; or thirsty people drawing near for refreshment, would find only a dusty basin and a rusty, silent, empty spout before them! [modified via deletions] [5]

The day will come when both Jew and Gentile realize that their acts of worship are no more than drinking at a dried up fountain. There is no refreshment to be found, only continual thirst for more of what they search for. What they need, and will ultimately find, is the Messiah Jesus.

Jesus will publish the Gospel to the heathen. The Greek word for "judgment" κρισιν signifies laws, precepts, and a whole system or body of doctrine. Jesus will show His laws, precepts, and a whole system of doctrine to the heathen.

Are we to understand that "some" of the heathens will be given the doctrine of the Gospel? That is not what this verse is saying, ". He shall not fail nor be discouraged, till he have set judgment in the earth: and the isles shall wait for his law." "in the earth: and the isles [nation of heathens] shall wait for his law."

It is obvious that his prophecy is yet to be fulfilled, but we have no doubt that it will happen. God is all-powerful, all knowing, all love, and there is no doubt that He will use all His attributes necessary to bring the heathen idolaters to Jesus.

---

[5] Living Illustrations by B. Carradine

Perhaps for some the transformation of the Jews and Gentiles will take place during the "Time of Jacob's Trouble", of that there is little doubt. Further conversions will undoubtedly take place during the battle between Satan's forces and Jesus. It is not unusual for a warrior on the losing side to decide to defect and join forces with the winning side.

There will also be many in the millennial era that have potential, but are not yet convicted in their spirit.

Those designated as kings and priests during that time will be instrumental in helping to fulfill this prophecy. Whatever method God chooses to use, we can be certain that it will not fail.

"Messiah Is Prophesied To Be Sought After By Gentiles As Well As Jews"

Chapter 50

"The King"

The Jews, and Pilate, likely considered Jesus to be no more than what we would term an itinerate preacher, one who went from place to place preaching His message. Jesus had walked the dusty roads of Israel bringing the Gospel of peace to humanity. Peace between man and their Holy God, which neither the Jew nor the Gentile had found.

In John the 18th chapter, we see Jesus confirming the words of Pilate as he asked, "Art thou a king?" "Then Pilate entered into the judgment hall again, and called Jesus, and said unto him, Art thou the King of the Jews? Jesus answered him, Sayest thou this thing of thyself, or did others tell it thee of me? Pilate answered, Am I a Jew? Thine own nation and the chief priests have delivered thee unto me: what hast thou done?

Jesus answered, My kingdom is not of this world: if my kingdom were of this world, then would my servants fight, that I should not be delivered to the Jews: but now is my kingdom not from hence. Pilate therefore said unto him, Art thou a king then? Jesus answered, Thou sayest that I am a king. To this end was I born, and for this cause came I into the world, that I should bear witness unto the truth. Every one that is of the truth heareth my voice." [1]

This was likely spoken in a mocking manner, as to say, "Are you really going to tell me you are a king?" Pilate did not believe Jesus when He acknowledges that His birth was to this end; He is the King, and will be so eternally.

---

[1] John 18:33-37

He even informed Pilate that His kingdom was not of this world; if it had been of this world, His servants would have rescued Him from the Jews.

Pilate did not pursue this line of thinking by asking Jesus where is this world from which you came, and where are you a king.

Pilate did not care to know anything more about Jesus and His presumed royal status, anymore than billions of persons worldwide today want to know.

If the saying "ignorance is bliss" is true, Pilate and billions of present day non-believers should be overflowing with happiness. Judging from what we see of nations in poverty, disease, famine, earthquake torn cities, deaths as the result of drug related murders, I cannot believe that ignorance is bliss. I am of the opinion that ignorance, in the area of spirituality, is devastating and eternally destructive.

Psalm the second chapter tells us that God has set His king on the Holy hill of Zion. "Yet have I set my king upon my holy hill of Zion." [2]

That prophecy is telling us that God has "set" [appointed] His King on the Holy hill of Zion. The first fulfillment was when King Jesus became man and dwelled among the Jews to set them free from Satan's power. Obviously, they enjoyed the services they provide Satan rather than to accept the freedom from God's appointed King.

The final fulfillment will be when King Jesus returns to plant His feet on Mount of Olives and declare Himself, once and for all time, King, and this time no one will successfully dispute His claim.

---

[2] Psalm 2:6

When Pilate first asked Jesus "Art thou the King of the Jews," Jesus asked him if he was saying this out of his own conviction, or was it something he had heard from another. Pilate snarled his answer, "Am I a Jew?"

Is it possible that if Jesus would speak to some today, who claim to be Christians, and ask them if they believe Him to be the King eternal, what would they say? Would they say, 'yes, you are the Savior?' Then Jesus might ask, 'Is this your own personal testimony, or are you simply mouthing words you have heard Christians say?' I fear that too many would have to admit they were no better spiritually than were the Jews and Gentiles of Jesus' day. Even some Jews believed Jesus to be the promised King, but after the Triumphal Entry scene, the crowd turned irate, believing the words of the chief priest and Pharisees. "He is no king, He is a fraud that works magic and is guilty of trickery by using evil spirits."

Timothy proclaimed Jesus to be the King of kings, and encouraged the people to keep faithful to the commandment he gave them to (v 12) "Fight the good fight of faith, lay hold on eternal life, whereunto thou art also called, and hast professed a good profession before many witnesses."

"I give thee charge in the sight of God, who quickeneth all things, and before Christ Jesus, who before Pontius Pilate witnessed a good confession;

That thou keep this commandment without spot, unrebukable, until the appearing of our Lord Jesus Christ: Which in his times he shall shew, who is the blessed and only Potentate, the King of kings, and Lord of lords;" [3]

---

[3] 1 Timothy 6:13-15

Timothy had no doubt that Jesus is the King of kings and proclaimed Him to be the only Royal Leader, the King of kings, and Lord of lords.

There is a day in the future when Jesus will erase all doubts from those who are of an unsettled mind concerning Him.

"And the ten horns which thou sawest are ten kings, which have received no kingdom as yet; but receive power as kings one hour with the beast. These have one mind, and shall give their power and strength unto he beast. These shall make war with the Lamb, and the Lamb shall overcome them: for he is Lord of lords, and King of kings: and they that are with him are called, and chosen, and faithful." [4]

In this revelation of Jesus, given to the apostle John, Jesus is described not only as the "Lamb", but also as the Lord of lords, and King of kings."

The final proof of His true identity comes to us in "And I saw heaven opened, and behold a white horse; and he that sat upon him was called Faithful and True, and in righteousness he doth judge and make war. His eyes were as a flame of fire, and on his head were many crowns; and he had a name written, that no man knew, but he himself. And he was clothed with a vesture dipped in blood: and his name is called The Word of God. And the armies which were in heaven followed him upon white horses, clothed in fine linen, white and clean. And out of his mouth goeth a sharp sword, that with it he should smite the nations: and he shall rule them with a rod of iron: and he treadeth the winepress of the fierceness and wrath of Almighty God.

---

[4] Revelation 17:12-14

And he hath on his vesture and on his thigh a name written, KING OF KINGS, AND LORD OF LORDS."[5]   When King Jesus appears in the sky with millions of His angels and millions of born again Christians who are now considered "saints", there will be no room left for doubt.

This study ends on a note of warning for those who have read these words, and still hold to their own confused belief system. [6]

"And I saw a great white throne, and him that sat on it, from whose face the earth and the heaven fled away; and there was found no place for them. And I saw the dead, small and great, stand before God; and the books were opened: and another book was opened, which is the book of life: and the dead were judged out of those things which were written in the books, according to their works. And the sea gave up the dead which were in it; and death and hell delivered up the dead which were in them: and they were judged every man according to their works. And death and hell were cast into the lake of fire. This is the second death. And whosoever was not found written in the book of life was cast into the lake of fire." [7]

The warning has now been given and now I will close this study on a note of hope and a promise of eternal peace and joy in the presence of our Holy God.

---

[5] Revelation 19:16   [6] Revelation 20:11-15
[7] Revelation 20:11-15

Just as Jesus said to His disciples many times during His ministry, He also says to the "whosoever" recorded in John "For God so loved the world, that he gave his only begotten Son, that whosoever believeth in him should not perish, but have everlasting life.

For God sent not his Son into the world to condemn the world; but that the world through him might be saved." [8]

You can appropriate this peace and joy, and make a reservation for your place in Heaven by obeying what Jesus said: "Jesus answered and said unto him, Verily, verily, I say unto thee, Except a man be born again, he cannot see the kingdom of God." [9]

Should you find it difficult to understand the concept of being "born again" feel free to contact me or any Bible teaching Evangelistic Pastor and you will soon find the mystery of being "born again."

It is my sincere prayer that any, and all, who have read the words of this study regarding the prophecies concerning the Messiah Jesus, will appropriate the salvation He provide for humanity.

I leave you with the word of the hymn written by Philip Paul Bliss (1838-1876). The words are as true today as they were the day he penned these.

---

[8] John 3:16 - 17
[9] John 3:3

"Man of Sorrows"

1   Man of sorrows! what a name
For the Son of God, who came
Ruined sinners to reclaim;
Hallelujah! What a Saviour.

2   Bearing shame and scoffing rude,
In my place condemned he stood,
Sealed my; pardon with his blood;
Hallelujah! What a Saviour!

3   Guilty, vile and helpless we,
Spotless Lamb of God was he;
Full atonement - can it be?
Hallelujah! What a Saviour!

4   Lifted up was he to die;
It is finished! was his cry;
Now in Heaven, exalted high;
Hallelujah! What a Saviour!

5   When he comes, our glorious King,
All his ransomed home to bring,
Then anew this song we'll sing:
Hallelujah! What a Saviour!

6068956R1

Made in the USA
Charleston, SC
10 September 2010